THE COMPLETE MANUAL OF
AIRBRUSHING

THE COMPLETE MANUAL OF
AIRBRUSHING

PETER OWEN & JANE ROLLASON

Alfred A. Knopf • New York 1988

THIS IS A BORZOI BOOK
PUBLISHED BY ALFRED A. KNOPF, INC.
First American Edition

Copyright © 1988 by Dorling Kindersley Limited, London
All rights reserved under International and Pan-American
Copyright Conventions. Published in the United States by
Alfred A. Knopf, Inc., New York.
Published in Great Britain by Dorling Kindersley Limited

Library of Congress 87-46100
ISBN 0 394 56852 4

The Complete Manual of
AIRBRUSHING TECHNIQUES
was produced by Nigel Osborne
38 Welbeck Street, London W1

Art Director Nigel Osborne
Editor Peter Brooke Ball
Design Assistants Fraser Newman & Kevin Swann
Photography Ian Howes & Mark French
Artwork Fraser Newman & Peter Owen

Printed in Hong Kong by Leefung Asco Printers Ltd
Reproduction by Universal Colour Scanning Ltd., Hong Kong

CONTENTS

SECTION ONE
EQUIPMENT & MATERIALS

SECTION TWO
ART TECHNIQUES

SECTION THREE
AIRBRUSH APPLICATIONS

REFERENCE SECTION

INTRODUCTION

The airbrush has a magical quality – it draws and paints without touching a surface, yet its effects are vibrant and polished, and the associated imagery is often beyond realism, following its own standards of invention and expression. But for the artist, the airbrush is a tool like any other, requiring specific knowledge and skill to be of significant value. It is important not only to appreciate but also to understand what the airbrush can do, and where it can be used appropriately.

Graphic images are all around us – in advertising and promotional materials, the packaging of consumer goods, illustrations for magazine covers and articles, album covers, and poster designs. Much of this work involves the airbrush, and in the major towns and cities of the industrialized world, most people are frequently exposed to a number of fine examples of airbrush art. Few of these people, however, could confidently identify airbrush technique, but they know the style – the clever three-dimensional illusionism, the high-gloss sleekness of the surface finish, the attention to shape, color, and detail.

These are elements of graphic presentation which the audience for this work has come to expect, and which reflect different aspects of visual communication – a sense of progress or nostalgia, dramatic impact and subtle humor, the evocation of affluence and style. The expectation of sophisticated imagery in all types of graphic art and illustration work has been promoted and supported by artists using the airbrush in many subtle and inventive ways. The impressive super-realism which the airbrush serves so well is only one of the many distinctive and wide-ranging styles of graphic work to which the airbrush contributes. Its creative power is now well established, and is being extended as more and more people come to recognize and enjoy the particular qualities of airbrush art.

THE GRAPHIC IMAGE

Despite the origins and early history of the airbrush, its primary functions and most widely known applications are now in the fields of graphic design and illustration. The flawless surface qualities and striking effects of super-realism which the airbrush can produce are naturally graphic in their expression. But the airbrush has many applications for two-dimensional design and illustration: on the simplest level, it can be used to lay areas of even, flat color into a diagrammatic line drawing; it is also useful for adding special effects to the last stages of an artwork which may have been done mainly by other methods—starbursts, for example, or thin veils of graded color.

Current trends for nostalgia often hark back to illustration styles of the 1930s and 1940s, and some of the original artists of that period used the airbrush in their work. Alberto Vargas, well-known for his pin-up posters

and magazine spreads, used airbrushing to round out the forms and provide subtle coloring. Herbert Bayer, moving from the Bauhaus in Germany to the US in the 1930s, used the airbrush both in illustration work and as a means of refining photographic collages. Advertising for products as diverse as chewing gum and bathing suits showed examples of airbrush art. In Europe, notable exponents of the technique included the French artist Cassandre, English designer Abram Games and in Italy, Paolo Garretto.

In the period following World War II, airbrushing was surprisingly neglected as a graphic skill. Commercial work for advertising and editorial illustration largely ignored the potential of the airbrush, and its use once again became more commonly associated with photo-retouching. But in major industrial drawing studios, particularly in the automobile and aerospace industries, airbrush art reached a new peak of expression in elegant technical renderings of engines, parts and giant machines. This has become a proud tradition of airbrushing which still continues today, although now carried forward by freelance artists rather than studio employees. The studios were also a training ground for artists who have subsequently moved into other fields of illustration and design, taking their expertise in air-brushing with them.

The 1960s was the decade of the revival of airbrush illustration. In America and Europe, artists discovered airbrushing equipment almost by chance in colleges and drawing studios and began to see its possibilities. In the USA, airbrush art was promoted by such artists as Charles White III, Dave Willardson, Bob Zoell and Doug Johnson, and in the UK by Philip Castle, Alan Aldridge and Michael English, among others. Particular images, such as Charles White III's glistening raw egg on black-and-white tiling, stuck in the minds of art directors and illustrators alike, for their glossy perfection and colorful detail. From there, the popularity of airbrushing escalated until airbrushed images became almost symbolic of the young, fast, affluent consumer society of the late 1960s and early 1970s. It has also been found useful for particular effects in animated film and cartoons associated with advertising and movie features, and this is another area where the capabilities of the technique have come to wider public attention.

The skills of airbrushing have been passed on by

example and by sheer hard work on the part of many self-taught illustrators. Many individuals have contributed new approaches to style and technique which have increased the versatility and practical value of the airbrush. Airbrushing is now established among new generations of artists as a significant artform in its own right: the profiles of major airbrush illustrators in the following pages demonstrate the current international status of this artform in the world of graphic arts.

THE BEGINNINGS OF AIRBRUSH ART

The airbrush has been around for almost a hundred years, during which period it has at some times been a favored and influential tool, and at others neglected and undervalued. It is currently widely used and popular with both professional and amateur artists, but many of the best-known airbrush illustrators of recent years were entirely self-taught. Not until the late 1960s was the versatility of airbrushing for graphic artists, illustrators and painters fully acknowledged, and even now there are few art courses which teach airbrushing as a specialist skill. In a sense, this has been the source of a great deal of creativity in airbrush art, as there has been no particular tradition of style or technique, and artists using the airbrush have been obliged to invent solutions to their various problems of representation by getting to know the capabilities of the tool, sometimes in unconventional ways.

The airbrush was invented in 1893 by Charles Burdick, a watercolor artist whose achievements as a painter remain unremarked, but who gave the art world a unique new tool which has been exploited in ways he could not have foreseen. Burdick's main aim was to develop a mechanical brush capable of laying an even, transparent layer of color more efficiently than the conventional paintbrush. Although the airbrush is now a precision instrument carefully designed and with every component tested for accuracy and efficiency, the basic principle is just as Burdick invented it and the physical appearance of the tool itself has changed little. It is, however, rather more sophisticated these days, benefiting from the elegance, as well as the improved mechanical performance, that modern technology can provide. As an instrument for applying a liquid medium, it seems to have more in common with a pen than with the traditional artist's brush – a streamlined shape with

an internal flow of medium coming from an inbuilt reservoir. For this reason it has commonly been regarded as quite separate from conventional painting techniques, and this has not always been helpful to promoting its more widespread use. Charles Burdick himself was not allowed to exhibit paintings at the Royal Academy of Art in London because the mechanical tool was frowned upon not being a painting instrument.

This attitude led to the airbrush finding its first major use in association with a trade or craft, rather than with fine art as its inventor had intended. At the turn of the century it was commonly used for photographic retouching and proved invaluable in this context. Subtle surface effects and gradual blending of tones are essential to retouching work, as the object is to add detail which should not look separate from the main image. Through airbrushing, the retoucher can add fine veils of opaque or translucent tone, develop detail or obliterate unwanted sections of the image, and add transparent color to a monochrome photograph without destroying the underlying structure of the picture. There are a number of different reasons for retouching a photographic image – to improve the quality of the picture and eradicate blemishes, to focus a specific area of detail and disguise other aspects, or, as is commonly the case in advertising and promotion work, to add a particular kind of detail and atmosphere that enhances the appearance of the product. The manipulation of photographic images today increasingly makes use of more complex processes of exposure and development, in the camera or the darkroom, but the traditional association of airbrushing and photography remains and is still an important aspect of photoretouching.

Another early use of the airbrush, now being revived in a more widespread context, was the decoration of fabrics and related products, such as fashion accessories and soft furnishings.

EXPONENTS OF AIRBRUSH ART

On the following pages there are examples of work of some of the leading exponents of airbrush art. Alongside the samples of work, brief biographies are also included and these provide useful background information on the development of the various styles. As can be seen, styles vary considerably and this goes to prove that there are no hard and fast rules.

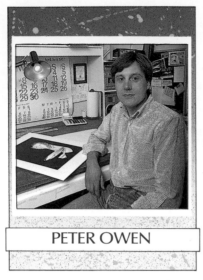

PETER OWEN

English illustrator Peter Owen has a comprehensive interest in airbrushing. His illustrations for advertising, album covers, film posters, book jackets and magazine articles have won him international awards and the originals are frequently exhibited; he receives commissions from throughout the UK and Europe, and from as far afield as Hong Kong. In addition, he runs The Airbrush Company from his studio base in Coventry, dealing with specialist airbrush equipment. His expertise in the technical side of airbrushing as well as his illustrator's skills have been displayed in his major contributions to practical books on the subject. The practical demonstrations of graphic imagery and illustration throughout Sections 1 and 2 of this book are Peter Owen's work.

Since his art school training in the late 1960s, when he learned to use the tool but was not formally taught airbrushing techniques, Owen has specialized in airbrush work. Early experience as a photographic retoucher allowed him to acquire the conventional practice of airbrushing, but it was not until he began work in London with illustrator Alan Aldridge that he fully discovered the potential of the airbrush, gradually developing the unique and distinctive style now so much in demand. Peter Owen uses Iwata airbrushes and equipment, and works in a broad range of media.

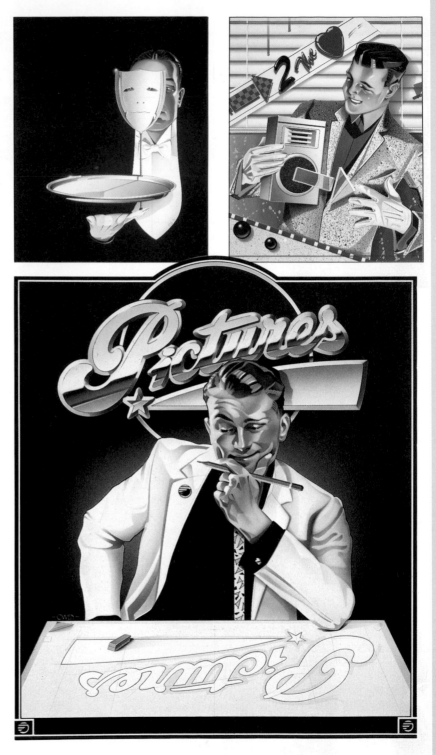

The mask image (top left) was commissioned for Playboy magazine. An illustration originally done by Owen as a sampler of airbrushing techniques (top right) has been taken up as a popular greetings card image. "Pictures" (above) is the picture logo for an artists' agency.

Owen's range of airbrush work covers (clockwise from left) handsome photorealism in the detailed painting of Christmas decorations; a lively new approach to a diagrammatic piece by Colin Elgie; and the traditional polished style of industrial studio work.

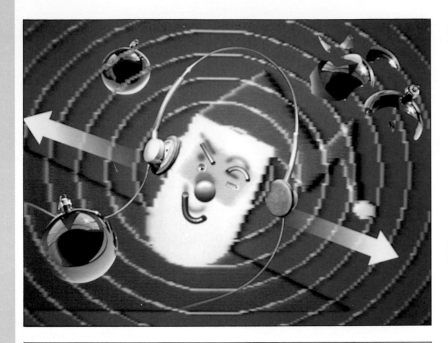

DAVE WILLARDSON

American illustrator Willardson could justly claim to be one of the pioneers of airbrush art. When he started to use the airbrush, in the mid-1960s, it was regarded as a mere mechanism mainly associated with photoretouching. Willardson persevered in using it as a painting tool in its own right, and continued to show his airbrush work around despite the initially dismissive reaction. When the illustrations were accepted and published, the sophisticated style of airbrushing seemed to catch the mood of the late 60s. Alongside Charles White III, with whom he later established a very successful illustration studio, Willardson promoted airbrush art toward the range and versatility it has today.

As well as being self-taught in the skills of airbrushing, he knows all there is about the operation of the tool – he uses a Thayer & Chandler model A – and considers it necessary to "become your own airbrush repairman". He prefers dyes to opaque media, enjoying the luminous colors and accepting the greater accuracy needed with a transparent medium that does not cover errors. His airbrush work has appeared in magazines and advertisements, on album covers and film posters.

The Willardson influence
Willardson was one of the first illustrators to produce pastiche artworks and his approach to airbrushing has encouraged others to experiment. Paul Allen combines airbrushed and computer-generated images (above left), while Bob Murdoch creates poster images in a 1930's style (left).

The range of Dave Willardson's work displays his typical high-gloss finish and tongue-in-cheek humor. The "Fork It Over" album cover (left), and magazine illustration "For Ears Only" (above) are works from the late 1970s. His poster for an exhibition by the Automotive Parts and Accessories Association (below) brings distinctive style to a popular motif of airbrush art – the gleaming auto.

1983 APAA SHOW

HAJIME SORAYAMA

A combined talent for figure work and the technical detail of machine mechanisms creates the impact of Hajime Sorayama's robots (below left). These surreal and unexpected images have become popular posters, attracting much attention for this freelance illustrator, both in his native Japan and internationally.

Sorayama remembers that he enjoyed drawing from his earliest years. His curiosity about the objects and images around him and a willingness to investigate different techniques of representation equipped him well for a career as an illustrator. While still at school he took a keen interest in technical subjects, making drawings of ships and airplanes. He acquired the discipline of commercial practice through art school training and by working as a comprehensive illustrator in an advertising agency, before going freelance in 1971. His agency work increased the range of his technique and subject matter – he was required to illustrate a variety of subjects using such media as pastels, markers, pens and paints.

The detail and high degree of surface finish in Sorayama's work make the airbrush a necessity for him, but he is both appreciative of its advantages and wary of its drawbacks. He uses it in combination with other drawing and painting skills, preferring not to rely on airbrushing alone as a means of achieving his glossy style. He works typically with acrylic paints, combining airbrushing with pencil drawing and brush painting.

Sorayama regards the masking process as a drawback of airbrush work, as he feels that covering the work with a mask makes it difficult for the artist to estimate color values. Consequently his technique is subtly controlled: he prefers to use the airbrush freehand and is only too aware of the practice required to perfect this approach.

Sorayama is perhaps unique among airbrush artists in that he doesn't use masks to create his images. As the illustrations on these two pages show, he has a fascination with chrome and its effects, all of which are painted freehand.

NORBERT CAMES

Much in demand for his high quality advertising illustrations, Norbert Cames has established a dramatic style of hyper-realist imagery. A self-taught airbrush artist, Cames acquired many skills of graphic presentation through early training as a lithographer and subsequent work in a design studio.

Cames has command of a broad range of techniques but appreciates the specific qualities of airbrush work. He owns airbrushes of all types, but often employs a single-action airbrush, which he feels to be an extension of his own hand. He has a disciplined and immaculate technique and stresses the importance of planning the work in detail beforehand to eliminate technical problems.

ABOUT THIS BOOK

The information and examples in this book are designed to cover the full range of airbrush work, from the simplest shapes and textures to complex pieces of graphic illustration, from operation of the airbrush itself to the different forms of masking and other technical expertise which the airbrush artist can put to use. The book is split into three main sections — Equipment and materials, Art techniques, and Applications — which concentrate on the various aspects of airbrush technique across the range of possible uses.

SECTION 1: EQUIPMENT AND MATERIALS

The basic principles of airbrushing are explained with detailed information about the different types of airbrush which are widely available, their modes of operation, and their technical capabilities. Fully annotated diagrams are included in profiles of 12 individual models, to illustrate the structure and function of each type and the accessories which go with them; their advantages and disadvantages are fully discussed, including reference to the suitability for different types of airbrush work in various media.

A similar approach is taken to the sources of air for the airbrush — from the spare auto tire to the most sophisticated multi-outlet compressor. The operation of each air source is fully explained, with its advantages or disadvantages in relation to the type of airbrush which you wish to use, and the scale and quality of work for which it is required.

An important sub-section explains how to clean and maintain airbrushing equipment, including a special feature on specific procedures for seven types of airbrush which represent all the possible components and structures you may find in the full range of airbrushes. A diagnostic fault-finding chart points to the problems commonly encountered in use of the airbrush: this enables you to identify the fault and the appropriate remedy to be applied.

Surfaces and supports, paint media, drawing accessories and studio materials are fully catalogued in relation to studio procedures and the specific techniques and applications of airbrushing.

SECTION 2: ART TECHNIQUES

This section proceeds through a graded series of techniques, from those required by complete beginners to advanced techniques for artists who have acquired some expertise with the airbrush.

To begin with, the basic control of the airbrush is explained with simple exercises for producing flat color washes, graded tones and vignetting, through to the construction of standard geometric forms shown in three-dimensional volume. Step-by-step examples show precisely the successive stages of the work and the techniques of realizing the required effect.

Techniques of masking basic shapes and different sections of a developing image are shown in full detail by means of practical examples, including highly finished artwork in realist and diagrammatic styles. The types of masking material from self-adhesive film through torn paper and board, loose plastic masks, liquid masking and found objects, are shown in use. They are applied to creating specific effects which exploit their particular properties and capabilities. It is explained how to plan the all-important sequence of masking to build up a detailed composite image, how to make use of special effects of hard and soft masking and the different textures which loose masks can create. In addition, this section explains how to adapt materials and equipment to the purpose in hand, how to correct errors and obliterate or erase mistakes where necessary.

An individual feature follows the technique of scaling up or down from a basic design construction or working drawing, followed by a series of advanced techniques which show you how to deal with sophisticated effects of shape, color and texture. This focuses on the way simple procedures can be combined to produce the complex pictorial images and diagrammatic conventions created by skilled airbrush illustrators. Finally, the disciplines of professional practice are introduced in the special circumstances of 'Working to a brief' and 'Working for print'.

SECTION 3: APPLICATIONS

Airbrushing has broad applications across a range of disciplines and is used in relation to a number of different crafts. Three-dimensional objects from various types of model to decorative foods are colored and finished with the airbrush. These applications are fully illustrated with step-by-step examples demonstrated by professional artists covering the range of three-dimensional work. Decorative fabrics and ceramics are also included in this section.

Special applications in the field of graphic art include photoretouching, technical illustration and medical illustration. Examples from all these areas are included with reference to the techniques commonly used and the special effects that evolved to solve particular problems. The same approach is shown in animation work, where the airbrush has made a unique contribution to movie features, cartoons and advertising films.

A profile of each of the various contributors is included to provide information about the background to their work and the way in which the airbrush is used in the context of professional practice. An extensive glossary and comprehensive index complete the book.

EQUIPMENT & MATERIALS

*"For me, the airbrush is a tool
not a style"*

DOUG JOHNSON

THE AIRBRUSH

The airbrush has had a checkered history, dating back to the late nineteenth century when the first airbrush was patented in America. The development of the airbrush into a practical tool happened simultaneously in Britain and America at the turn of the century. It was designed initially for laying down flat washes of watercolor, but its application as a photoretouching tool was quickly realized and exploited by the newspaper business.

The fine or graphic art capabilities of the airbrush were first seriously explored in the 20s and 30s by artists in the vanguard of new artistic direction and technique, as the works of Wasily Kandinsky and Paul Klee and surrealists Man Ray and Max Ernst show. The airbrush was the perfect tool for graphic representation of the spirit of the age — the age of the machine aesthetic. Edward McKnight-Kauffer, a leading graphic designer and innovator, brought airbrush art to millions with his posters for London Transport and Shell, where he used the airbrush to achieve the flat planes of color characteristic of his Cubist-inspired approach. The airbrush fully came into its own in popular terms as Art Deco flourished — it was used for artwork, decoration, figurines, fashion art, posters and design.

Its fortunes faded with those of Art Deco and didn't pick up until the late 40s and 50s, when the great boom in American car manufacturing created a new demand for retouching and glossy representation of vast expanses of chrome and bodywork in car advertising.

The airbrush was ideally suited to rendering the psychedelic art of the 60s and was widely used in the graphic art of the period. As psychedelia fell from favor, the airbrush was relegated to the studios of the professional photoretoucher and technical illustrator, the car customizer and the model maker.

It has been widely taken up again during the last decade or so and airbrushes are now used for many different purposes, including the traditional areas of graphic art, photoretouching and modeling, and the newer areas of special effects and animation, fabric design, ceramics, glass etching and food decoration. Airbrush art is all around us today, on movie posters, magazine covers, book jackets and consumer packaging designs, and the airbrush seems set to enjoy its longest flush of popularity yet.

Charles Burdick's patent design
The two old De Vilbiss airbrushes (below) bear the patent stamp of Charles Burdick, the man who invented the airbrush. The basic design and appearance has changed little over the years.

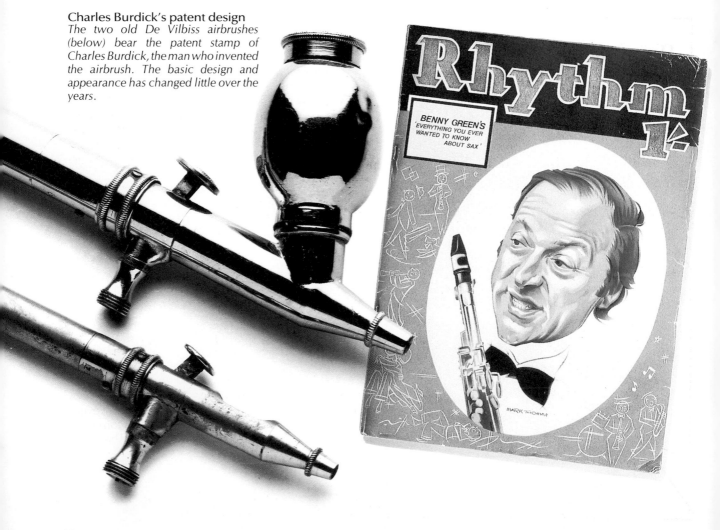

TYPES OF AIRBRUSH

In order to exploit the full potential of your airbrush, you need to understand what's happening inside. There are several different types of airbrush, ranging in complexity from the simple single action external mix to the independent double action, but they all work on the basic principle of atomization. Paint and pressurized air are channeled separately through the body of the airbrush and meet at the tip. As the air mixes with the paint, the paint is atomized and expelled through the nozzle of the airbrush as a fine spray. Control of this spray, in terms of paint:air ratio, color and consistency of paint, and the distance of the nozzle from the surface, is the key to airbrush art. The level of control built into the airbrush is what distinguishes one type from another.

Airbrushes can be divided into two main categories – single action and double action. In general terms, a single action airbrush is ideal for the limited purposes of the model maker, but if you want to produce serious airbrush art, such as detailed graphic work, it is better to invest in a double action airbrush right at the start. Double action models offer all the versatility and refinement required for professional illustration.

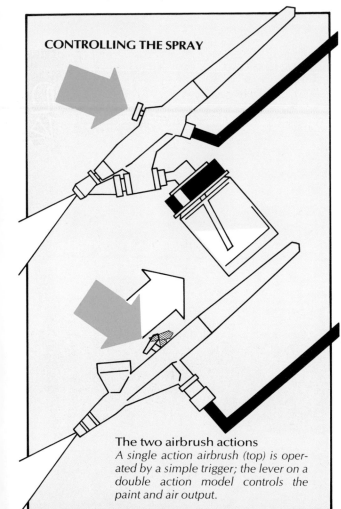

CONTROLLING THE SPRAY

The two airbrush actions
A single action airbrush (top) is oper-ated by a simple trigger; the lever on a double action model controls the paint and air output.

SINGLE ACTION AIRBRUSHES

The simplest type of airbrush is operated by depressing a trigger which acts like an on/off switch to the air supply – in other words, the trigger has a single action. Paint is drawn up into the airbrush and is atomized by the rush of air as it passes through the nozzle. Although detailed artwork is hard to achieve with a single action airbrush, they are highly regarded by modelers.

External mix spray gun

This is the most basic airbrush available. It is really a sophisticated spray gun with a minimally adjustable spray. Despite its limitations, this model is very popular. It can be used wherever large areas of flat color with-out detail are required. Detail can be achieved by skilful masking, although this is unnecessarily time-consuming when a slightly more sophisticated model can be used instead. It is suitable for stenciling, covering large expanses with color, spraying thinned chemical substances such as rustproofer and ceramic underglaze, and basic model painting.

Major brands are the Badger 250 and the Humbrol Modeler's airbrush (see page 23).

External mix with needle

A more robust design than the first type, this airbrush produces a finer and more controllable spray. The spray is still relatively coarse, however, creating a stippled or large dot pattern.

This airbrush is capable of achieving the high finish required in modeling, and is the popular choice among hobbyists. It is also widely used in the ceramics industry for spraying simple patterns on porcelain. Additional uses include fabric design, simple retouching, basic graphic work and textured work.

Major brands are the Badger 350 (see page 24) and the Paasche F#l for use with light media, and the more refined Paasche H. None of these single action airbrushes needs adaptation for left-handed users.

Internal mix

This model is the most sophisticated of the single action airbrushes. It is capable of producing a much finer and more professional spray than other single action models, because the paint is atomized within the body of the airbrush and is thoroughly diffused by the time it meets the surface being sprayed.

It is very popular among hobbyists, and its uses include fabric spraying, fine lettering, custom painting cars and bikes, taxidermy, ceramic decoration, and modeling. Once you are in this price range, however, the cheaper end of the double action range becomes an alternative. For not very much more, you could have the facility of controlling both air and paint supply while spraying and all the versatility that double action airbrushes offer.

Major brands are the Badger 200 and the Thayer and Chandler Models E (see page 25) and G.

DOUBLE ACTION AIRBRUSHES

Double action airbrushes are in a different league from the single action models. Their distinction lies in their versatility. Finger-operated control of both the air and paint supplies enables you to determine exactly the width and density of the spray, and to produce art of photographic quality.

Fixed double action

Only a few models are made to this slightly oddball design. As with independent double action airbrushes, the paint and air supply are both regulated by the finger-operated lever, but in the fixed double action model, the paint:air ratio is preset. It is not possible, for example, to expel a small amount of air with a large amount of paint. It is easier to operate — you simply draw the lever back and the paint and air flows are increased — and the spray quality is excellent, but its repertoire of effects is limited. Extremely fine work can be produced if you have the patience to work out the ratio which will produce exactly what you want.

This airbrush is used mainly for illustration which could perhaps be described as accurate rather than creative. The very fine lines which it can produce also make it suitable for porcelain restoring and other very detailed work.

The two brands of fixed double action available are the Efbe range and the Conopois (see page 26).

Independent double action

Models in this category represent the top of the professional airbrush range. The dexterity required to operate this airbrush cannot be learned overnight, but that should not prevent the committed beginner from investing in one. Downward pressure of the lever regulates air supply and backward pressure regulates paint supply. This variable paint:air ratio makes an unlimited range of effects and finishes possible.

A wide range of features and accessories is available and it is really a matter of identifying your needs and choosing a model that meets them — ask for advice from a local specialist airbrush dealer.

Independent double action airbrushes can be put to almost any use, but they are essential for technical illustration, photoretouching, medical illustration, acrylics on canvas and precision model making.

Among the major manufacturers of independent double action airbrushes are Badger (see page 31), de Vilbiss (see page 29) , Paasche (see page 27) and Iwata (see page 28).

SPECIAL CATEGORY AIRBRUSHES

These include the jumbo models for large-scale work (see page 32), the spray gun (see page 33) for heavy duty spraying and the ultimate airbrush option — the Paasche AB Turbo (see page 34).

CHOOSING THE RIGHT AIRBRUSH

Before investing in an airbrush, consider what you want to use it for and what you want it to achieve. Generally speaking, the more sophisticated — and expensive — an airbrush is, the more time and skill are needed to use it successfully.

THE MAJOR TYPES

This survey of twelve of the major brands of airbrush provides an overview of the range of models to consider when you buy an airbrush and is designed to help you identify the airbrush best suited in both design and sophistication to your particular purposes. Before buying, consider also the range of air sources (see pages 38 to 45) and other accessories (see page 36) on offer.

A thorough investigation of the airbrushes on the market today would turn up hundreds of different brand names and many different countries of origin from Taiwan to Spain, but a practised eye could match any of them almost exactly to one of these twelve models.

THE BRUSHES FEATURED

HUMBROL MODELER'S
Single action external mix spray gun

More a spray gun than an airbrush, the Humbrol Modeler's airbrush is the most basic design included in this section. It is ideal wherever large areas of flat color without detail are required, and is widely used for working with stencils, decorating stage scenery, spraying oil or rustproofer, preparing ceramic underglazes, simple illustration and, true to its name, applying basic color to models.

This type of spray gun can be bought for a fraction of the cost of more complex designs. If you are completely new to airbrushing, having a go with a Humbrol is an inexpensive way of introducing yourself to the feel of an airbrush.

The Humbrol Modeler's airbrush features simple air and paint controls which allow the spray pattern to be varied. Enamels, artist's colors and any liquid that can be thinned to the consistency of milk can be sprayed through it.

How it works

The design is simple. The air and paint meet outside the head of the airbrush, the paint is atomized and roughly diffused, and the result – compared to that produced by more sophisticated models – is a fairly coarse spray. To operate, you hold the airbrush as if it were a pen and press downward on the air release lever with your forefinger. There are three adjustable features: the air supply can be pre-set within a range of 6 settings, setting 1 for a soft, spattery spray and setting 6 for a hard, blocked spray; the paint supply can be regulated with the paint jet adjustment ring; and the air jet can also be adjusted to create different spray patterns. No adjustments can be made while spraying. If the airbrush is being used for long periods, the paint tip may need resetting from time to time.

Features

- Spray pattern range from a width of ¾ in/18 mm to 2 in/5 cm
- Screw-on paint jar
- Operates on 15 to 50 psi/1 to 3.3 bar, normal operating pressure 30 psi/2 bar
- Compatible with all air systems
- Suitable for use with all correctly thinned media
- Accessories provided with the airbrush include a spare paint jar, and a 50 in/127 cm length of air hose with an air volume control fitted

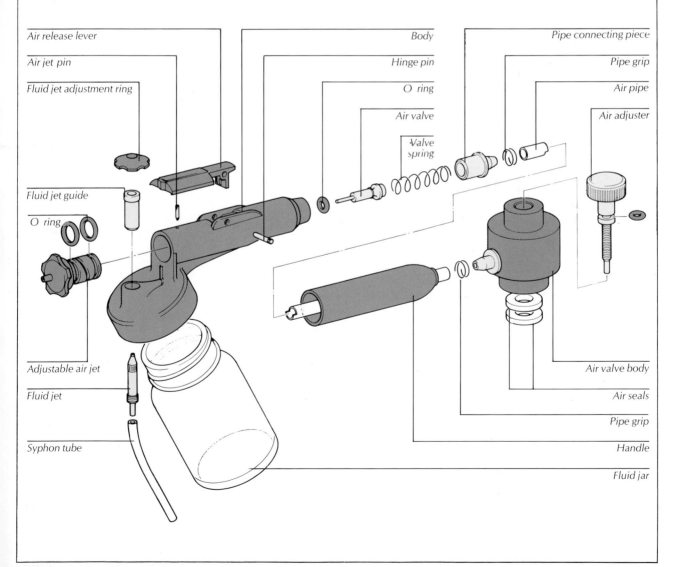

Air release lever

Air jet pin

Fluid jet adjustment ring

Fluid jet guide

O ring

Adjustable air jet

Fluid jet

Syphon tube

Body

Hinge pin

O ring

Air valve

Valve spring

Pipe connecting piece

Pipe grip

Air pipe

Air adjuster

Air valve body

Air seals

Pipe grip

Handle

Fluid jar

BADGER 350
Single action external mix with needle

This is one of the most popular single action airbrushes. It is capable of achieving the high finish required in modeling and is widely used in the ceramics industry for spraying simple patterns on porcelain. Other uses include fabric design, simple retouching, basic graphic work and textured work. It falls in the middle of the single action range, between the more basic external mix model with no needle and the internal mix model, which is capable of a finer spray.

The Badger 350 is easy to maintain. The body is constructed of molded high impact nylon resistant to solvents and paint chemicals. The air tip and head assembly are the main components.

Spare tyre valve adapter
With the modeling or car customizing enthusiast working in a garage in mind, Badger produce a spare tyre valve adapter which attaches to the tyre and the air hose (see page 40). The tyre should not be inflated above 40 psi/2.6 bar.

How it works
This robust external mix with needle airbrush is simply operated by depressing the control lever (see diagram). The air and paint are separately propelled and meet outside the head of the airbrush, producing a relatively coarse spray with a stippled or large dot pattern. The air tip directs the air jet and the needle delivers the paint, and both are adjustable. They have to be preset, however, and it is not possible to adjust the spray pattern while working.

Features
● Produces a coarse or stippled spray pattern, ranging in width from $\frac{1}{8}$ in/3 mm to 2 in/5 cm
● Adjustable head assembly for different widths of spray
● Three alternative head assemblies
Fine (example below left) sprays a line $\frac{1}{8}$ in/3 mm to l in/2.5 cm wide. For use with thin media, e.g. inks, dyes, water-colors, gouache
Medium (example below center) sprays a line $\frac{1}{4}$ in/6 mm to $1\frac{3}{8}$ in/3.5 cm wide. For use with medium viscosity media, e.g. thinned down lacquers and enamels
Heavy (example below right) sprays a line $\frac{1}{2}$ in/12 mm to 2 in/5 cm wide. For use with heavy viscosity media, e.g. ceramic underglazes and oil paints
● Suction feed, with a choice of $\frac{3}{4}$ oz/22 cc and 2 oz/60 cc quick-change paint jars or $\frac{1}{4}$ oz/7 cc color cup
● Compatible with all air systems
● Operates on 15 to 50 psi/1 to 3.3 bar. pressure

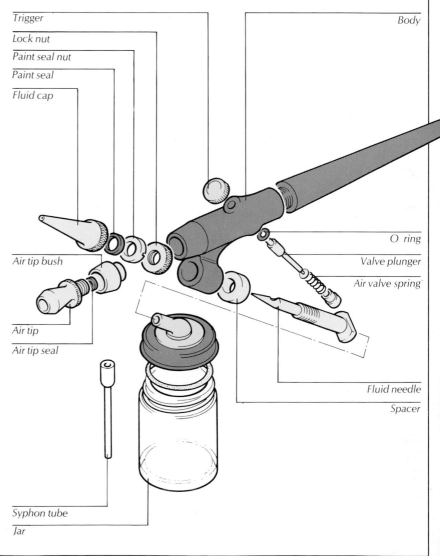

Trigger

Lock nut

Paint seal nut

Paint seal

Fluid cap

Air tip bush

Air tip

Air tip seal

Syphon tube

Jar

Body

O ring

Valve plunger

Air valve spring

Fluid needle

Spacer

THAYER & CHANDLER E Single action, internal mix

The Thayer and Chandler Model E is an internal mix design and represents the top end of the single action range. It was originally designed for industrial use, where touch-up or closely confined spray was required.

It can produce a much finer and more professional spray than external mix models and is particularly popular among hobbyists. Its uses include fabric spraying, fine lettering, car and bike customizing, taxidermy, ceramic decoration and modeling. All types of lacquer and enamel can be sprayed through this airbrush, and its metal construction is resistant to chemicals and solvents.

How it works

The color is atomized within the body of the airbrush and is thoroughly diffused by the time it meets the surface being sprayed. A needle adjuster on the handle can be preset to control the amount of color expelled and the width of the spray. When the trigger is depressed, the preset amount of color is released. The color cannot be regulated while spraying, however, and fine graduated work is not possible.

Features

● Spray pattern ranges from 1/16 in/1.5 mm to 2 in/5 cm.
● Suction-feed, with a choice of three colour jars in 1oz/30 cc, 2 oz/60 cc and 4 oz/120 cc sizes
● Compatible with all air systems
● Suitable for all types of water-based media, lacquers and enamels
● Accessories supplied with airbrush: 1 oz/30 cc color jar, color tube and brush hanger

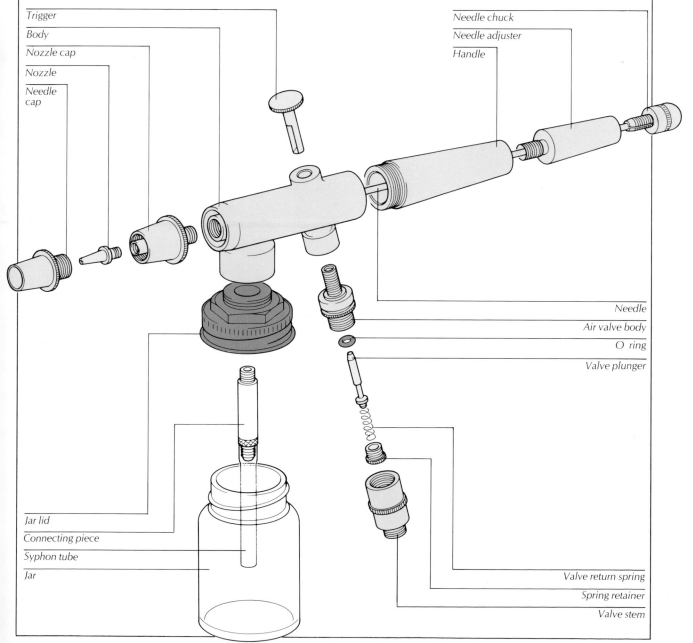

Trigger
Body
Nozzle cap
Nozzle
Needle cap

Needle chuck
Needle adjuster
Handle

Needle
Air valve body
O ring
Valve plunger

Jar lid
Connecting piece
Syphon tube
Jar

Valve return spring
Spring retainer
Valve stem

CONOPOIS F
Fixed double action

This popular airbrush, hand-made in Britain, is one of a small group of fixed double action airbrushes. It is easier to handle than an independent double action brush, but does not offer the same versatility in the range of effects it can create. It is widely used by illustrators for accurate, precise work. The very fine lines that it can produce make it suitable for technical illustration and other very detailed work.

How it works

As with independent double action airbrushes, the paint and air supply are both regulated by the finger-operated lever, but in the fixed double action model, the paint:air ratio is preset. It is not possible, for example, to expel a small amount of air with a large amount of paint. The Conopois offers greater flexibility than other fixed double action models – it features a needle adjusting ring, which allows the amount of color to be predetermined. The air pressure can then be adjusted while spraying to create a finer or coarser spray pattern.

Gentle depression of the control lever with the needle guards at the end of the body brushing the surface being sprayed will produce a fine line. Draw the brush back from the surface for a softer line. Firmer depression of the lever will broaden the spray.

Features

● Spray pattern width from a hairline to 2 in/5 cm
● Two alternative color housings – a color cup and a larger $1/16$ oz/2 cc color pot, offering a quick change facility
● Suitable for all media
● Normal operating pressure 30 psi/ 2 bar
● Stipple cap available
● Needle adjusting ring to predetermine the amount of color expelled
● Adjustable for left and right handed users.

Quick color change using the Conopois

Decide which colors you will need for the job in hand. Premix each one in a color pot and put all the color pots in the covered stand. If you are working in monochrome, for example, you might use process white and black with four intermediate grays numbered 1 to 4.

Select a color pot and hold it, but do not press it in, to the color cup socket. Depress the lever, and a charge of color will be drawn into the airbrush. Replace the pot and spray. Repeat the process if more color is needed or go on to the next tint in the same way. If you are covering a broader area with one of the colors, insert the color pot right into the airbrush.

Flushing with water between each pot change will only be necessary for color work. Keep a water filled color pot in the stand and charge the brush with water by holding the pot to the color cup socket and spraying for a moment.

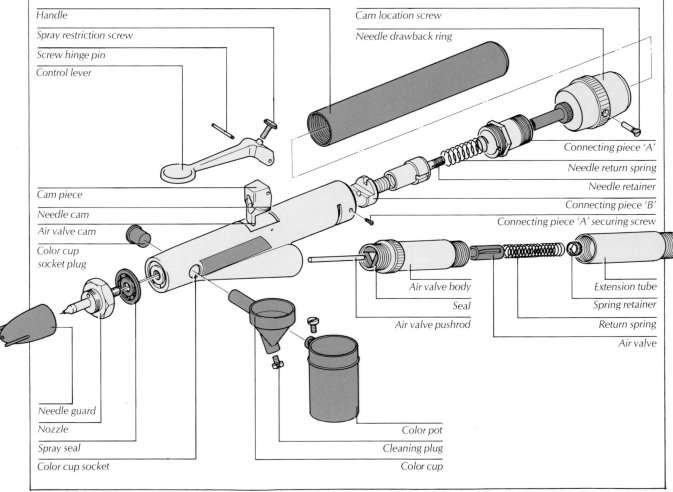

Handle
Spray restriction screw
Screw hinge pin
Control lever
Cam piece
Needle cam
Air valve cam
Color cup socket plug
Needle guard
Nozzle
Spray seal
Color cup socket
Cam location screw
Needle drawback ring
Connecting piece 'A'
Needle return spring
Needle retainer
Connecting piece 'B'
Connecting piece 'A' securing screw
Air valve body
Seal
Air valve pushrod
Extension tube
Spring retainer
Return spring
Air valve
Color pot
Cleaning plug
Color cup

PAASCHE V
Independent double action

The Paasche V is the ideal airbrush for detail, shading and tinting. It is a favorite among technical illustrators, graphic artists, photoretouchers and restorers, indeed any artist who wants a wide range of fine spray patterns.

Two interchangeable nozzle sets are available — a fine nozzle for smaller spray patterns and a medium nozzle for larger patterns and rapid coverage.

How it works

The trigger on the Paasche V allows fine control of both the air and paint supplies. You push the trigger down for air and pull backwards for paint. This model has a presetting wheel which can be adjusted to limit the minimum amount of paint sprayed from the nozzle.

Features

● Two alternative nozzle sets
Fine produces a spray ranging from 1/64 in/0.4 mm to I in/2.5 cm
Medium produces a spray ranging from 1/32 in/0.8 mm to I in/2.5 cm,
● Suction-feed, with a choice of 1/8 oz/3.5 cc side color cup or I oz/30 cc color jar
● Accessories provided with airbrush: 1/8 oz/3.5 cc metal color cup, I oz/ 30 cc color jar

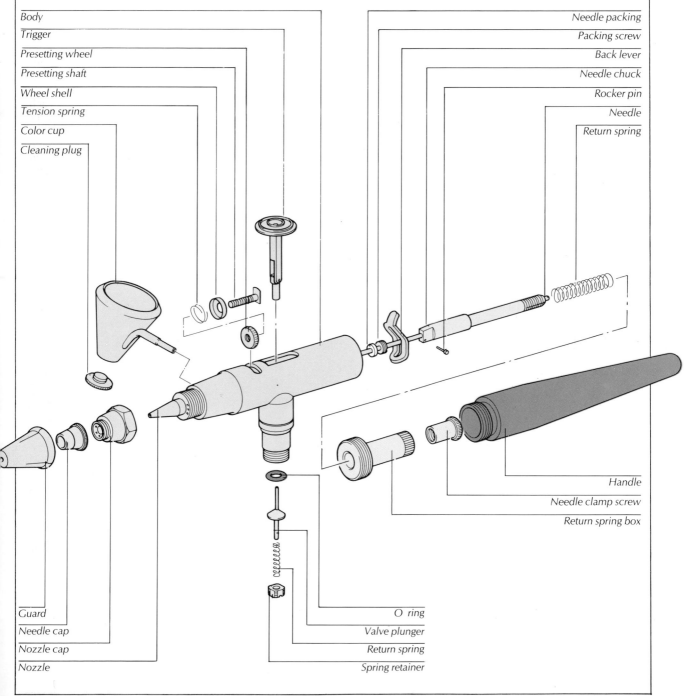

Body
Trigger
Presetting wheel
Presetting shaft
Wheel shell
Tension spring
Color cup
Cleaning plug

Needle packing
Packing screw
Back lever
Needle chuck
Rocker pin
Needle
Return spring

Guard
Needle cap
Nozzle cap
Nozzle

O ring
Valve plunger
Return spring
Spring retainer

Handle
Needle clamp screw
Return spring box

27

IWATA HP-B Independent double action

The Iwata HP-B is a top quality professional airbrush, designed for fine to medium detail work. Whatever your field of airbrush art, if you need to produce precise, fine work, a model of this quality is worth investing in.

The HP-B is a gravity feed model with a built in color cup. This has the advantage of being less prone to clogging and easier to clean. A suction feed side cup version – the HP-SB – is also available. This was developed in response to requests for a quick color change facility.

The body of the HP-B is constructed of chrome-plated brass and can be used with acrylics, gouache, transparent watercolors, dyes, inks, etc.

How it works
The principle is the same as for all double action models. To spray, you press down on the control lever and pull back with forefinger or thumb. To stop spraying, you push the control lever forward and remove your finger. If you draw the lever back, but not down, a large drop of color may jet out.

Features
● Built-in ¹⁄₁₆oz/1.5 cc color cup
● Nozzle diameter 0.2 mm
● Normal operating pressure 30 psi/2 bar
● Optional preset adjustment handle, which limits the backward movement of the needle
● Accessories provided with the airbrush include a nozzle wrench, a parts list and an instruction leaflet

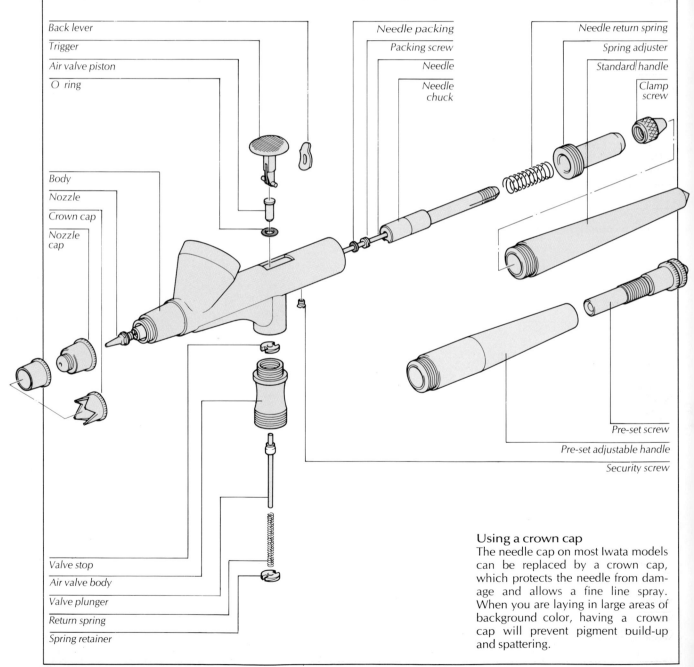

Back lever
Trigger
Air valve piston
O ring
Body
Nozzle
Crown cap
Nozzle cap
Valve stop
Air valve body
Valve plunger
Return spring
Spring retainer

Needle packing
Packing screw
Needle
Needle chuck

Needle return spring
Spring adjuster
Standard handle
Clamp screw

Pre-set screw
Pre-set adjustable handle
Security screw

Using a crown cap
The needle cap on most Iwata models can be replaced by a crown cap, which protects the needle from damage and allows a fine line spray. When you are laying in large areas of background color, having a crown cap will prevent pigment build-up and spattering.

DE VILBISS SUPER 63A Independent double action

De Vilbiss is a long established company, which has been going since the turn of the century. Their hard-wearing independent double action models – the Super 63A, Super 63E and Sprite – are widely used in Europe.

The 63A is a professional tool, particularly suitable for photoretouching and other delicate work – it can produce a hairline of color in the hands of a practiced artist. The color is housed in a paint well in the body of the brush, rather than a color cup. The 63E produces a slightly thicker line than the 63A, and has a larger reservoir – a ⅙ oz/5 cc color bowl. It is more suitable for spraying large areas. Both models are gravity feed.

How it works
De Vilbiss models are slightly differently constructed from most other airbrushes. They feature different components, such as the floating tip nozzle assembly rather than a screw-in assembly.

Downward pressure on the lever allows compressed air to enter the airbrush. The air pressure is controlled by a mushroom valve. Backward pressure on the lever controls the amount of color sprayed, by withdrawing the needle. The cam control can be pre-set to regulate the amount of color released. The needle return spring shuts off the color cleanly and instantly.

Features
● Suitable for use with watercolor, ink, acrylic, enamel – any medium of the consistency to pass through a strainer
● Matched nozzle and air cap are available as a set
● Compatible with all types of air source
● A rubber washer at the end of the air hose ensures an airtight seal between the hose and airbrush, eliminating loss of pressure. However, if this model is used a great deal with enamels and thinners, the washer is liable to perish and need replacing

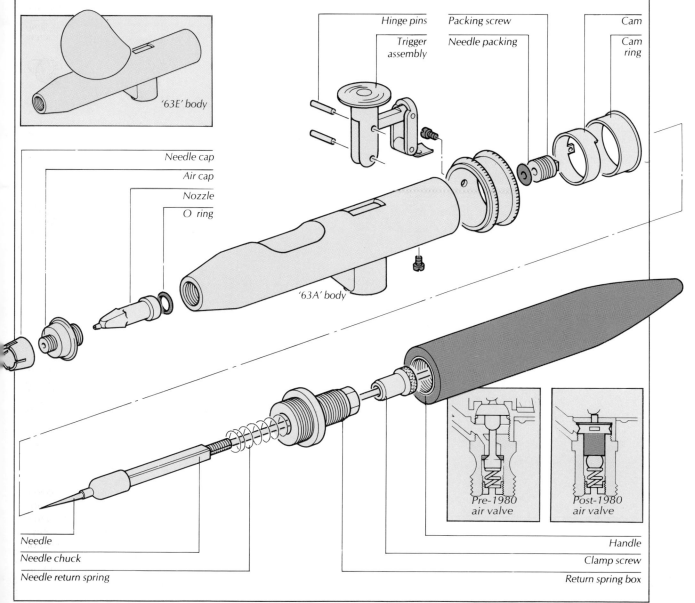

'63E' body

Hinge pins
Trigger assembly
Packing screw
Needle packing
Cam
Cam ring

Needle cap
Air cap
Nozzle
O ring

'63A' body

Pre-1980 air valve
Post-1980 air valve

Needle
Needle chuck
Needle return spring

Handle
Clamp screw
Return spring box

EFBE CI HINGED "DESIGNER" Fixed double action

The German-made Efbe C1 Hinged airbrush, also known as the "Designer", is one of six Efbe airbrushes, each developed for a particular function ranging from retouching to light industrial models. It is distinguished from the de Vilbiss Super 63, Paasche V and other airbrushes in its class by its paint housing – a swivel color cup which can be positioned at any angle – and by

its fixed action operating lever (described below).

How it works

The inner workings of the Efbe C1 Hinged are very similar to those of other double action airbrushes. The difference is that you don't press down on the finger lever to open the air valve – the backward action of the finger lever releases both air and medium in a pre-set ratio. The volume of air and medium increases as you draw the lever back.

Features

● Five interchangeable color cups for quick color change work, making the "Designer" a good choice for multi-color, multi-tone work
● Adjustable ¼ oz/6 cc capacity suction-feed swivel color cup – you can work at any angle without danger of the paint spilling out
● 0.3 mm nozzle
● Normal operating pressure 22–30 psi/1.5 – 2 bar
● Tempered nickel silver alloy needle for durability and strength

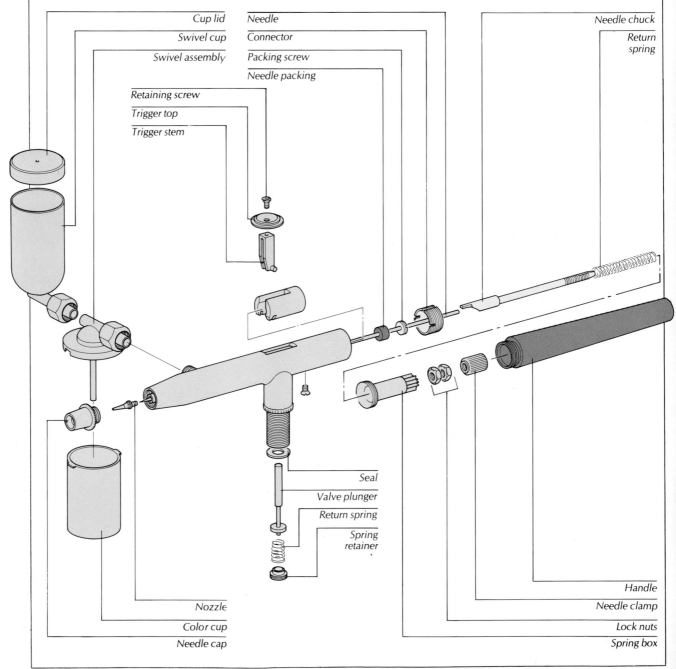

Cup lid
Swivel cup
Swivel assembly
Retaining screw
Trigger top
Trigger stem

Needle
Connector
Packing screw
Needle packing

Needle chuck
Return spring

Seal
Valve plunger
Return spring
Spring retainer

Nozzle
Color cup
Needle cap

Handle
Needle clamp
Lock nuts
Spring box

BADGER 150
Independent double action

The Badger 150 is a very versatile airbrush, which is particularly suitable for illustrators and for any large-scale work. It can be used with any medium that is reducible to the consistency of double cream – ceramic glazes, inks, dyes and so on. It is a suction-feed model, enabling you to make quick changes of color.

It is available in three head assembly/ needle sets – fine (XF), medium (IL) and large (HD) nozzles – which are interchangeable. It is constructed of metal, except for the Teflon needle bearing and head assembly seal. The seal prevents air escaping into the paint passage and causing a jerky spray.

How it works

The Badger 150 is operated much like any other double action airbrush – press the trigger down for air and backward for paint. However, it features a presetting screw which can be used to regulate the minimum amount of paint emitted.

Features

● Three interchangeable paint housings are available – 3/4 oz/22cc and 2 oz/60cc color jars and a 1/4 oz/7 cc color cup
● Three alternative head assemblies
Fine (XF) sprays from a pencil line to l in/2.5 cm wide. For use with low viscosity media, e.g. very thin acrylics, watercolors, gouache, inks and dyes
Medium (IL) sprays a line from 1/16 in/1.5 mm to 1⅜ in/3.5 cm wide. Can handle medium viscosity media, e.g. thinned hobby lacquers and enamels
Large (HD) sprays a line 1/8 in 3 mm to 2 in/5 cm wide. Designed for use with high viscosity media, e.g. automotive paints, ceramic glazes and acrylic
● Line-adjusting nut, which is used to lock the control lever in position
● Perforated air cap to reduce the risk of color spreading when spraying close to the support
● Self-lubricating needle preventing metal to metal contact and ensuring smooth lever action
● Accessories included in the Badger 150 set: 2 sizes of jar and color cup, protective cap, spare needle, wrench for head, airbrush holder, instruction booklet and plastic case

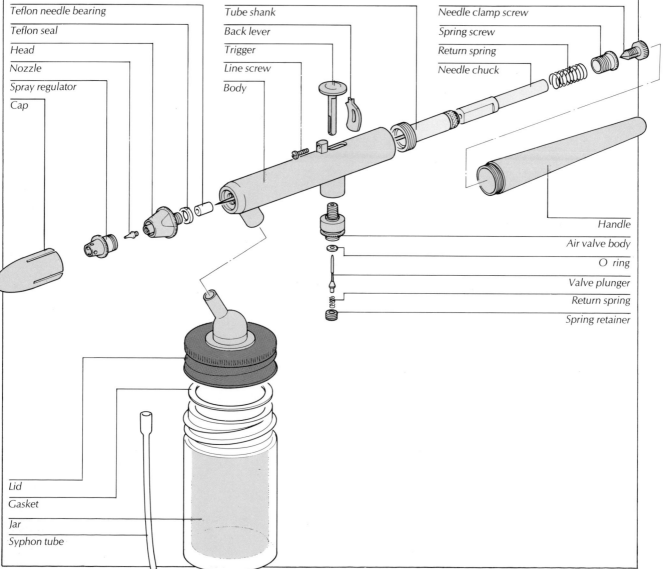

Teflon needle bearing
Teflon seal
Head
Nozzle
Spray regulator
Cap

Tube shank
Back lever
Trigger
Line screw
Body

Needle clamp screw
Spring screw
Return spring
Needle chuck

Handle
Air valve body
O ring
Valve plunger
Return spring
Spring retainer

Lid
Gasket
Jar
Syphon tube

IWATA JUMBO HP-E Independent double action

The Iwata HP-E Jumbo is a heavy duty independent double action airbrush designed for working on a large scale. It combines the covering capacity of the smaller spray guns with the refinement of the double action airbrush. It is the ideal airbrush for working on a large scale – for photoretouching, fabric art, airbrushing posters and large artwork, mural painting and modeling.

The HP-E is a gravity-feed model but the same design is also available with suction-feed color housing. The gravity-feed airbrush has two advantages – the flow of color to the needle is more immediate and positive, and it is easier to clean. The HP-BE suction-feed ver-

sion has a bottle system, and the great advantage here is that you can change color very quickly by simply unscrewing and replacing one paint jar with another.

As well as having a greater covering capacity, the Jumbo model can cope with heavier paints than a standard double action airbrush.

How it works

The design is the same as that of the other Iwata independent double action models – you press the control lever down to release air and pull it back to release paint. Because it is de-

signed for use with high viscosity paints it has additional features making it easier to strip down and clean the internal components. The fluid cup is fastened with a taper-nut and can be easily removed.

Features

- Interchangeable larger nozzle sizes – 0.6 and 0.8mm
- Removable 40 cc color cup with lid to prevent spillage
- Available in both gravity-feed (HP-E) and suction-feed (HP-BE) designs
- Suitable for higher viscosity media, including lacquers and enamels

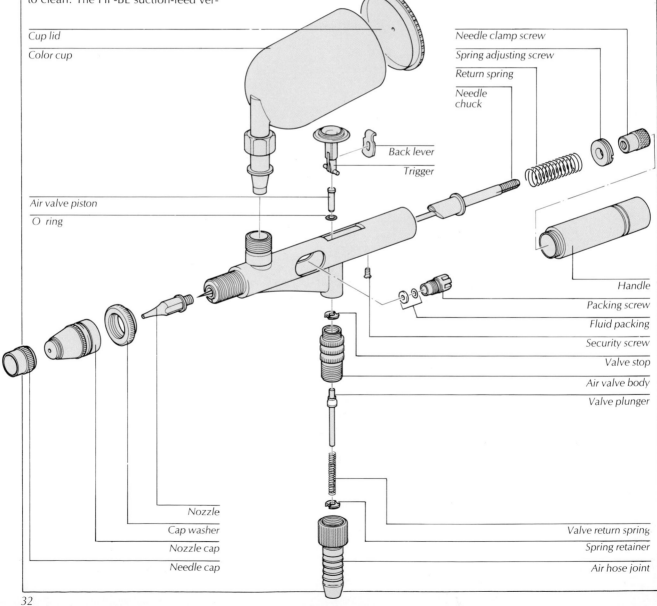

Cup lid
Color cup
Needle clamp screw
Spring adjusting screw
Return spring
Needle chuck
Back lever
Trigger
Air valve piston
O ring
Handle
Packing screw
Fluid packing
Security screw
Valve stop
Air valve body
Valve plunger
Nozzle
Cap washer
Nozzle cap
Needle cap
Valve return spring
Spring retainer
Air hose joint

IWATA RG2 SPRAY GUN
Special category

This spray gun is a special category brush. It is larger than an airbrush, but smaller than an industrial spray gun. It is made by the Japanese airbrush company, Iwata, as part of their range of professional airbrushes.

It is particularly suitable for car customizing and touch—up work, for textile spraying on a large scale, and for signwriting. Many professional airbrush artists have an RG2 as well as an independent double action model, which they use for laying in large areas of background color.

How it works
The RG2 spray gun works on the same principle as fixed double action airbrushes — paint and air are released in a preset ratio. A trigger beneath the body of the brush releases first air as it is gently depressed and then air and color. The amount of color can be preset to a wide range of settings using the fluid adjusting screw. The large capacity color cups have a swivel design, and can be turned away from either a vertical or horizontal work surface. The recommended spraying distance is 15 to 20 cm.

Features
● Three alternative needle and nozzle sets, which produce a wide range of spray patterns from $\frac{5}{8}$ in/15 mm to $1\frac{3}{8}$ in/3.5 cm.
● 3 large capacity color cups with covers to prevent spillage — 130 cc, 220 cc, 250 cc
● Normal operating pressure 40 psi/ 2.6 bar
● Runs off a large air compressor
● Fluid adjusting knob to preset amount of color expelled

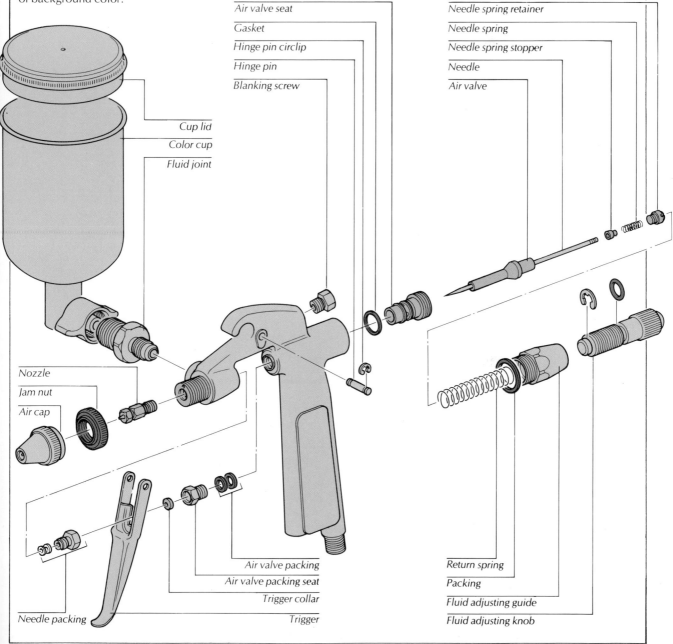

Air valve seat
Gasket
Hinge pin circlip
Hinge pin
Blanking screw

Needle spring retainer
Needle spring
Needle spring stopper
Needle
Air valve

Cup lid
Color cup
Fluid joint

Nozzle
Jam nut
Air cap

Air valve packing
Air valve packing seat
Trigger collar
Trigger

Needle packing

Return spring
Packing
Fluid adjusting guide
Fluid adjusting knob

PAASCHE AB TURBO
Special category

If you have mastered the techniques of the conventional double action air-brush, an even more sophisticated option is open to you – the Paasche AB Turbo. It is expensive, temperamental and highly sensitive, but for producing the finest detailed work it has no equal. Because it is such a special tool, it is not recommended for the beginner.

The Paasche AB Turbo is an independent double action gravity feed model. It gives the artist the ability to control the speed of the spray – a unique feature in airbrushes. The Turbo can only be used with water-based paints, inks and dyes – it is not suitable for the hobbyist's lacquers or the ceramist's enamels. Skilful and practiced handling of the Turbo can produce the most subtle of effects, as well as grades of fine line, shades and tints. In order to create these effects, however, it must maintained in perfect working order.

If you do consider buying a Turbo, be prepared to spend a lot of time simply handling and experimenting with it.

How it works
What makes it a turbo is its air-driven turbine wheel, which rotates at a speed of up to 20,000 rpm.

The turbine vibrates the needle back and forth at high speed. Color is drawn through a slot in the needle bearing along which the needle oscillates. This action creates surface tension and causes the color to cling to the needle. The back and forth motion of the needle forces the color into the path of the air jet. On each oscillation, pressurized air blasts the needle clear , the needle then returns for more color and the process is repeated in a very high-frequency action. The spray emerges to one side of the airbrush body and not directly in line with it, as in other airbrushes. The AB throws a very directed spray so only limited masking is necessary.

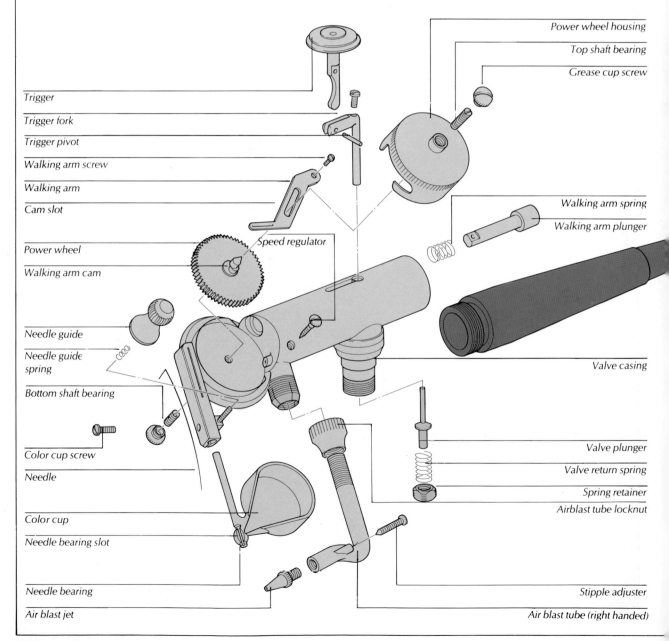

Trigger

Trigger fork

Trigger pivot

Walking arm screw

Walking arm

Cam slot

Power wheel

Walking arm cam

Needle guide

Needle guide spring

Bottom shaft bearing

Color cup screw

Needle

Color cup

Needle bearing slot

Needle bearing

Air blast jet

Speed regulator

Power wheel housing

Top shaft bearing

Grease cup screw

Walking arm spring

Walking arm plunger

Valve casing

Valve plunger

Valve return spring

Spring retainer

Airblast tube locknut

Stipple adjuster

Air blast tube (right handed)

Features

● Gravity feed, with built in color cup and color cup adjusting/regulating screw

● Self-feeding grease cups to lubricate the turbine

● Stipple adjustment screw at the air nozzle, controlling the amount of air coming through and hence the degree of spatter

● Turbine speed control

● Left and right hand models available

● Suitable for use with water-based paints, inks and dyes only – not lacquers or enamels, even if thinned down

● Accessories supplied with the brush: 6 ft/180 cm air hose, 12 spare needles, screwdriver, tweezers, bench hanger and instruction booklet

The capabilities of the Turbo

This example of airbrush art was executed almost entirely without masks which are usually considered essential when creating an image containing such detail. The artist has exploited the Paasche Turbo's ability to spray extremely fine lines – something only made possible by its design and the unique role played by the needle. A soft, paintbrush-like quality can be achieved using this technique.

CLEANING AND LUBRICATING TOOLS AND EQUIPMENT

You do not normally need special tools or materials for cleaning and lubricating an airbrush – most of what you require can be bought in a genera store.

Petroleum jelly is the best material for lubricating the needle; use a light engineering oil to keep other moving parts in good condition. If you have an airbrush with a screw-in nozzle, you may need a sealing compound that will guarantee an airtight seal.

A selection of straight and angled brushes is useful.

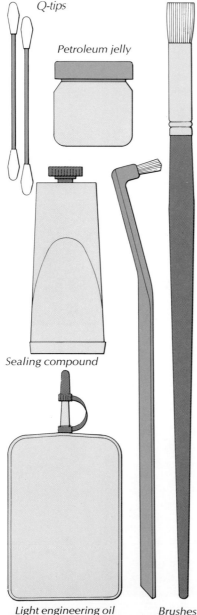

Q-tips

Petroleum jelly

Sealing compound

Light engineering oil   *Brushes*

USEFUL TOOLS

If you are stripping down an airbrush completely, you will almost certainly need special tools, that have been purposely made for the job by the manufacturers. However, if you are just carrying out a routine maintenance, you can almost always improvise using standard tools.

Pliers are undoubtedly useful for stripping down and assembling an airbrush but they can also be ruthless on soft metals and should be used gingerly. Parallel-grip pliers are less likely to tear or damage an airbrush but needle-nosed pliers are useful for gripping small or awkwardly sited pieces.

An adjustable wrench is invaluable if you are stripping down an airbrush. Choose a good quality type which doesn't allow any play between the jaws.

Adjustable wrench

Parallel-grip pliers

Tweezers

Needle-nosed pliers

Screwdrivers

SPECIALIST TOOL KITS

For anyone planning a complete strip down of an airbrush, a specialist tool kit is essential. Virtually all airbrush manufacturers make special tool kits which are specific to certain models and, although they are relatively expensive, they are a worthwhile investment if you plan to do all your own servicing. The reason why special tools are needed for complete strip downs is because they are less likely to damage vulnerable parts than standard tools which are found in the normal tool bag.

Most tool kits contain wrenches and sockets for removing delicate items like nozzles and valves – without these you run the risk of damaging the soft metals which are used to make many of the most delicate components.

The range of tools you get in any one kit will vary according to the complexity of the airbrush, but in each case, they should enable you to dismantle all the moving parts completely.

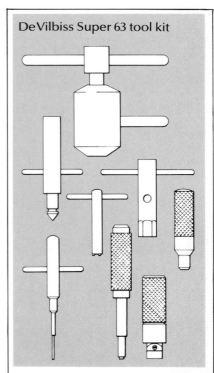

DeVilbiss Super 63 tool kit

This tool kit is specially designed for the DeVilbiss Super 63. It contains such items as a blanking off tool and a wrench for removing the valve. Without a tool kit like this, stripping down an airbrush completely is extremely difficult to do without damaging the most delicate components.

AIR HOSES

The air hose is a vital piece of equipment that connects the airbrush to the air source. Three types are generally used in airbrushing—the clear plastic hose, the braided rubber hose, and the curled coil hose. Whichever you choose, remember that neither airbrush nor compressor air hose connector has a standard thread size. Check that the connectors at each end of the hose you are buying are compatible with your equipment. If not, adapters are always available.

Hoses come in various lengths from 4 ft/1.2 m to 12 ft/3.6 m. Anything longer becomes potentially dangerous and impractical if it means you are a long way from your air source; consider installing a piped-in system that will bring the air regulator up to your work station. Suitable lengths for use with an air can are 4 ft/1.2 m and 8 ft/2.4 m. With a compressor beneath your work surface an 8 ft/2.4 m hose gives the greatest flexibility.

You can make up your own hose length, but it is tricky and not recommended. On a safety note, check your air hose regularly for leaks and particularly if it gets snagged under a chair or caught in some way. If there are any leaks, your compressor will be overworked trying to compensate. In fact you should check your whole system regularly for leaks.

TYPES OF AIR HOSE

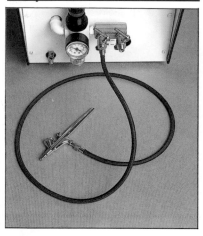

Braided rubber hose
This is the most popular type of hose. Although it is expensive, it is hard-wearing and durable.

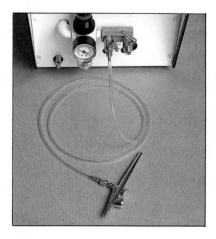

Clear plastic hose
This type of hosing is relatively inexpensive but is easily damaged. It has the advantage that you can see if moisture forms inside it.

Curled coil hose
Made from polythene, this type of hose is a newcomer to the market and is also the most expensive. It is very strong and curls away safely when you don't need it. It is also lightweight.

Quick-release fittings
Thanks to the introduction of quick-release fittings, connecting air hoses to compressors and airbrushes no longer relies on wrenches, washers and thread adapters. Quick-release fittings operate on the "bayonet" principle: a simple push and a twist ensures an airtight seal. Some pieces of equipment are fitted with quick-release fittings as standard but with others you may have to buy them separately. They are a good investment as they save time and anguish. Your local airbrush supplier should have a stock of fittings, but, if not, contact the manufacturer direct.

DIAPHRAGM COMPRESSOR ADAPTER

If you buy your diaphragm compressor new it should bear a warning label saying that the compressor is only designed to be used with "bleeder type instruments". For safety reasons there must be an air bleed hole between compressor and air hose. If not you may get a terrific build-up of air in the compressor. This adapter has a pin-sized bleed hole and should be fitted between compressor and air hose. It is an apparently insignificant piece of equipment that should never be forgotten.

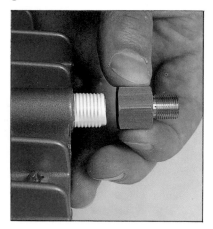

AIR SOURCES

After the airbrush the most important piece of equipment for the airbrush artist is the air source. It is compressed or pressurized air that atomizes the paint and propels it through the brush. As with airbrushes, there is a wide choice of air propellants, ranging from the inexpensive and basic air can to the highly sophisticated, professional silent storage compressors.

Choosing the right air source

Several factors will influence your initial choice of air source. You may have invested in a high-quality double action airbrush and it may seem pointless to team it with a cheap, erratic propellant, such as an air can or a diaphragm compressor. You may want the best air supply right from the start to ensure that you produce the best results. On the other hand, you may not want to invest in both top-quality airbrush and air source all at once. Cheap air sources are certainly an option for the amateur or occasional airbrush user. If you do go for a cheaper air source, always take into account its limitations and their effect on your work. When you are making your choice, there are many considerations.

WORK ENVIRONMENT

Space
Air sources vary in size from the hand-held propellant can to an oxygen cylinder to a heavy-duty industrial compressor, which needs a permanent housing site.

Noise
The extremely popular small diaphragm compressor, for example, makes a great deal of noise for its size, which you or those working around you might find distracting or disruptive.

Power supply
Propellant air cans can be used on site – for example, in a client's office for last-minute corrections. Mains-fed compressors can't be carried in a briefcase.
The full-time airbrush artist will need at least a small diaphragm model, whereas the occasional user may make do with a propellant can. Think of the long term, however. The cost of using propellant cans on a regular basis soon overtakes the initial investment in a small diaphragm model, and once you've bought it, it should give you a lifetime's service.

Price

Air sources vary in price as much as quality, from the spare tyre, which costs only effort, and the cheap propellant can, to the whole range of sophisticated storage compressors. Bear in mind that the cost of roughly 30 propellant cans is equal to that of a diaphragm compressor. And for perhaps half as much again you could buy a small silent compressor, with all the advantages of a constant air source and the peace and quiet that that brings.
This is perhaps the most decisive factor of all, particularly for the illustrator, photo retoucher and fine artist. The best-quality spray is produced using a non-pulsing silent compressor, where the air supply is automatically replenished as necessary. The poorest quality comes from the spare tire, where the air pressure is dropping from the moment you start using it.

Multi-user set-up

If you work alongside other airbrush artists, you should consider the larger silent compressors, which can run more than one airbrush at the same time.

COMPRESSED AIR CYLINDER

A very popular propellant in the US, large air cylinders can be difficult to service in the UK and Europe – you need to be near a supplier who can refill your tank. The compressed air tank has a metering valve on top and provides a steady air supply. However, it is cumbersome and extremely heavy.

What you need
A compressed air tank, a pressure regulator and measuring gauge, an air hose, and a trolley or set of wheels for moving it around.

Advantages
- Running costs: nil
- Lasts a long time
- No power supply needed
- Provides fairly constant air pressure until the air begins to run low
- Quiet
- Maintenance-free

Disadvantages
- Initial outlay: usually a hefty deposit on the canister
- Very heavy to move
- Takes up a lot of room
- Supplier to replenish air must be within reach

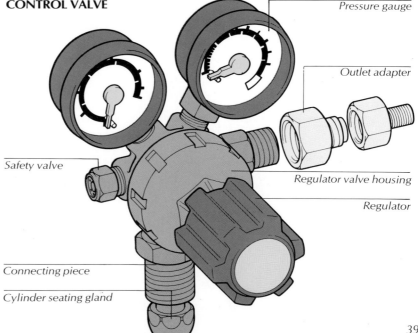

CONTROL VALVE

Pressure gauge

Outlet adapter

Regulator valve housing

Regulator

Safety valve

Connecting piece

Cylinder seating gland

PROPELLANT AIR CAN

For many beginners, this is the first choice. The initial outlay is very low in return for an adequate quality of air supply. Air cans are also widely used among the professionals, favored for their lightness, portability and flexibility. A recently developed accessory makes the air can an even more attractive option – a metered valve which shows how much air is left in the can. As the air is used up, the pressure falls and without this valve, the can will suddenly run out altogether, leaving the artist high and dry. If you don't have a metered valve, it is a case of getting to know by trial and error when the air level is falling below workable pressure. You can reckon on the pressure staying constant until the can is between a half and two-thirds used. At this point it is worth replacing the can, and setting the old can aside for producing spatter effects.

Another useful accessory for the air can is a control valve that varies the air pressure. This option allows you, for example, to drop the air pressure to produce a coarser dot pattern rather than working always at the same air pressure. Non-variable control valves are either open or closed – there is no intermediate setting.

What you need
Either a 12 oz/340 g or 20 oz/571 g air can (the 20 oz/571 g can is the more commonly used size), plus a spare, a control valve (adjustable if possible), and a flexible air hose. The metring valve is optional.

Advantages
● Inexpensive in the short run
● Widely available from graphic suppliers – buy it along with your paints and masking film
● Highly portable
● Power supply not required – can be used on site
● Quiet
● Ideal for the beginner
● Invaluable for any last-minute touch-up corrections

Disadvantages
● Expensive in the long run – 30 air cans equals a mini compressor
● Air pressure begins to drop once the can is a half to one-third empty
● Air supply may run out or become erratic in the middle of a piece of work, perhaps even ruining the work

Air can connection

1 To connect an air can to an airbrush you need a propellant control valve and a standard hose.

2 Make sure the control valve is in the closed position before fitting it to the can. Screw the valve into the can as far as possible – the control valve operates the self-sealing valve in the can. Because the cans are self-sealing, you can remove the control valve without losing any air remaining in the can.

3 Finally fit the air hose to the airbrush. Air cans are filled with non-flammable, non-toxic liquid gas, which is perfectly safe to work with. Empty cans should always be disposed of carefully.

FOOT PUMP AND STORAGE TANK

A surprisingly large number of airbrush artists still depend on this somewhat primitive and certainly exhausting air supply. Its early use dates back to the Second World War when it was used as an alternative to an electric compressor. It has survived since then in many graphic design studios, long after it could have reasonably been expected to have become extinct. To operate the system you fill the tank with air using a foot pump. You can then sit down to your work. The air pressure will gradually drop all the time you are spraying. When the air is exhausted, work stops and pumping begins again. The tank holds a fair amount of air, however, and filling it once should see you through a medium-sized job. While you may well invest in a secondhand model or welcome a cast-off from a fellow airbrush artist, think twice before buying this system new – sophisticated versions fall into the same price range as the mini-compressor.

What you need
The foot pump and storage tank, a pressure gauge, an air hose, a valve, and strong leg muscles

Advantages
● Running costs: effort only
● No power supply required
● Quiet

Disadvantages
● Air pressure cannot be kept constant
● Work interrupted as the air runs out
● Exhausting, time-consuming, and distracting to replenish the air supply
● Cost new equivalent to the cost of an electric mini compressor

SPARE TIRE

Just as the most simple airbrush is ideal for certain jobs, so the most basic air source has its place – usually for rough jobs in the garage. The tyre continues to be a favorite among modellers, who are not looking for, say, the perfect flat tone that the illustrator wants.

What you need
A spare tire still on the wheel rim, access to the air pump at a local gas station or your own foot pump, an air hose, and a pressure regulating gauge. If you are using a foot pump, you also need a great deal of energy for reflating the tire.

Advantages
• Initial expense: tire only
• Quiet and reasonably efficient for work in a garage
• Doesn't require mains power supply – in theory it could be used anywhere, but in practice is cumbersome and dirty

Disadvantages
• Uneven, poor quality air supply – the air pressure is continuously dropping from the moment you start spraying
• Dirty and damp
• Exhausting if you use a foot pump
• Heavy to move around
• Inexpensive alternatives are available, such as the propellant air can

Spare tire connection

1 If you use an inner tube as an air source, it must be inside the tyre and the tire must be on a rim. An inner tube on its own is not safe – it can be easily punctured and may explode if over-inflated.

Inflate the tire to 40 psi/2.6 either with a foot pump or at your local garage. Remove the dust cap that protects the valve on the tire.

2 Fit a special adapter that matches the tire valve thread size to the propellant control valve thread size.

3 Making sure the control valve is in the closed position – screw in as far as possible – connect it to the valve adapter on the tire.

4 Connect one end of a standard airbrush hose to the propellant control.

5 Open the control valve and you are all set to go. You can vary the pressure slightly with this set up, but there is no gauge, it is simply trial and error.

valve (still in the closed position) and the other end to airbrush.

DIAPHRAGM COMPRESSOR

There are at least twenty different versions of this smallest and cheapest of the compressors. They are all very similar: the basic design has not been changed or developed, although a variety of accessories are available to improve its efficiency. This is the first of the air sources described so far which allows work to continue uninterrupted – a constant air supply can be maintained by deft operation of a footswitch on the mains lead.

The main disadvantage of this type of compressor is the unevenness of the air flow, described below. High on the professional airbrush user's list of priorities is a constant, regular air flow, essential for producing an even, flat finish. Although the diaphragm compressor cannot be said to provide this, it is suitable for the purposes which do not require a flat finish.

How it works
The diaphragm compressor supplies instant air – you switch it on as you start to spray, and off when it is not in use. A fan pulls air into the compressor and pushes it into the cylinder. A rubber diaphragm then compresses the air and feeds it into the air hose. It is the action of the rubber diaphragm and the lack of an air reservoir that causes pulsing in the air flow. The effects of this irregularity can be sudden spatters interrupting a flat tone, or a fine line becoming broken. If you want to produce accurate detail, therefore, whether on ceramics, models, fabrics or artboard, you will either need something more sophisticated than this model or the whole gamut of accessories listed below.

What you need
The compressor and mains lead (as it comes).
A footswitch positioned on the mains lead within reach as you sit or stand at your work station. Otherwise you will be constantly getting up to turn the compressor on and off.

An anti-pulsation tank This is a bolt-on tank which is used to store air between the compressor and the air hose, in an attempt, as its name suggests, to sidestep irregularities in the air supply. It comes with a pressure regulator and a pressure gauge. The anti-pulsation tank was developed in response to demands from diaphragm-compressor owners for a regular air supply.

A moisture trap with pressure regulator and pressure gauge, which bolts on to the front of the compressor. A moisture trap is an essential accessory (see page 45). If the compressor is used a lot, however, and gets hot, heat is absorbed by the moisture trap rendering the filter less than a hundred per cent effective. To counteract this problem, a cooling hose and bracket attachment is available which mounts the moisture trap away from the body of the compressor – an accessory to an accessory.

The accumulated cost of the compressor with all these bolt-ons attached, brings it into the price range of a small storage compressor, which you might feel is a better investment. But, if your airbrush work doesn't involve fine detail and the pulsing air supply is not a problem, the diaphragm compressor will be perfectly adequate for your needs.

Advantages
- Maintenance-free
- Never needs oiling
- Robust and long lasting
- Inexpensive compared to storage compressors
- Compatible with all types of airbrush
- Small and lightweight (weight depends on the model, but will be between 5 and 12lb/2.3 and 5.5kg.

Disadvantages
- Power supply essential
- Pulsing air supply, or a complex arrangement of accessories
- Overheats if in constant use
- Noisy (imagine a lawn mower in an enclosed space)

Warning: It is essential with this type of compressor either to fit an air bleed-off valve or to drill a tiny hole (1/64 in 0.4 mm minimum) in the airbrush hose adapter to ensure a constant air bleed. This allows the motor to operate efficiently and prevents serious overheating.

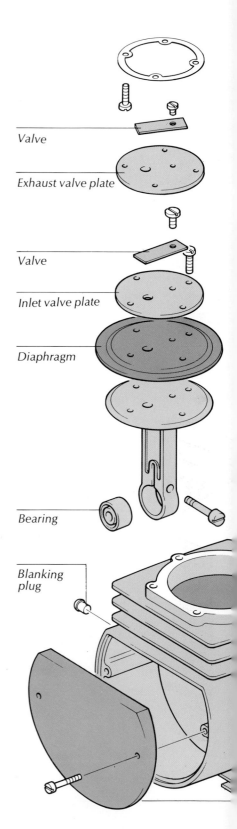

Valve

Exhaust valve plate

Valve

Inlet valve plate

Diaphragm

Bearing

Blanking plug

DIAPHRAGM COMPRESSOR ACCESSORIES

Pulse eliminators
Diaphragm compressors don't always produce a steady flow of air and this can be frustrating. One way of dealing with the problem is to fit a pulse eliminator (above) between the airbrush and the compressor. A pulse eliminator is essentially a valve which steadies the air flow.

Automatic switching
Some advanced diaphragm compressors like the Badger model (left) have an automatic switching system – as soon as the airbrush trigger is released, the compressor switches off.

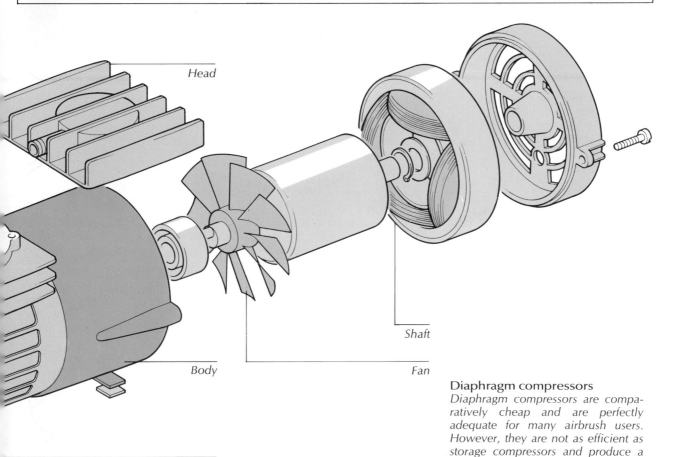

Head

Body

Shaft

Fan

Cover plate

Diaphragm compressors
Diaphragm compressors are comparatively cheap and are perfectly adequate for many airbrush users. However, they are not as efficient as storage compressors and produce a less regular air flow.

SMALL STORAGE COMPRESSORS

This is an extremely popular model used by top class illustrators around the world. The design is neat with boxed-in components, which include a small, silent refrigerator motor, a storage tank, and a pressure regulator with moisture trap. It generates an excellent air supply and will provide years of dependable service. Because the pressure in the tank is always higher than the pressure required to operate the airbrush, the air supply can be exactly regulated to a constant pressure. The pressure regulator has a built-in moisture trap which effectively filters off any impurities in the air delivered to the brush.

This compressor also features a safety valve, which lets off excess air if the pressure build-up is too great, and a check valve, which ensures that air cannot flow back from the tank toward the pumping system.

It is a piston machine and relies on oil for cooling and lubrication. There is an oil level glass, which indicates maximum and minimum levels and how much oil is in the piston chamber. Maintenance is therefore fairly simple.

The small compressor can be used with all types of airbrush, including spray gun and turbo models, but should not be operated at above 40 psi/2.6 bar.

It is ideal for running a single airbrush, but doesn't really have the capacity to run two airbrushes at full steam simultaneously.

How it works
There are manual and automatic versions of this compressor. With both types, when the motor is turned on, air is pumped into the tank. As you work, air is drawn into the air hose from the storage tank. The pressure regulator ensures that the air is supplied to the brush at a constant pressure enabling you to produce an even spray. When it reaches a pressure of 80 psi/5.2 bar, the automatic version switches off; the manual type has to be switched off by hand. The air pressure slowly drops as you use the brush, although always remaining at a higher pressure than the airbrush operating pressure. When the pressure drops to 60 psi/4 bar, the automatic compressor switches back on; the manual version has to be switched by hand. If you have a manual version,

remember to switch it off when it is up to pressure or it will be in danger of overheating.

What you need
The compressor as it comes. No accessories are required.

Advantages
- Reliably constant air supply
- Very compact – small enough to be desk-top
- Quiet and dependable

Disadvantages
- Relatively expensive
- Some maintenance involved, although little more than wielding an oil can
- Manual versions need switching on and off, interrupting work flow

Safety note. If you are working at high pressure with a storage compressor, make sure that you do not direct the spray at your hands or any part of your body. The pressure can sometimes be powerful enough to force pigment particles through your skin. If the pigment is toxic, this can be very dangerous.

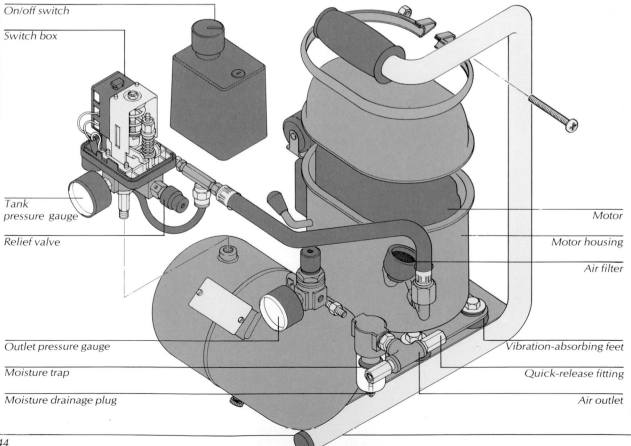

On/off switch

Switch box

Tank pressure gauge

Relief valve

Outlet pressure gauge

Moisture trap

Moisture drainage plug

Motor

Motor housing

Air filter

Vibration-absorbing feet

Quick-release fitting

Air outlet

SILENT STORAGE COMPRESSORS

The most sophisticated air sources are silent storage compressors. The smallest of all is a fairly new design which slots in between the mini or diaphragm compressor and the storage compressors. It is a silent compressor without a storage tank, in some models air is stored in the handle long enough to eliminate the pulsing problems associated with the mini compressor.

Silent storage compressor
This ¼ HP silent compressor is capable of powering a single airbrush.

LARGE STORAGE COMPRESSOR

The design of the larger model is almost identical to the small storage compressor already described. Both sizes are widely used in schools, colleges and studios but, among professionals, the larger version is perhaps the most popular model of all.

- It has a greater capacity storage tank, and the tank is laid out beside the motor rather than being boxed in.
- It stores a greater volume of air – the motor doesn't have to work so hard and therefore the compressor has a longer working life.
- A spray gun, for example, can be operated at up to 60 psi/4 bar with this more powerful compressor. The air pressure in the tank builds up to 120 psi/8 bar and comes down to 80 psi/5.2 bar before switching itself on again.
- It is not much bigger than its less powerful cousin, but it does sit more happily on the floor than on a desk.
- Up to four airbrushes can be run off this type of storage compressor simultaneously.
- It switches on and off automatically.

INDUSTRIAL COMPRESSOR

In large studios, art colleges and other big set-ups, where, say, 20 to 30 airbrushes may be in use at one time, the best option is an industrial compressor. It needs a permanent housing site and air has to be piped from it around the room. Each artist can have a separate air regulator on his or her desk and can therefore work independently.

Moisture traps

A moisture trap or filter is an essential feature of a compressor, but is not always built in. You may have to buy one as an accessory and bolt it on. Air contains moisture, and the function of the trap is to filter the moisture out before the air is pulled into the air hose for delivery to the brush. If moisture does get into the air hose, it will work its way up into the airbrush and spit out while you are spraying. This would be unwelcome at any time, but if you were just finishing spraying a perfectly even wash of color or adding final highlights to a piece of artwork, hours of work could be wasted.

Large storage compressor
This type of compressor is favoured by professionals because it has a large storage capacity and can power several airbrushes at the same time.

COMPRESSOR MAINTENANCE

Compressors are not particularly demanding machines and should give years of dependable service in return for very little attention. All types of compressor should be kept upright, whether on a desk or on the floor, and well ventilated with space for air to circulate on all sides.

Different models have different needs. The diaphragm compressor, for example, is virtually maintenance free. The silent storage compressor runs on oil – maintenance amounts to little more than regularly checking the oil for level and changing it from time to time.

Safety is an important consideration when working with any powered machinery. A new compressor should carry a test certificate but, if you are buying a second-hand compressor, try to choose a reputable make and check with your supplier if you are unsure about its worthiness.

Never use a compressor that seems to have developed a fault, such as frequent overheating, a whining motor, or an air leakage. Always have serious faults repaired by an authorized dealer rather trying to attempt them yourself.

ADAPTERS

A huge range of adapters is available and enables you to link up almost any airbrush with any air source. So, if you change your airbrush, it doesn't follow that you have to change your compressor.

Adapter uses
Adapters can be used to deal with awkward situations. The adapter below shows two different types of hose attached to an outlet manifold.

The range of adapters
A small selection of the huge range of airbrush adapters is illustrated on the right. Some adapters enable you to match the bores between air hoses and compressors, others compensate for differences in thread patterns.

Standard adapters
Most compressors have a standard metal fitting adapter for attaching the air hose – the air hose simply screws on (below).

Standard Adapters

Compressors have a standard metal fitting adapter for attaching the air hose — the air hose simply screws on.

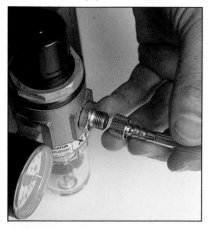

FITTING TO A QUICK-RELEASE CONNECTOR

Various quick-release or quick-fit connectors are available for running more than one airbrush off a compressor. The connector divides the air supply according to the number of airbrushes being run off the compressor — five is really the maximum number for a storage compressor, any more and you need to consider two compressors or an industrial set-up (see page 45).

Quick-release connectors are useful if you have to use different hoses for different airbrushes. Some airbrushes can only be used with a particular hose — for example, the Badger range uses a thin hose with a thin thread that is not compatible with other airbrushes.

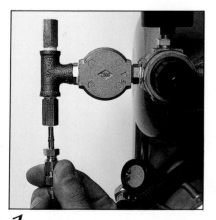

1 A quick-release connector has two parts — one for the compressor and one for the air hose.

2 Simply insert the jackplug attached to the end of the hose into the connector and screw it tight.

DIAPHRAGM COMPRESSORS General maintenance procedures

One of the great selling points of the diaphragm compressor is that it is virtually maintenance free — unlike the storage models, it doesn't run on oil. No machine should be completely ignored, however.

1 Check that the bleed hole is free of dirt — it must never be allowed to get blocked.

2 Check the electrics including the plug, from time to time.

3 Make sure that the compressor doesn't overheat — if it does, use it for shorter periods.

4 If it starts to make unusual whining noises, it may be nearing the end of its life, so have it checked by an authorized dealer.

Connecting to a regulator gauge

1 The gauge shown here is a combined pressure regulator and moisture filter gauge fitted to a storage compressor. With this system, the air hose attaches to the front of the regulator. Unscrew and remove the cap.

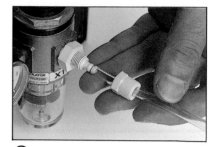

2 Push the air hose through the cap and screw the cap back on to the regulator unit.

Pressure adjustment

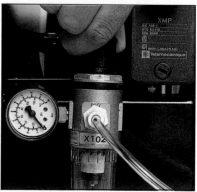

On a combined moisture filter and pressure regulator unit (above), the pressure can be adjusted by loosening the control knob locking ring on the regulator — clockwise to increase the pressure, and counterclockwise to decrease the pressure.

Draining off moisture

1 Excess moisture gathers in the bowl beneath the moisture trap. To drain it off, push up the plunger pin. The air pressure will force any moisture out.

2 A layer of water will gradually build up in the tank of a storage compressor. It should be drained regularly – if not, the base of the tank could rust through eventually, especially if it has high air pressures behind it. Simply unscrew the drain tap to let the water out – a piece of paper towel should be enough to mop it up.

STORAGE COMPRESSORS
Filling with oil

A storage compressor is like any other piece of expensive machinery in that it needs regular maintenance. The emphasis is on regular maintenance rather than just occasional maintenance.

One of the most important things to check frequently on a storage compressor is the oil level. This is usually easy to do on most machines because they have an oil level gauge which is easy to read. If the oil level should drop below the prescribed line, top up the reservoir immediately or else the moving parts won't be lubricated properly.

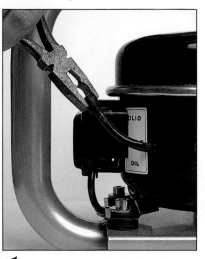

1 New compressors are supplied empty of oil for safety in transportation, and the first thing to do with a new compressor is to fill it with oil. The sight glass indicates the correct oil level (right).

2 With a pair of pliers carefully remove the rubber cap that protects the spout. The model shown here has one spout but some models have two. On a two-spout version, attach the air filter to either spout and seal the other with a rubber cap.

WATT/AMP.	135/0,96
VOLT/HZ	220·240/50
LIVELLO NIVEAU LEVEL PEGEL	

3 Fill with approved oil – supplied with a new compressor or available in quart containers from your supplier – to the level indicated on the sight glass.

4 Attach the air filter provided onto the spout. On a two-spout version, choose either spout and fix a protective cap to the other.

General maintenance procedures

Weekly/after each use

1 Check that the compressor is switched off and drain any moisture from the outlet filter.

2 Check that the reservoir tank is empty of air and drain off any moisture in the tank.

3 Clean the air intake filter.

4 Check the oil level and top up if necessary. Only use the special oil supplied by the manufacturer.

Every 6 to 12 months depending on frequency of use

1 When the compressor is switched off, replace the outlet filter element.

2 Clean the bowl with warm soapy water.

3 Change the oil – every six months if used daily. First remove the sight glass carefully. Put a container to collect the oil beneath the opening and tilt the compressor until all the oil has poured out. Replace the sight glass and refill with special oil. You can get additional oil from your supplier.

4 Check the condition of all pipes, hoses, and connectors for air leaks. Do not use the compressor until any air leaks have been sealed.

Note: always keep the compressor upright and in a well ventilated space.

Adjusting the pressure
The air pressure is simply adjusted on a storage compressor by loosening the locking ring (above).

MOISTURE TRAP
Changing the filter

As with any filter system, the filter or element will eventually clog up in a moisture trap. It acts like a sponge to collect impurities in the air passing through it. After, say, a year of fairly regular use, the filter will not be one hundred per cent effective and will need replacing.

2 With a small wrench, unscrew the locking nut.

1 To change the filter or element on the moisture trap, first unscrew the bowl and remove it.

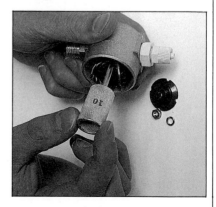

3 Remove the filter. Discard and replace.

EQUIPMENT COMPATIBILITY

It follows that the more sophisticated an airbrush is, the better its air source should be. At one end of the scale there is the compressed air can which is adequate for powering a simple, single action airbrush but would hardly do justice to a professional, double action airbrush — a compressed air can contains a limited amount of air and the pressure can drop, causing unpredictable splattering. At the other extreme, the facilities on a large, silent compressor, complete with a pressure gauge and moisture trap, would be wasted on a simple airbrush.

It is also worth bearing in mind that if you plan to use a diaphragm compressor, add-ons like an anti-pulsation tank can help to make it more efficient.

The six pairings illustrated on these pages are purely suggestions — obviously much will depend on the depth of your pocket and the type of artwork or models you intend to produce.

Compressed air can and single action external mix airbrush

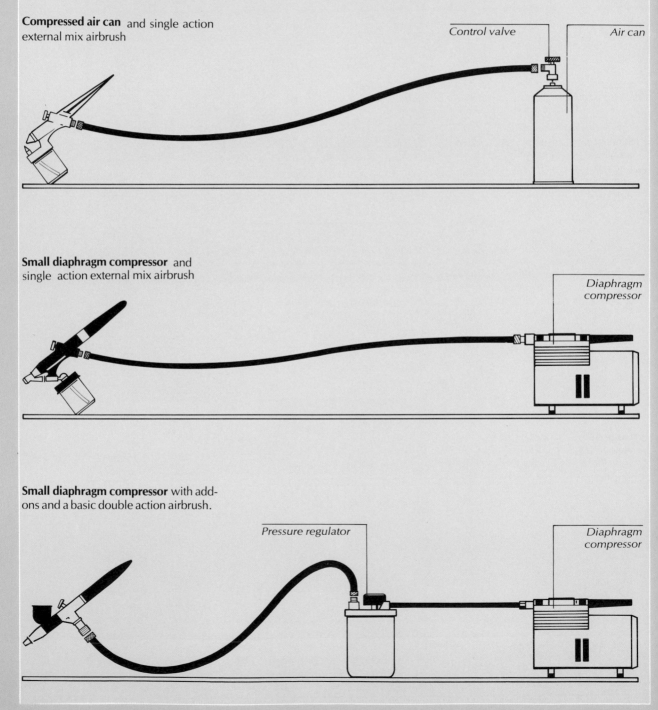

Control valve

Air can

Small diaphragm compressor and single action external mix airbrush

Diaphragm compressor

Small diaphragm compressor with add-ons and a basic double action airbrush.

Pressure regulator

Diaphragm compressor

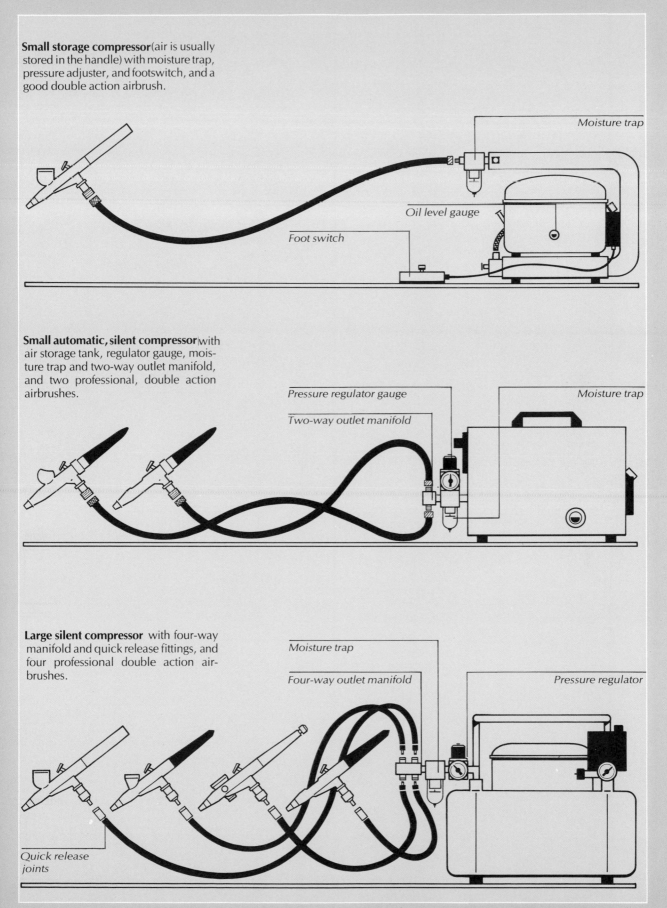

Small storage compressor (air is usually stored in the handle) with moisture trap, pressure adjuster, and footswitch, and a good double action airbrush.

Moisture trap

Oil level gauge

Foot switch

Small automatic, silent compressor with air storage tank, regulator gauge, moisture trap and two-way outlet manifold, and two professional, double action airbrushes.

Pressure regulator gauge

Two-way outlet manifold

Moisture trap

Large silent compressor with four-way manifold and quick release fittings, and four professional double action airbrushes.

Moisture trap

Four-way outlet manifold

Pressure regulator

Quick release joints

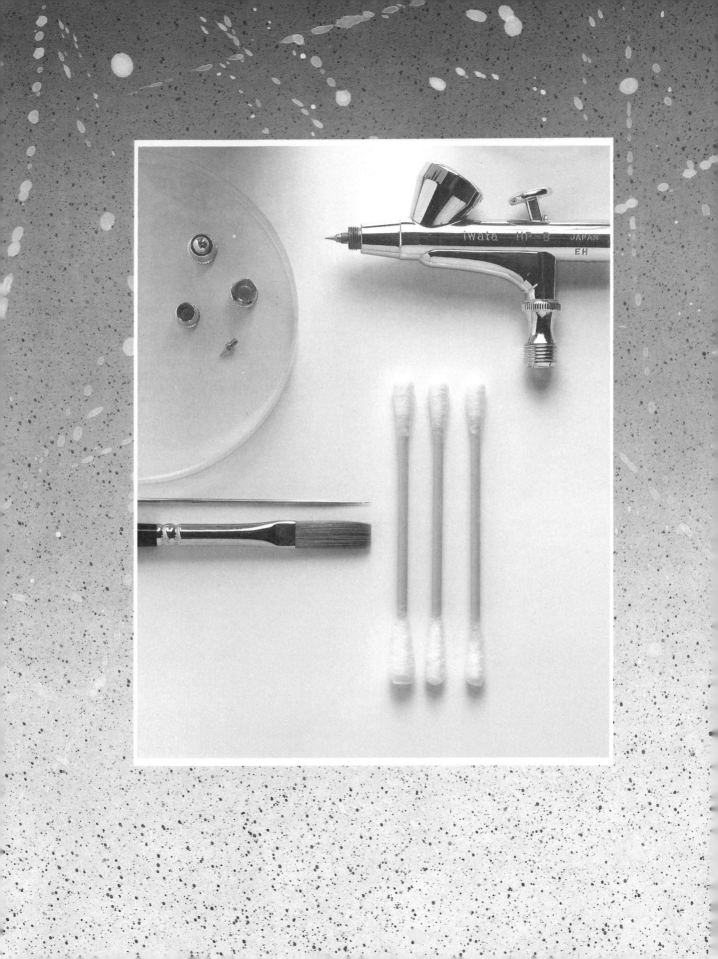

BASIC CLEANING PROCEDURES

The airbrush is an expensive, finely crafted, precision instrument with many accurately machined parts. If these delicate bits and pieces are allowed to become dirty or clogged, not only will the performance of the airbrush be impaired, but irrevocable damage may be caused.

As with any mechanical instrument, your airbrush will probably need professional servicing now and again, but trips to the repair shop can be kept to a minimum if you regularly clean and flush out your instrument. Most of the cleaning procedures are simple and soon become routine – it's as well to form a cleaning habit as soon as you start using your airbrush. There are no hard and fast rules but, generally speaking, the thicker the medium you are using, the more often the airbrush should be flushed out – regular flushing will avoid having to spend time on major cleaning sessions.

FLUSHING OUT THE AIRBRUSH

At regular intervals while spraying, say every hour over the period of a day, and between color changes and at the end of each spraying operation, fill the color cup or well with appropriate cleaner and squirt it through the airbrush into a jar or rag.

1 Cleaning fluid is best applied from a plastic bottle fitted with a plastic nozzle. Various cleaning agents can be used with water-based media, including technical pen cleaning agent, water, water mixed with a small amount of mild detergent, and airbrush aerosol cleaner containing a fine oil which lubricates as it cleans.

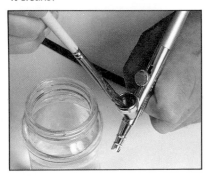

2 For quick cleaning between colors, keep a glass jar filled with water and a paintbrush close to hand. Use the brush to load water into the color cup or well, then swirl the water around and spray it out through the airbrush. Repeat the process if necessary.

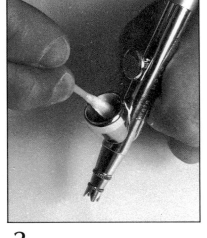

3 Q-tips are very useful in so many ways to the airbrush artist, can be used to clean out the color bowl quickly and to soak up drops of color or water.

4 To ensure that absolutely nothing gets in to contaminate the new color if, for example, you are doing photoretouching work that requires one hundred per cent pure color, use a high quality stiff paintbrush rather than a Q-tip.

FLUSHING THE COLOR BOWL

Many airbrush users rely on this simple but effective method of flushing out the color bowl and needle chamber with water or cleaning fluid.

1 First retract or, better still, remove the needle.

2 Load the color cup or well with water. Put your finger, or, better still, a piece of cloth over the end of the air cap and blow a small amount of air through the brush. The fluid will be forced to bubble back into the color cup, cleaning out the system.

Keeping the needle in top condition
A light coat of petroleum jelly applied to the back of the needle helps it to slide back and forth easily, cutting down on friction and wear and tear. A small dab of jelly can also be applied to each side of the finger lever to smooth its action.

CLEANING THE NEEDLE

Follow this simple procedure to check and clean your needle. If your airbrush is spluttering or blotting, the cleaning procedure outlined below will prevent this from happening.

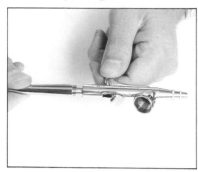

1 Unscrew and remove the handle of the airbrush.

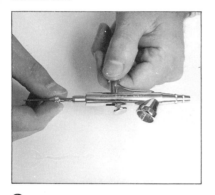

2 Unscrew the needle locking nut which is located at the back of the needle chuck assembly in the majority of models. It is not necessary to remove this nut but only to slacken it.

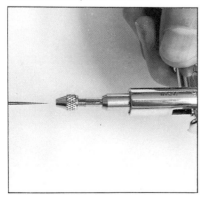

3 With the locking nut loose, draw the needle out. Take especially good care not to damage or bend the needle, which is extremely fragile, as you work it out of the main body of the brush.

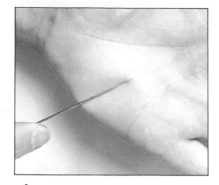

4 If the needle is dirty rather than damaged, it can be cleaned in two ways. One way is to pull it gently across the palm of your hand, turning it as you go. Alternatively you cal pull the needle across a sheet of blotting paper while twisting it with your fingers. Whichever way you clean the needle, try to avoid bending it.

5 If you do accidentally bend the tip of your needle, or if it has been damaged inside the brush, you may be able to straighten it on a hard, flat surface like glass or melamine. Place the needle flat and put your fingertip on the point. Roll the needle back and forth across the surface – with the right amount of pressure, this should correct the curve.

Replacing the needle

Reverse the procedure for replacing the needle.

If the needle is damaged rather than dirty, it is best to replace it with a new needle. Needles are not expensive and it is not really worth the trouble of filing down an old needle to reuse it.

CLEANING THE NOZZLE

The procedure for cleaning an airbrush nozzle is slightly different for the two types of nozzle assembly – the fixed nozzle is common to most airbrushes; the floating nozzle is found in the de-Vilbiss and Paasche models. The main point to remember is the same for both types – the nozzle is the most delicate component of your airbrush and should be handled with great care.

Removing a fixed nozzle

1 Start by retracting or removing the needle and carefully unscrewing the needle cap. Follow this by removing the needle and nozzle caps to expose the fluid nozzle.

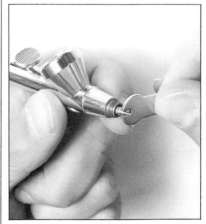

2 Using the small wrench supplied with the airbrush or one designed for the purpose, unscrew the nozzle. Check the nozzle for damage or clogging (see page 55).

When you replace the nozzle or fit a new one, reversing the procedure above, screw it firmly to make an airtight seal. If your airbrush is quite old or worn, you may need to use a little petroleum jelly to ensure the seal is airtight.

Removing a floating nozzle

1 Retract or remove the needle. Unscrew and remove the needle/air cap and check the inside for any paint.

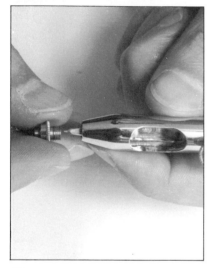

2 Remove the nozzle cap, exposing the floating nozzle.

3 Gently pull out the floating nozzle with your fingers.

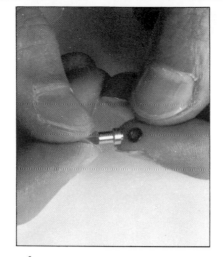

4 There is a small black rubber washer fitted to the end of the floating nozzle, which forms an airtight seal around the nozzle. Remove this and check that it hasn't perished. Check the nozzle for damage or clogging.

Reverse this procedure for replacing the nozzle or fitting a new one.

Types of nozzle

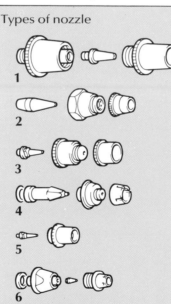

All airbrush nozzles serve the same purpose but they come in many different shapes and sizes. Here are some of the many different designs.

1 Thayer and Chandler
2 Paasche
3 Iwata
4 DeVilbiss
5 Efbe
6 Badger

Cleaning with a reamer

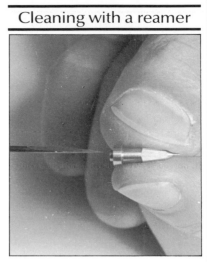

If the nozzle is very badly clogged, use a reamer – a flat ended needle – to clean it out, exercising the greatest of care. A reamer is supplied with some makes of airbrush. If not, you can buy one from a graphic supplier or improvise by filing down the sides of an old thick needle.

Soaking

Soak all the nozzle components overnight in water or an appropriate solvent. Don't soak the rubber washer from the floating nozzle type airbrush, however – it probably won't need cleaning and you risk damaging it by soaking. Reassemble all the components the next day and blast air through the brush before loading with color.

STRIP DOWNS: MAJOR TYPES OF AIRBRUSH

This section shows in clear detailed step-by-step sequences how to strip down and reassemble seven different types of airbrush, from the simple single action external mix to the most sophisticated of all, the Turbo. Even if your airbrush is not the same brand as any of those featured, you should be able to identify and match the type and use the sequence as a guide.

Note that the manufacturer's terms are used for each airbrush, and the same component may therefore appear under a different name in consecutive strip-down sequences. This is to avoid confusion if you use these sequences in conjunction with the manufacturer's literature.

Many airbrushes available on the market today are not all they seem – you may find that an obscurely named model is an exact copy of a leading brand. Together with the survey of major brands (see pp. 22-35), these sequences will help you determine whether you have one of these frequently found "pirate" models.

Before you attempt to take your airbrush to pieces, it is important to realize what you are embarking on. Removal, cleaning and replacement of the needle and nozzle assembly is as far as most amateurs will either want or be able to go. Read through the sequence in detail first to establish whether what you want to do to your airbrush is something simple that you can happily attempt yourself, or whether you would be better off going to a specialist. Beware of finding yourself confronted with a bench top full of bewilderingly similar or unidentifiable components which then have to be swept into a plastic bag and surrendered to your local dealer for reassembly.

Some repairs require specialist tools which may be either very expensive if they are only used occasionally, or not even available to the public. These are identified in the sequences, and again – although ingenuity will help you out in some cases – you are referred to your dealer.

The featured airbrushes
The seven airbrushes featured in this section have been carefully selected to illustrate seven different strip down procedures.

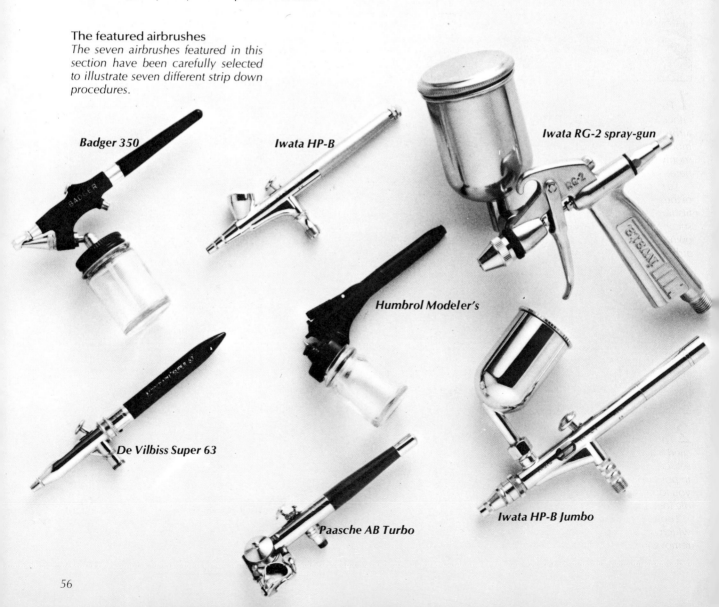

Badger 350

Iwata HP-B

Iwata RG-2 spray-gun

Humbrol Modeler's

De Vilbiss Super 63

Paasche AB Turbo

Iwata HP-B Jumbo

PAASCHE H

This sequence demonstrates a complete strip down of the relatively simple Paasche H single action airbrush, similar to the *Badger 350* (see page 24). Single action airbrushes have a limited number of components and are much easier to maintain and repair yourself than double action models. Regular cleaning is important to keep a single action airbrush in good working order, however, particularly if you use it with any of the oil or spirit-based media such as enamels or lacquers.

Complete strip down

1 The Paasche H can be fitted with either a jar or a side cup. Because this airbrush is particularly popular with modelers, however, it is more commonly used with a jar, as demonstrated here.

To remove the jar, pull the jar stem out of the airbrush body (the side cup push-fits in a similar way). This model has a suction-feed system which creates its own seal as paint is pulled up into the airbrush.

2 The needle and nozzle assembly are sited outside the body of the airbrush. A set screw holds the needle and paint tip in position. This is the same screw that you loosen or tighten to adjust the needle for a broader or finer spray pattern.

Loosen the screw with the wrench which is supplied with the airbrush and remove it.

3 The needle and paint tip are either side of the body and have to be removed at the same time. Holding the tip in one hand, unscrew the needle with the other and both parts will come away. Ensure that the needle and paint tip are clean.

Three alternative head assemblies – needle plus air cap – are available for this type of airbrush, with fine, medium or broad spray patterns.

4 Unscrew and remove the air cap. Check that it is clean and undamaged. Clean or replace as necessary.

5 The front section of the airbrush is now dismantled. Clean off any stray bits of dried paint. Unscrew the lever assembly.

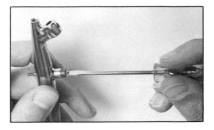

6 Unscrew the air valve nut with a screwdriver.

7 Having loosened the air valve nut, remove it with your fingers.

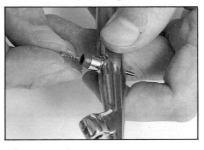

8 Remove the air valve spring with your fingers – it sits in position.

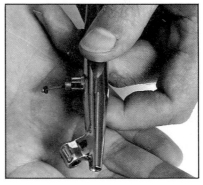

9 Remove the air valve plunger and washer with your fingers – they also sit in place. The washer will need replacing from time to time – check its condition.

Reassembly

Simply reverse the procedures outlined for the strip down.

IWATA HP-B

The Iwata HP-B is a top quality Japanese-made professional airbrush (see page 28). Handle all its components with the greatest of care. For regular maintenance and cleaning purposes, you will only need to follow this sequence as far as removing the needle and nozzle assembly. Unless you are very experienced, any more complex repairs or servicing should be referred to an authorized dealer if at all possible.

Removing the needle

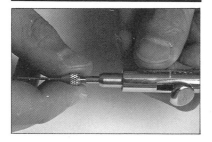

First unscrew and remove the handle. To remove the needle, first loosen the needle chucking nut (or needle locking nut) on the needle clamp. The function of this nut is to hold the needle securely in position. Gently pull the needle backward , taking great care not to damage it. You may want to remove the needle to clean or check it, or to allow you to work on the nozzle. It is important to remember that you should never work on the nozzle while the needle is still in position – you can only damage it.

Removing the nozzle

1 Remove the needle cap. If you are not taking the needle out and simply want to give the nozzle a visual check, withdraw the needle by ½ in/5 mm. The tip of the nozzle will now be visible. The needle cap needs fairly regular cleaning with a Q-tip dipped in an appropriate solvent.

2 Unscrew the nozzle cap. This protects the nozzle and, when reassembling, must be screwed in tightly to form an airtight seal.

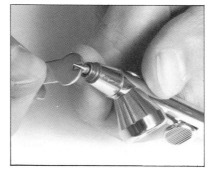

3 Carefully loosen the nozzle with the small wrench supplied with airbrush. It is important to use the correct wrench because the nozzle is a very delicate component. Trying to loosen the nozzle with any other tool, such as a small pair of pliers, is very likely to damage it.

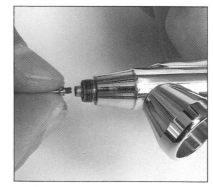

4 Remove the nozzle with your fingertips – it is very small so take care not to lose it. Check it for damage and dirt, and replace if necessary. Clean it by soaking separately in solvent, or unblock it with an old airbrush needle or reamer, always handing with care. For day-to-day purposes, this is as far as the strip down need be taken. Read Reassembly (page 59) before starting to replace the nozzle.

5 Unscrew the needle clamp body from the airbrush. If it is jammed, tap the body of the airbrush with a small screwdriver.

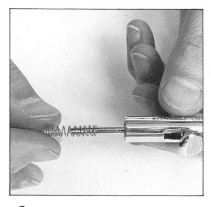

6 Slide the needle spring gently off the needle clamp. The spring should be lightly greased on a fairly regular basis. Check that the spring isn't broken or tired. Withdraw the clamp itself from the main body of the airbrush.

7 Remove the auxiliary lever with tweezers. You will need to turn it slightly to get it through the top slot. Remove the main lever with your fingertips. Check that the pin pivot inside the airbrush body is not bent. If it is, reshape it carefully with a small pair of pliers.

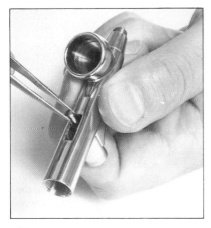

8 Pull out the piston carefully, again using tweezers. A stiff lever action while spraying will indicate that the piston needs lubricating. This may happen fairly regularly. The piston sits in the piston O ring, whith is removed next with tweezers. Check the O ring for damage.

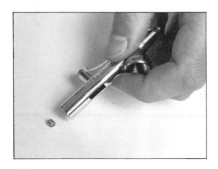

9 The needle packing screw is located between the color cup and the needle clamp to prevent liquid flowing back into the main body of the airbrush. Use a small screwdriver to remove it. The needle packing screw holds in position the needle packing or O ring.

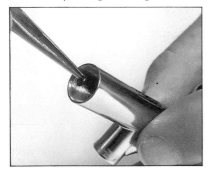

10 Remove the needle packing with tweezers. Check it carefully because it will occasionally need replacing. In all Iwata models, this O ring is made of low friction neoprene.

Stripping the valve

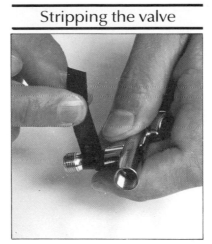

1 The air valve assembly is the focus of the rest of the strip down. To prevent damage to the assembly, when removing it from the body of the airbrush, wrap insulation tape around the outside of the assembly.

2 Grip the valve assembly with a mole wrench and unscrew it from the main body of the airbrush. Gently does it.

3 Remove the air valve guide from the air valve assembly with a pair of tweezers. Be warned – this component is spring loaded.

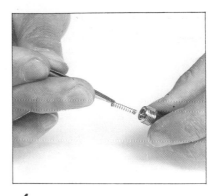

4 Remove the air valve guide spring with a pair of tweezers. Check that it isn't damaged or tired. Lightly grease if necessary.

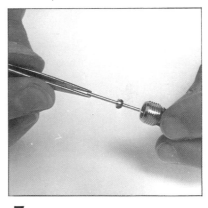

5 Finally, remove the air valve with tweezers. Check that the seal isn't worn or damaged.

Reassembly

You. now have a large number of different-sized components spread before you. To reassemble your Iwata, simply reverse the procedure, starting at the last step and working back to the beginning.

When you are replacing the auxiliary lever, check that it goes in the right way round. The airbrush won't work if it is the wrong way round. Use the spare parts drawing supplied with your airbrush, or a photograph of it, as a guide.

Replacing the nozzle must be done *with great care. Use the wrench to* tighten it, but bear in mind that it has a very fine thread and just a little too much pressure will break the thread. Remember to screw the nozzle cap in tightly to form an air seal.

DEVILBISS SUPER 63

This sequence demonstrates a complete strip down of the DeVilbiss Super 63 independent double action airbrush, which has a more complicated design than most other models. For the purposes of regular maintenance and remedying common faults such as color blockages, you will only need to follow these steps as far as the removal of the needle and nozzle. Consider carefully whether you want to attempt any more serious repairs or maintenance before you start taking your airbrush apart. Specialist tools become necessary (although with a bit of ingenuity enthusiasts can always manage without) and it is all too easy to find yourself surrounded by thirty components and not quite remembering which bit is which. It can be done, however, and carefully following these steps will help. If you feel at all out of your depth, take the airbrush to an authorized dealer for repair or servicing – it is better to play safe, even if it does cost you money.

In May 1980, DeVilbiss changed the design of the air valve system of the Super 63 – separate sequences for taking apart the old diaphragm air valve assembly and the new stem and seal air assembly are included. Check the date of manufacture of your Super 63 before you start.

The technical terms used throughout this sequence are those used by the manufacturers and will sometimes differ from terms used elsewhere in this book or in sections dealing with other brands of airbrush.

Removing the needle

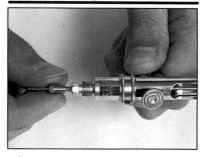

1 Unscrew and carefully remove the handle of the airbrush, exposing the back of the needle.

2 Loosen the needle locking nut with your fingers – this nut holds the needle in position.

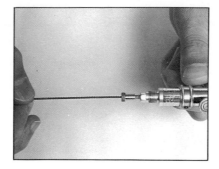

3 Leave the needle locking nut where it is and carefully withdraw the needle. Always remove the needle before attempting any maintenance – it is all too easy to damage. Check that the needle is not bent or damaged and clean it (see page 53) or replace it is necessary.

Removing the nozzle assembly

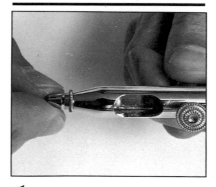

1 The nozzle assembly is the most delicate part of any airbrush and should be handled with great care. Start dismantling the assembly by unscrewing and removing the air cap guard with your fingertips.

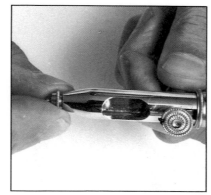

2 Removing the air cap guard exposes the air cap. Unscrew the air cap with your fingers and remove.

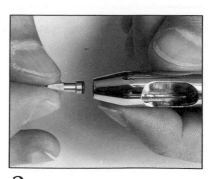

3 The function of the air cap is to hold the nozzle in place. Remove the nozzle carefully with your fingers.

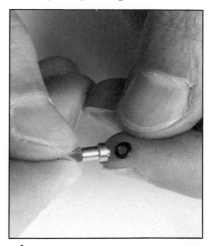

4 A nozzle washer – or rubber O ring – push-fits on to the end of the nozzle. Remove the washer with your fingers and keep it in a container of some kind until you are ready to replace it, so that it doesn't get lost. This is an important item and the airbrush won't work without it – keep some spares handy because they do wear out and you're bound to lose one sooner or later. Spares can be bought from an airbrush specialist but you can also get them direct from the manufacturer.

5 Check the nozzle for blockages or damage and clean or replace as necessary (see page 54). You can try to unclog a blockage using a reamer and the greatest of care – insert the reamer into the broad end of the nozzle (never into the fine hole) and attempt to hook out the dried medium. Alternatively try soaking the nozzle in an appropriate solvent.

You may not want to proceed beyond this stage in which case, reassemble the nozzle assembly and replace the needle by reversing the steps outlined above.

Removing the needle spring box assembly

The major strip down of the Super 63 starts here – from this point on specialist tools are required (although ingenuity can always replace them) and you should consider taking your airbrush for a professional service or repair.

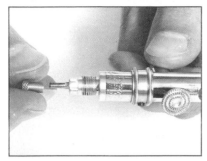

1 Unscrew and remove the needle locking nut which holds the needle in place and attaches to the needle spring box assembly. Don't force the screw and handle it with the utmost care.

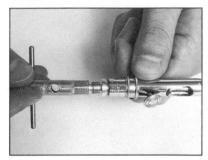

2 Using the box wrench from the De Vilbiss specialist tool kit, loosen the needle spring box. A small adjustable wrench should also be able to do this job but is more likely to scar the box.

3 Carefully remove the needle spring box along with the needle spring and the square piece. The spring is likely to jump.

4 Remove the needle spring from the square piece with your fingers. It is a simple push fit.

The needle spring box assembly is now disassembled. Check all the components. The spring may need retensioning or replacing – it is invariably better, in the long run, to get a new spring. The needle spring box, which is made of very soft metal, may have corroded and need replacing. Clean all the components by carefully wiping them (no medium should have penetrated this section). Lubricate with light machine oil or grease, such as petroleum jelly. It is important to keep this section well lubricated because grime can easily build up, causing it slowly to seize up and become inefficient.

Removing the stem and seal air assembly

The following steps only apply to models made after 15.5.1980.

1 A stud driver is used to remove the air valve assembly.

2 The air valve stem and seal are left in the airbrush when the air valve assembly is removed. With tweezers or small pliers, gently remove the stem and seal.

3 With a very small screwdriver remove the air valve screw from the air valve assembly.

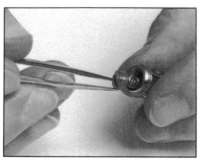

4 Hold the air valve as shown in the photograph – inside it are a spring and a ball bearing which may otherwise fall out and get lost.

5 With tweezers carefully remove the air valve spring.

6 Tip up the air valve into the palm of your hand or a container and the ball bearing will drop out.
The air valve assembly is now disassembled. Check all the components for damage or corrosion.

Removing the diaphragm air valve

The diaphragm air valve assembly is only found on airbrushes made before 15.5.1980 and to strip it requires a special set of tools.

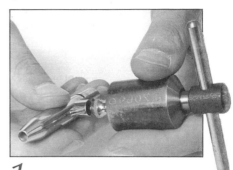

1 Use a stud driver from the specialist tool kit to remove the air valve assembly. No substitute tool can safely be recommended.

2 Remove the diaphragm nut with the special key from the specialist tool kit. Another case where you need the right tool.

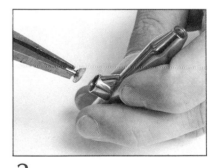

3 Remove the diaphragm – which is shaped like a mushroom – with a small pair of pliers, picking it up by its solid stem. The washer part was originally made from leather, but more recently from plastic. These plastic diaphragms are known to harden or rot and shatter, or else they become distorted .

4 To dismantle the air valve assembly, first loosen the air valve spring retainer with a small screwdriver.

5 Remove the air valve spring retainer with tweezers and care.

6 Remove the air valve spring with tweezers.

7 Remove the air valve stem with tweezers.
continued. . .

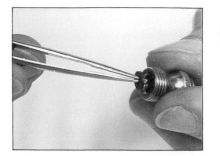

8 *Along with the air valve stem comes the air valve washer, which is seated in the top of the air valve body. Carefully pull it out with tweezers. This rubber washer forms the airtight seal in the valve assembly. If it perishes or becomes distorted, air will leak. Check it and replace it if necessary – it will need replacing from time to time.*

Removing the lever assembly screw

1 *Two fixing screws are located on the body of the airbrush – one on the underside and the other on the cam ring. With a small screwdriver, loosen and remove the screw on the underside of the airbrush body which holds the lever assembly in position.*

2 *With the small screwdriver, loosen and remove the screw on the cam ring – this is a familiar screw which is used when operating the airbrush to change the position of the lever, presetting the amount of air released by the lever.*

3 *Remove the cam ring by pulling it gently. The cam locks the lever into a set position.*

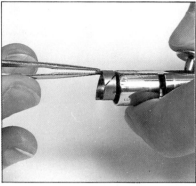

4 *Gently pull out the cam, normally held in position by the cam screw, with a pair of tweezers.*

Removing the lever assembly

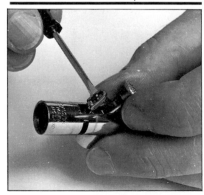

The lever assembly comes out in one piece in a complicated manoeuvre that takes a certain amount of practice. Hook the rear part of the lever assembly with a small screwdriver and gently pull it up through the hole. Watch it coming out, and when it reaches the point where it can't come any further, twist the assembly so that it will come out – judging by eye – and remove it with your fingers. You can easily damage it if you try to force it.

Removing the needle packing gland

The airbrush body is now empty except for the needle packing gland and washers. The function of these components is to prevent paint going the wrong way back up the needle and into the body of the airbrush. It is crucial that they make a perfect seal. The needle moves constantly back and forth through the washers, subjecting them to continuous wear, and they do need regular replacement. They are made of leather in the Super 63, rather than neoprene rubber as in other makes, and need regular replacement. This is a tricky operation that you might consider leaving to an authorized dealer. If you attempt it yourself, have some spare needle packing washers to hand before you start – you may damage them simply in the process of removing them.

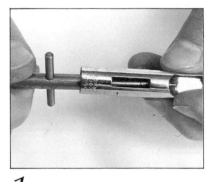

1 *A special key is included in the specialist tool kit for the purpose of removing the needle packing gland, which is a small screw. Insert the key right into the body of the airbrush and unscrew the needle packing gland. This is almost impossible without the proper tool.*

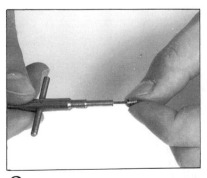

2 *Carefully remove the key from the body of the airbrush. You should find that the needle packing gland has come out on the end of it.*

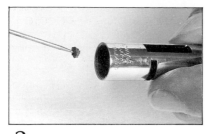

3 Using an old bent airbrush needle, try to hook into the leather washers and pull them out. De Vilbiss recommend using two washers sandwiched together to make a perfect seal, but if your airbrush has been serviced or is second-hand, you may find only one.

Before replacing the washers or inserting new ones, impregnate them lightly with castor oil – this will enable the needle to run smoothly through them. If the old washers have actually shattered inside the airbrush, take it to an authorized dealer for cleaning – small bits will have lodged solidly in the body of the airbrush and will be impossible to remove yourself. Regularly replacing these washers will reduce the chances of this happening.

Although two washers will make a tighter seal around the needle, it may prove extremely difficult to get two in and one will do if necessary.

Reassembly

Reassembling the various parts of the Super 63 is a matter of reversing the procedures for disassembly. These additional steps will help with some parts of the sequence, however.

Replacing the lever assembly

A special tool – called the trigger linkage location tool – is included in the specialist tool kit. This tool temporarily holds the lever assembly in position while you replace the screw in the underside of the airbrush body which holds it there permanently (see Removing the lever assembly screw).

Replacing the diaphragm air valve system

The following steps only apply to models made before 15.5.1980.

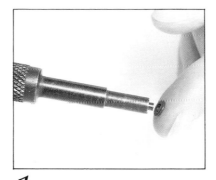

1 There is a useful but not essential special tool available for replacing the air valve washer.

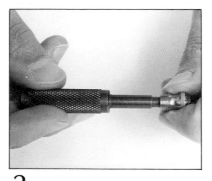

2 Insert the tool, with the washer attached, into the air valve. Bed the washer in to make an airtight seal. Use a small screwdriver to ensure that the valve is properly bedded in.

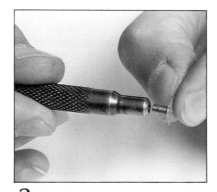

3 Bedding in a new diaphragm to make an airtight seal can also be difficult. A tool, called a forming tool, is available for making this job easier. When in position, the diaphragm is shaped like a mushroom cap. A new diaphragm is flat. Push the new, flat diaphragm on to the forming tool.

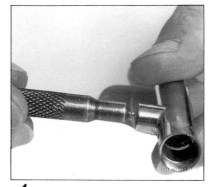

4 Insert the tool, and diaphragm, into the airbrush body – the doming inside the body matches that of the forming tool exactly – and bed in the diaphragm.

5 Remove the forming tool and replace the diaphragm nut which holds the diaphragm in position.

Testing for air leaks

DeVilbiss make a very useful tool, called a blanking off tool, which can be used to test for air leaks before you replace the needle nozzle assembly.

Reassemble the airbrush so that just the needle and nozzle assembly remain to be fitted. Screw the blanking off tool into the front of the airbrush, blocking off the air passage. Connect the airbrush to the air source and check whether the air valve assembly is working properly. If it isn't correctly reassembled or there is some other fault, you will hear air escaping up through the lever, and you will have to disassemble the air valve system to find out what is wrong. You will at least have been saved the time spent putting back the nozzle assembly and needle.

HUMBROL MODELER'S

This very simple model has very few components and very little is required to maintain it.

1 Unscrew the color jar.

2 The pipe through which the paint is delivered to the air jet is now exposed. Remove and clean. Check that the hole to which the pipe is attached and through which the paint is sucked is clear. Again, this must be kept free from any build up of paint – if it becomes completely blocked, there is a remote danger that the jar might explode. The air jet should also be kept free from paint.

3 Clean the paint jet with a pointed needle to clear any blockages.

4 Clean the air bleed hole carefully with a needle.

Routine adjustments

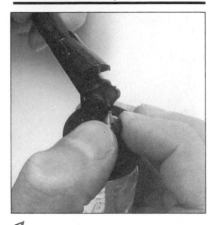

1 The paint jet adjustment ring regulates the relative positions of the paint supply and the air supply. Rotate it upward to increase the width of the spray line and downward for a narrower line.

2 The air jet is also adjustable and enables you to produce a variety of spray patterns.

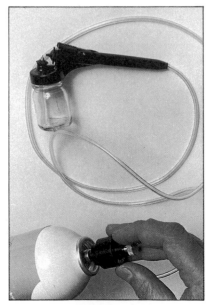

3 You may need an adapter to screw the hose to an air can.

IWATA RG2 SPRAY GUN

This strip down and reassembly sequence demonstrates the removal of the needle and nozzle only of the RG2 spray gun. Anything more complex should not be attempted by an amateur because it is too complicated. Fewer things will go wrong with this model than with a more delicate double action airbrush, and proper needle and nozzle maintenance should ensure trouble-free service. It is an on/off system with no precision parts. The trigger mechanism can be taken apart, but there shouldn't be any reason to do so and a demonstration is not included here.

Removing the fluid bowl

Unscrew and remove the fluid bowl. Not only can the bowl be removed completely but its angle can be adjusted as well.

Removing the needle

1 Using the wrench supplied with the spray gun, loosen the fluid adjusting guide.

2 Remove the fluid adjusting guide, which holds the needle in position, with your fingers to expose the air valve spring.

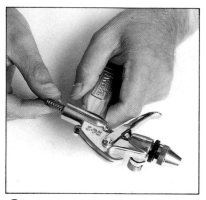

3 Extract the air valve spring with your fingers.

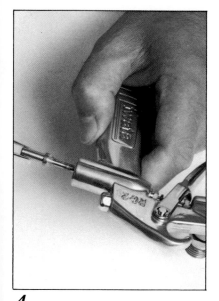

4 The fluid needle and air valve form one unit – remove it carefully with your fingers or a pair of tweezers.

5 You will have to remove the needle from the air valve in order to inspect and clean it. Do this by unscrewing the needle spring stopper.

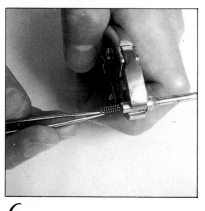

6 Remove the needle spring. Clean the needle or replace it if necessary.
The spray gun needle is tough compared to a finer double action airbrush needle. It shouldn't get bent and won't need replacing as often, although it is inevitable that it will do from time to time.
Three different sizes of needle, giving different width spray patterns, are available.

Removing the nozzle

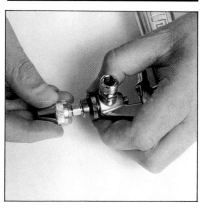

1 Using your fingers, unscrew and remove the nozzle cap by hand from the end of the spray gun.

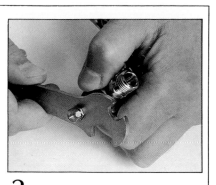

2 Using the special wrench supplied with the spray gun, carefully loosen the nozzle.

3 Remove the nozzle with your fingers. It is much larger than an airbrush nozzle and less delicate, but it still needs handling and cleaning with care.

REASSEMBLY

Simply reverse the procedures outlined in the strip down sequence.

IWATA JUMBO HP-E

The Iwata Jumbo is very similar in design to the Iwata HP-E and other independent double action models in the range, except that everything is on a larger scale. It is designed for use with high viscosity paints, and the strip down and reassembly procedures are deliberately made easier to do yourself than on the smaller Iwata models because you will probably need to follow them more regularly. If you lack confidence on the maintenance side, however, just stick to cleaning the needle and nozzle assembly, and refer anything more complicated to an authorized dealer.

Removing the needle

1 The Jumbo comes with a small wrench. Use the wrench to loosen the color cup. Remove the cup.

2 Unscrew and remove the handle from the body of the airbrush. This exposes the needle.

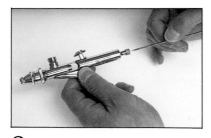

3 Carefully remove the needle from the body of the airbrush. Although the needle is much thicker than needles used in ordinary airbrushes, it is still a very delicate component and needs handling with great care.

Removing the nozzle assembly

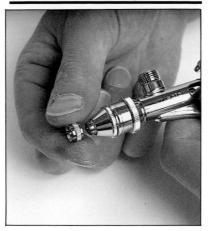

1 Unscrew and remove the needle cap. This small component needs fairly regular cleaning with a Q-tip dipped in an appropriate solvent.

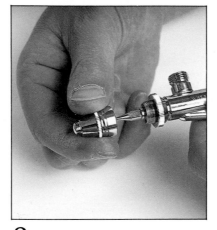

2 Unscrew and remove the nozzle cap. The nozzle cap protects the nozzle and when reassembling, must be screwed in tightly to form a seal.

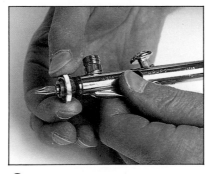

3 Before removing the nozzle itself, carefully unscrew and remove the cap washer.

4 Using the wrench supplied with the Jumbo, loosen the nozzle. It is important to use the correct tool here because the nozzle is a very delicate component and is easily damaged by mishandling.

5 Remove the nozzle with your fingertips. Check it for damage and dirt and replace it when necessary. Clean it by soaking separately in solvent.

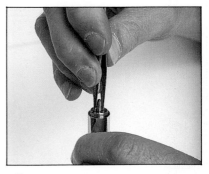

6 Using a small pair of tweezers, unscrew and remove the spring adjusting screw.

7 *Remove the needle spring and chucking guide with your fingers.*

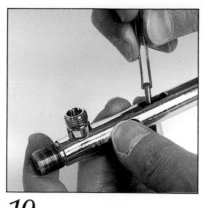

10 *The piston is located in the airbrush body beneath the main lever. Remove it carefully with the small tweezers. The piston may need lubricating if the lever action is stiff.*

13 *Remove the needle packing screw and the needle packing with your fingers. The Jumbo is now completely disassembled.*

Reassembly

Check each component for dirt, hardened color |or damage as you remove it. Clean and replace all components as necessary.

To reassemble the Iwata Jumbo, simply follow the procedure in the reverse order. When you are replacing the auxiliary lever, check that it goes in the right way round. The airbrush won't work if it's in the wrong way round. Use the spare parts drawing supplied with the Jumbo or a photograph of it as a guide.

Replacing the nozzle must be done with great care. Use the spanner to tighten it, but remember that it has a very fine thread and just a little too much pressure will break the thread. Remember to screw the nozzle cap in tightly to form an air seal.

8 *Use the small tweezers to remove the auxiliary lever behind the main lever.*

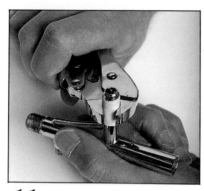

11 *Wind a piece of masking tape around the air valve assembly to protect it. Using a wrench, carefully loosen and remove the air valve assembly.*

9 *Remove the main lever from the body of the airbrush with your fingertips.*

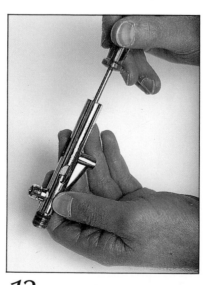

12 *Unscrew the needle packing screw which is located inside the body of the airbrush. Use a small screwdriver.*

PAASCHE AB TURBO

The sequence of photographs below shows the main adjustments that can be made to the Turbo and the very simple maintenance that you can undertake yourself. It is not recommended, however, that you attempt to strip down a Turbo yourself — for serious repairs return it to an authorized dealer.

The AB Turbo toolkit
Three essential tools are included with the AB Turbo when you buy it.

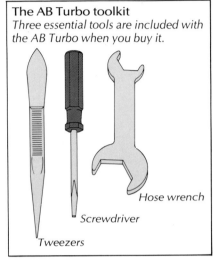

Hose wrench

Screwdriver

Tweezers

Adjusting the speed regulator screw

1 You will probably find yourself adjusting the speed regulator screw more often then any other adjustable component on the Turbo. Its function is to control the speed of the needle and consequently the spray pattern, by regulating the amount of air reaching the power wheel and the walking arm. Using the screwdriver supplied with the Turbo, turn the speed regulator screw

clockwise to slow the needle (for a coarser pattern) and counterclockwise to increase its speed (for a finer pattern).

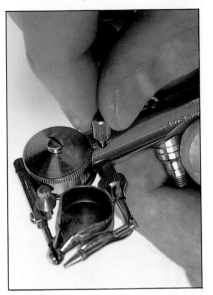

2 An extra attachment with a finger adjustment is available so that you don't need to get the screwdriver out each time you want to adjust the screw.

Cross-section of head section
On the AB Turbo, the needle is operated by a walking arm which is driven by a power wheel located in the body of the airbrush.

Cam slot

Cam

Power wheel

Walking arm

Needle

Trigger

Air blast tube locknut

Air blast tube

Stipple adjuster

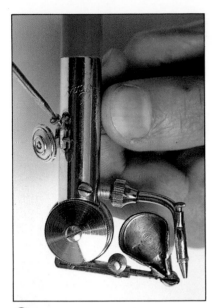

the brush itself rather than at the air source end.

The more you use your Turbo, the more you will begin to appreciate its finesse. It takes time to get to know the instrument and much is learned through trial and error.

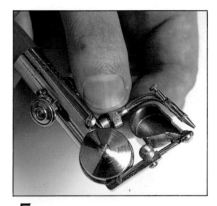

3 As the finger lever is pressed down, the main air valve is opened. It is useful to be able to preset this lever action, by turning the lever adjustment screw.

4 The stipple adjuster controls the volume of air that flows through the air blast tube. It can slow the air supply to give a spatter effect. Use the screwdriver or your finger to turn the stipple adjuster. The Turbo is the only airbrush which allows you to adjust the air pressure on

5 Before you start spraying, you can alter the angle of the air jet by loosening the air blast tube locknut. This nut can be turned right round so that the air jet hits either the thickest or the thinnest part of the needle. The position of the needle itself cannot be changed.

Needle maintenance

Dealing with the needle can be a major problem with the AB Turbo. If the needle is not fitted properly, it can suddenly fly out when the air source is activated.

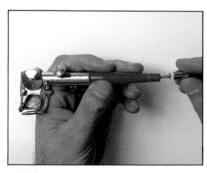

Spare needles
Unscrew the endcap to reveal the 12 spare needles which it houses. Always keep a good stock of spare needles.

THE NEEDLE ASSEMBLY

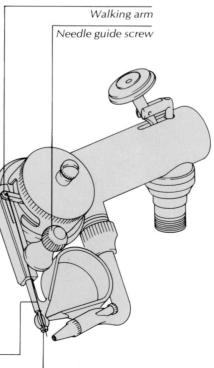

Walking arm

Needle guide screw

Needle

Needle bearing

1 Using the tweezers supplied with the airbrush, grasp the needle.

2 Lift the needle out of its bearing.

continued . . .

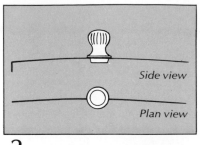

Side view

Plan view

3 *The correct shape of an AB needle is slightly bowed as in the illustration. Clean the needle carefully with your fingers or cotton – don't put it in solvent.*

If you are replacing the needle, you may need to bow it yourself. Lay the needle across your first two fingers and apply a little pressure with your thumb to create a bow.

4 *The needle bearing is a friction-fit part that will need cleaning from time to time. Use the tweezers to remove it carefully.*

5 *To replace it, push it back in, taking care not to push too hard or you may flatten it. It is essential to realign the needle bearing when you replace it. Align the small hole on the needle bearing with the hole in the color cup as you push it in – once in position, it cannot be adjusted.*

Replacing the needle

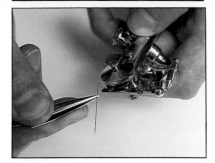

1 *Replacing the old needle or fitting a new one requires care. It must be fitted all the way under the lip of the needle guide screw.*

2 *The needle guide screw should hold the needle snugly and not allow the needle to vibrate too much. TAKE CARE – if the needle is not properly positioned, it may fly out of the needle bearing and cause an injury.*

Sharpening the needle

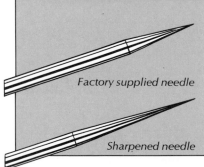

Factory supplied needle

Sharpened needle

The AB Turbo is renowned for its ability to spray very fine lines but you can actually improve on this by sharpening the needle and by extending the taper.

The easiest way of sharpening and tapering the needle is to use fine emery paper. Make sure the taper is even right the way round the needle, otherwise you may get an uneven spray.

3 *The color cup can be completely detached from the body of the airbrush by unscrewing the color cup screw on the front side of the color cup support. Soak the color cup separately in an appropriate solvent. The angle of the color cup can be altered with a little finger pressure.*

General hints on the AB Turbo

- Before you start doing any maintenance work on your airbrush, always remove the needle.
- When you are using your AB Turbo, it should sound something like an electric dentist's drill. If the pitch alters or if the sound fluctuates, the chances are that the walking arm or power wheel are binding.
- If you do dismantle your airbrush, label each screw carefully. One good way of doing this is to stick each screw to a piece of labelled masking tape. The screws on the AB Turbo are very specific but they tend to look alike. If you have to replace a screw, make absolutely certain that you order the right type by referring to its name and number.
- When you are adjusting your airbrush, don't be tempted into forcing the screws – they are made of brass and it is all too easy to damage the threads.
- Never use lacquers in a Turbo.

FAULT-FINDING CHART

This exhaustive fault-finding chart deals with all the mechanical and handling faults you are likely to encounter with your airbrush, whether it's a single action external mix or an independent double action model.

The faults are arranged in two main sections: mechanical and handling. The mechanical faults are further divided into two broad categories: faults to do with the needle, nozzle assembly, and paint reservoir; and faults to do with the control lever assembly and the air valve assembly. The illustrations are designed to help you identify and defects.

HOW TO USE THE CHART

Identify the fault from the descriptions and/or examples in the left-hand column, establishing whether you have a mechanical or a handling fault. The key in the right-hand column will tell you which types of airbrush each fault applies to. Check through the list of possible causes and isolate the most likely suggestion. Solutions are given for each problem which are safe for you to attempt yourself. You may be referred to the relevant information elsewhere in this book. Some solutions are not recommended for doing yourself.

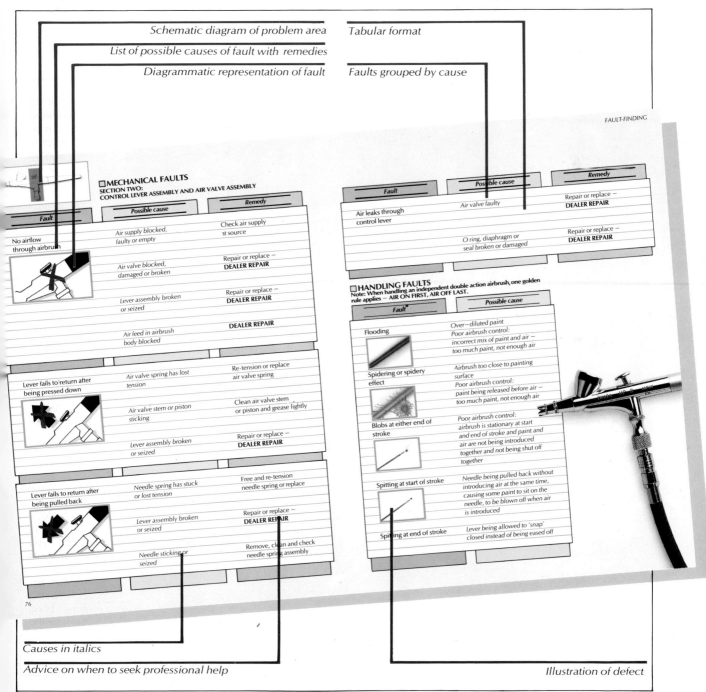

Schematic diagram of problem area

List of possible causes of fault with remedies

Diagrammatic representation of fault

Tabular format

Faults grouped by cause

FAULT-FINDING

☐ **MECHANICAL FAULTS**
SECTION TWO:
CONTROL LEVER ASSEMBLY AND AIR VALVE ASSEMBLY

Fault	Possible cause	Remedy
No airflow through airbrush	*Air supply blocked, faulty or empty*	Check air supply at source
	Air valve blocked, damaged or broken	Repair or replace — **DEALER REPAIR**
	Lever assembly broken or seized	Repair or replace — **DEALER REPAIR**
	Air feed in airbrush body blocked	**DEALER REPAIR**
Lever fails to return after being pressed down	*Air valve spring has lost tension*	Re-tension or replace air valve spring
	Air valve stem or piston sticking	Clean air valve stem or piston and grease lightly
	Lever assembly broken or seized	Repair or replace — **DEALER REPAIR**
Lever fails to return after being pulled back	*Needle spring has stuck or lost tension*	Free and re-tension needle spring or replace
	Lever assembly broken or seized	Repair or replace — **DEALER REPAIR**
	Needle sticking or seized	Remove, clean and check needle spring assembly

Fault	Possible cause	Remedy
Air leaks through control lever	*Air valve faulty*	Repair or replace — **DEALER REPAIR**
	O ring, diaphragm or seal broken or damaged	Repair or replace — **DEALER REPAIR**

☐ **HANDLING FAULTS**
Note: When handling an independent double action airbrush, one golden rule applies — AIR ON FIRST, AIR OFF LAST.

Fault	Possible cause
Flooding	*Over–diluted paint*
	Poor airbrush control: incorrect mix of paint and air — too much paint, not enough air
Spidering or spidery effect	*Airbrush too close to painting surface*
	Poor airbrush control: paint being released before air — too much paint, not enough air
Blobs at either end of stroke	*Poor airbrush control: airbrush is stationary at start and end of stroke and paint and air are not being introduced together and not being shut off together*
Spitting at start of stroke	*Needle being pulled back without introducing air at the same time, causing some paint to sit on the needle, to be blown off when air is introduced*
Spitting at end of stroke	*Lever being allowed to 'snap' closed instead of being eased off*

76

Causes in italics

Advice on when to seek professional help

Illustration of defect

71

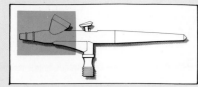

☐MECHANICAL FAULTS
SECTION ONE:
NEEDLE, NEEDLE ASSEMBLY & PAINT RESERVOIR

Fault	Possible cause	Remedy
No medium being sprayed	*No medium in paint reservoir*	Fill reservoir
	Medium too thick, blocking flow from reservoir	Empty reservoir and clean. Remix medium to correct consistency
	Dried medium in nozzle	Clean nozzle and needle, removing first if necessary
Position of jar feed tube	*Jar feed tube not in contact with medium*	Add more medium to jar
	Hole in jar lid blocked	Unblock and clean jar lid
	Needle wedged in nozzle	Remove, clean and reset needle
	Needle not operating correctly	Check needle locking nut and needle spring assembly
Common damage	*Spray regulator too tight*	Open up spray regulator one or two turns
	Nozzle or nozzle assembly damaged	Replace nozzle or nozzle assembly
	Needle damaged	Replace needle

Fault	Possible cause	Remedy
Bubbles of medium leaks from nozzle assembly and paint reservoir	*Nozzle assembly not assembled or seated correctly*	Strip down, check and refit nozzle assembly
	Nozzle assembly mismatched	Replace with correct parts
	Nozzle washer missing or damaged	Replace nozzle washer
	Nozzle or nozzle assembly damaged	Replace nozzle or nozzle assembly
	Needle damaged or not seated correctly	Replace or refit needle
	Nozzle and needle mis matched	Replace nozzle and/or needle
Air leaks through nozzle	*Air valve assembly faulty*	Repair or replace air valve assembly – **DEALER REPAIR**
	Lever assembly faulty	Repair or replace lever assembly – **DEALER REPAIR**
Needle sticking	*Build up of medium on needle*	Remove needle, clean and replace
	Needle packing washers or O ring faulty	Replace needle packing washers or O ring – **DEALER REPAIR**

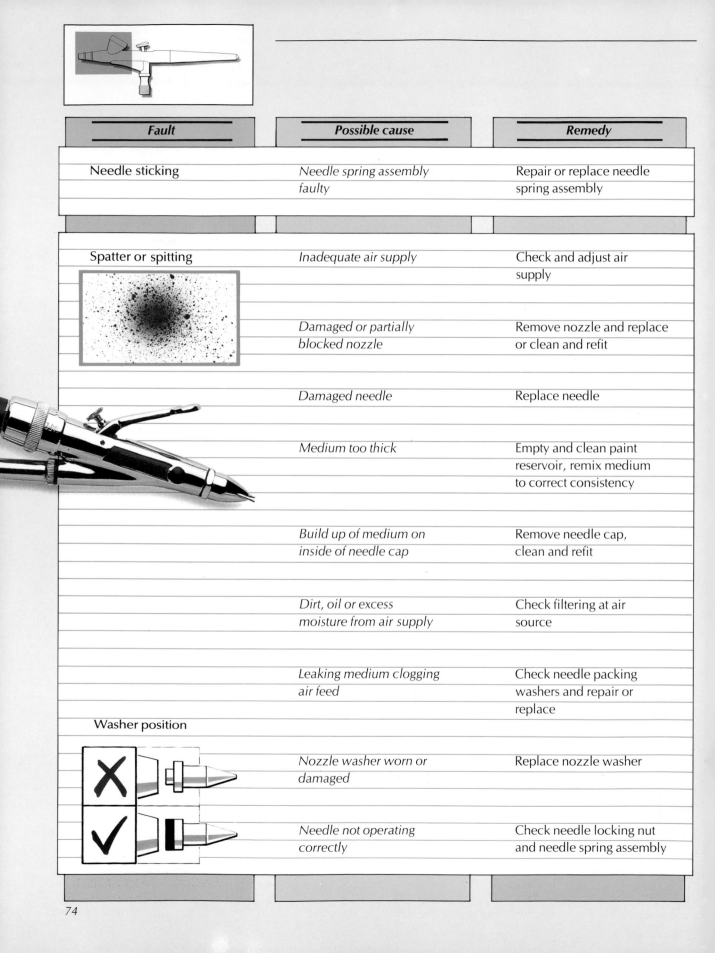

Fault	Possible cause	Remedy
Needle sticking	*Needle spring assembly faulty*	Repair or replace needle spring assembly
Spatter or spitting	*Inadequate air supply*	Check and adjust air supply
	Damaged or partially blocked nozzle	Remove nozzle and replace or clean and refit
	Damaged needle	Replace needle
	Medium too thick	Empty and clean paint reservoir, remix medium to correct consistency
	Build up of medium on inside of needle cap	Remove needle cap, clean and refit
	Dirt, oil or excess moisture from air supply	Check filtering at air source
	Leaking medium clogging air feed	Check needle packing washers and repair or replace
Washer position	*Nozzle washer worn or damaged*	Replace nozzle washer
	Needle not operating correctly	Check needle locking nut and needle spring assembly

Fault	Possible cause	Remedy
Coarse spray	*Low air pressure*	Check and adjust air supply
	Medium too thick	Empty and clean paint reservoir, remix medium to correct consistency
	Damaged nozzle	Replace nozzle
	Damaged needle	Replace needle
Uneven or broken line spray	*Damaged needle*	Replace needle
	Damaged or partially blocked nozzle	Remove nozzle and replace or clean and refit
	Obstruction in needle cap/guard	Remove needle cap/guard, clean and refit
	Nozzle assembly not correctly assembled	Strip down, check and refit nozzle assembly
Spray emitted at an angle	*Damaged or bent needle*	Replace or straighten and refit needle
	Damaged or split nozzle	Replace nozzle
Regular pulse pattern	*Pulsating air supply*	Fit reservoir to air supply

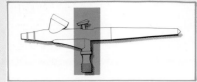

▢MECHANICAL FAULTS
SECTION TWO:
CONTROL LEVER ASSEMBLY AND AIR VALVE ASSEMBLY

Fault	Possible cause	Remedy
No airflow through airbrush	*Air supply blocked, faulty or empty*	Check air supply source
	Air valve blocked, damaged or broken	Repair or replace — **DEALER REPAIR**
	Lever assembly broken or seized	Repair or replace — **DEALER REPAIR**
	Air feed in airbrush body blocked	**DEALER REPAIR**
Lever fails to return after being pressed down	*Air valve spring has lost tension*	Re-tension or replace air valve spring
	Air valve stem or piston sticking	Clean air valve stem or piston and grease lightly
	Lever assembly broken or seized	Repair or replace — **DEALER REPAIR**
Lever fails to return after being pulled back	*Needle spring has stuck or lost tension*	Free and re-tension needle spring or replace
	Lever assembly broken or seized	Repair or replace — **DEALER REPAIR**
	Needle sticking or seized	Remove, clean and check needle spring assembly

Fault	Possible cause	Remedy
Air leaks through control lever	Air valve faulty	Repair or replace — **DEALER REPAIR**
	O ring, diaphragm or seal broken or damaged	Repair or replace — **DEALER REPAIR**

☐HANDLING FAULTS
Note: When handling an independent double action airbrush, one golden rule applies — AIR ON FIRST, AIR OFF LAST.

Fault	Possible cause
Flooding	Over diluted paint
	Poor airbrush control: incorrect mix of paint and air — too much paint, not enough air
Spidering or spidery effect	Airbrush too close to painting surface
	Poor airbrush control: paint being released before air — too much paint, not enough air
Blobs at either end of stroke	Poor airbrush control: airbrush is stationary at start and end of stroke and paint and air are not being introduced together and not being shut off together
Spitting at start of stroke	Needle being pulled back without introducing air at the same time, causing some paint to sit on the needle, to be blown off when air is introduced
Spitting at end of stroke	Lever being allowed to "snap" closed instead of being eased off

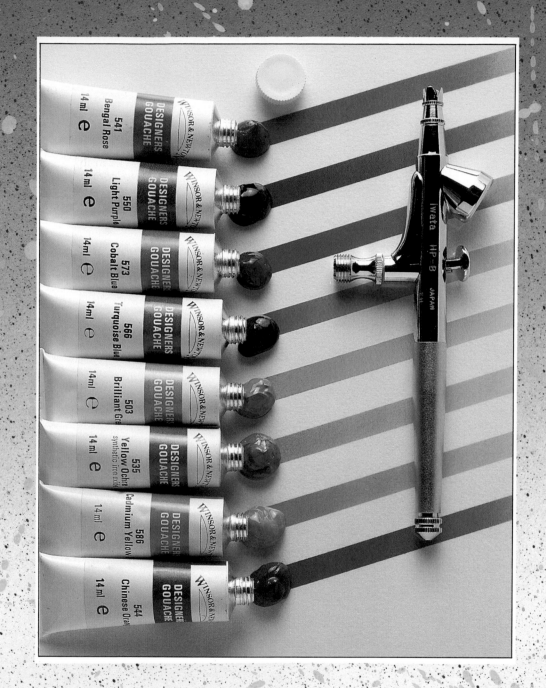

MEDIA AND MATERIALS

There is surprisingly little restriction on the painting media and surfaces which can be used for airbrush work. The nature of the work is occasionally limiting—in fabric painting or vehicle customizing, for example, it makes sense to use specialist products—but most airbrush artists have a variety of media to choose from, and supports can be stiff or flexible, smooth or textured, and come in different weights and thicknesses. This range is an advantage, but it may take some time to establish the different properties and suitability of the materials on offer.

The scale of the work is important. Many boards and papers are manufactured to fixed dimensions, while certain types of paint and ink are typically packaged in small amounts. These inks are fine for most small-scale artworks and illustrations, but for large scale work there may be more suitable materials. The intended perman-ency of the work is a consideration; some artwork for reproduction may be relatively short-term and dispos-able, but some original work may need to be durable and colorfast; many media manufacturers code their paints and colors to indicate permanence.

Surface effects depend partly on expertise in using the airbrush, but also on the texture of the support and the quality of the painting medium. Transparent colors gain brilliance from the underlying whiteness of the support, and subtle tones and hues can be built up by layering the colors one upon the other. With opaque paint, you can obliterate and rework any area of an image, but color mixing is done on the palette, and the color key is set by the surface reflectiveness and density of the paint. With experience it is possible to combine them to create particular effects.

Acrylics
This artwork exploits all the characteristics of acrylic paint. It has been thinned for delicate areas like the threads.

Gouache
Gouache is the traditional airbrush medium. It is ideal for creating fully realized artworks like this car key.

Watercolor
This artwork demonstrates a classic use of watercolor – the powerful pen and ink drawing has been allowed to show through the translucent washes.

SURFACES

In the field of airbrush art, a surface to spray on can be almost anything. If it is able to receive paint and is properly prepared, then try it. Some people have to choose their surfaces and others have the choice made for them. The illustrator, painter and graphic artist have a wide choice of boards, papers and canvases. The modeller may work on metal, plastic, clay, resin or wood. The automotive customizer works on fiberglass or metal. The ceramist works on clay and china, and on filler for restoration work. The photoretoucher deals with photographic surfaces. There is icing for the food decorator, fabric for the textile designer and fish scales for the taxidermist. And so the list goes on. Whatever surface you choose, always test your medium on a small area or small sample before starting on a large piece of work.

There is a vast choice of papers and boards available. The best way to find the surface which suits you, your airbrush, your medium and the style of your work is to experiment. There are some golden rules to follow, such as never spray acrylic paint on to an oil-primed canvas, but a little time and money spent in an artist's suppliers will teach you more about surfaces than reading about them. The smooth, shiny finish of much airbrush art is best achieved on smooth, shiny artboard, whereas a more grainy effect needs a softer, rougher surface. For detailed technical work, a fine, smooth surface is essential — if the surface is too textured it will interfere with your precision. Transparent media, such as inks and dyes, may sit better on a smooth surface, whereas opaque media, such as gouache or acrylic, may respond better to the key of a textured surface.

Artboard

Artboard is the best surface for graphic work and technical illustration. It is also good for mixed media work, where you might combine airbrushing with line work using a technical pen, brushwork, and graphite pencil drawing. It responds well to scratching back with a scalpel blade to create highlights or texture.

CS10 is a particularly good board — it is completely smooth but careful alteration or rubbing out will not damage its surface. It is expensive, however, and for practice work cheaper boards are a good alternative. Another option is to mount CS10 paper on board yourself, using the dry-mounting method (for information on dry-mounting, see page 82).

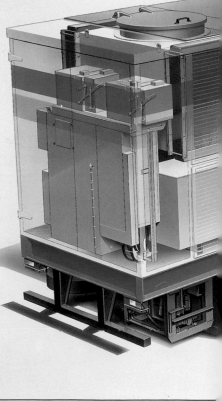

Hard-pressed artboard
The fine detail in this very technical artwork demanded a smooth, stable surface. If a coarse paper had been used, much of the subtlety would have been lost.

Textured paper
This artwork was done on a grainy paper to make it appear as if it was traditionally painted with watercolors. The artist has exploited the texture of the paper.

CS10 is not always recommended if the work is intended for reproduction. The reproduction process increasingly uses the scanner in place of conventional color separation, and involves wrapping artwork around a drum. If the reproduction house receives an inflexible CS10 artboard, they may well lift the top layers of paper with the artwork off the compressed paper base of the artboard. The artwork itself may be damaged, and it will certainly not be returned to you in perfect condition. A flexible artboard, such as a Bristol board, is a good alternative, available in different weights and stiffnesses.

Watercolor Paper

Watercolor paper is worth trying for a textured or fairly freestyle type of work. It is much cheaper than artboard, but it does have its problems. Unless it is very good quality or is pre-stretched, it will need stretching before you start spraying to prevent it cockling or buckling as it becomes saturated with medium. Masking film has to be used with the greatest of care. Because the surface of the paper is bumpy, the adhesion of the mask is not airtight and medium can seep underneath. It may also damage the surface of the paper and any painted areas beneath it as you remove it. Liquid masking applied with a paintbrush is a good solution to both of these problems. When liquid masking is removed, however, it may take with it your carefully rendered graphite drawing. Always test masking film or liquid on a spare piece of watercolor paper first. The fibrous quality of watercolor papers can be a diasadvantage if your style includes technical pen work or creating highlights with a scalpel blade — either of these techniques may pull fibers from the paper or board and spoil the finished work.

Pre-stretched watercolor paper is widely available and will save you time. If you do need to stretch your own paper, it is a fairly simple process. Soak the paper for a minute or so in clean water, remove, and shake off any excess water. Lay it on a wooden drawing board, smooth it out carefully and fix all four edges with gummed tape. The best way to wet the tape is by dipping it in the water. Push a thumbtack through tape and paper into the board at each corner to prevent the tape ripping as it shrinks slightly during drying. It will take anything from an hour upward to dry.

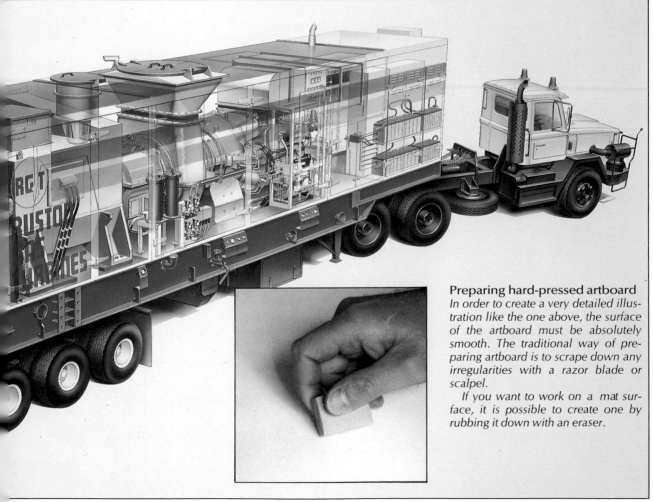

Preparing hard-pressed artboard
In order to create a very detailed illustration like the one above, the surface of the artboard must be absolutely smooth. The traditional way of preparing artboard is to scrape down any irregularities with a razor blade or scalpel.

If you want to work on a mat surface, it is possible to create one by rubbing it down with an eraser.

Photographic Papers

Photographic papers present the airbrush artist with a glossy, fine and non-absorbent surface. Dyes, watercolors and inks are particularly good media to use — their brilliance is accentuated by the glossy brightness of the paper. There are two types — resin-coated, which has a tougher finish, and bromide. Bromide is the better choice if your style involves scratching back or brushwork.

Photographic papers have a surface layer of emulsion, which can crack or bend if not handled with care. You need to wet-mount resin-coated paper and wet-or-dry-mount bromide paper before starting work.

For wet-mounting, you will need a mounting board and a rubber-based adhesive. Apply the adhesive solution to the back of the photographic paper and the mounting board and allow both surfaces to dry. Affix the top 1 in/2.5 cm of the paper to the mounting board, and place a piece of ordinary paper between photographic paper and board. Carefully pull the paper out, gently but firmly rolling the paper onto the mount. Wipe off any excess adhesive from the board.

Dry-mounting involves more equipment, including a dry-mounting machine. First cut a piece of dry-mounting tissue to the exact size of the photograph and tack it to the back of the photograph with a tacking iron. Place the photograph on the mounting board, cover it with a piece of paper, and put in the dry mounting machine for 10 seconds. Resin-coated paper cannot be dry mounted because it will melt.

Mask cutting must be done with great care to avoid cutting through the emulsion on the paper. Cuts in the emulsion are difficult to disguise. Mask the edge of the photograph with masking tape to protect it.

Canvas and Masonite

These are excellent for spraying oils and acrylics. A canvas can be made from cotton, linen or synthetic fabric stretched over a wooden frame. You can either buy a ready prepared canvas or buy the material by the yard/meter and stretch it yourself. **Masonite** is a much cheaper alternative, but many artists find that the responsive feel of a stretched canvas cannot be sacrificed. Wood is a traditional artist's surface but is expensive and may warp. Canvases and masonite need either sizing with animal-glue size and then priming, or, more simply, priming with an acrylic primer. If you are working with acrylics, use acrylic primer. For oils, you can use either oil-based or acrylic primer.

Acetate and Cel

Acetate and cel are used in different areas of illustration — by medical illustrators to render a series of changes to a single base artwork, by animators and for use with overhead projectors. They come in pads, rolls and sheets. Low tack masking film should be treated with care on acetate. If it is left on too long, say overnight, it will be impossible to remove the next day.

PREPARATION OF SURFACES

All surfaces must be free from grease, dust and fingerprints. Any or all of these will prevent fine airbrush spray being accepted by the surface and may show through a finished piece of work. Minor blemishes on any surface to be painted will be accentuated by airbrushing, so careful preparation of whatever you are spraying on before starting work is essential. Avoid imprinting fingermarks on your surface. Some artists wear cotton gloves when handling clean artboard and when transferring a drawing on to it. Some modelmakers wear rubber gloves to ensure their models stay clean.

Mounting Board
Not recommended — as mounting board is saturated with color, the layers that make it up may separate and fall apart.

Metal
Ensure it is free from dust and grease, then prime and apply a base coat.

Canvas and Masonite
Size and prime.

Foam Rubber (example below)
Spray with prosetic adhesive.

China and Clay
Smooth any irregularities in the surface with very fine grades of sand or glass paper, wash with a little water and detergent, then leave to dry.

Plaster
Leave molded|plaster to dry out for at least a couple of days either in sunlight or in a warm place. Then seal with a coat of polyurethane or shellac.

Plastic
Clean with a soft bristle toothbrush in warm water with a few drops of **dish detergent** then rinse in clean water. Leave to dry naturally for several hours or overnight. Alternatively wipe over with a clean rag dipped in lighter fuel. To avoid fingerprints once it is clean, wear rubber gloves or handle only on the underside. Prime with an appropriate primer.

Wood
Sand down with coarse sandpaper, seal with shellac, and then fine-sand to a smooth finish.

Fabric
Iron, mount on a wooden frame, stretching taut and taping, and iron lightly again.

Photographic Papers
Remove all fingerprints and grease with a tissue dipped in water.

Watercolor Paper
May need to be stretched — see page 81 for method.

WATER-BASED MEDIA

WATERCOLOR

Watercolor — the original airbrush medium for which the first airbrush was designed — is highly prized by fine and graphic artists for its luminosity and brilliance, especially when sprayed on to a white ground. It is made from finely ground pigment and gum arabic or a synthetic substitute, and it will not clog or block your airbrush. An excellent range of colors is available in this classic medium. Tone and depth are built up in layers of color, worked conventionally from light to dark. Pure watercolors are transparent and have no covering power, so dark colors cannot be lightened by overspraying. For techniques involving dark to light spraying, use gouache, also known as body color, or give watercolor body by mixing in a little zinc white gouache. Watercolor can be more difficult to control than gouache because it will saturate artboard or paper more quickly and more thoroughly than gouache. Watercolor paper must be pre-stretched (see page 81) to prevent it cockling.

Watercolor comes in several forms and in different quality grades: in liquid form, in tubes, as dry cakes, and as semi-moist pans and half-pans. Liquid watercolor is a good choice for the airbrush artist — it can be used straight from the bottle, or transferred with a dropper (usually fitted in the lid) for accurate color mixing. It is very concentrated and bright but not always permanent, so check on the colorfastness of a particular brand and hue if permanence is a required quality. If you use tubes or pans, invest in the more expensive artist's quality colors — student's or ordinary quality are no match for their permanence, translucency and subtlety.

USING WATERCOLOR

Dilution techniques
Liquid watercolor requires no dilution and is used straight from the bottle. Tube and cake color should be diluted in the approximate ratio of one part watercolor to one part water. To ensure that no solid matter creeps into the mixed color, use distilled water. Always mix up more than enough color to complete the job — it is impossible to recreate a tone exactly — or measure the ingredients of the mixture accurately with a dropper, and record the formula.

Fixing technique
A watercolor varnish is specially produced which provides a water-resistant, glossy, protective coating to finished artwork. It dries in a few hours and is colorless, although the original colors may appear slightly darker through it. Ethyl alcohol is used to thin and clean watercolor varnish. Ordinary fixing varnish may cause watercolors to bleed and is not recommended.

Cleaning
Cleaning your airbrush and any other tools after spraying watercolor could not be easier — simply immerse the tip and paint housing in clean water. Spray a little water through the airbrush to clean it out thoroughly before putting it away at night.

Work environment
Working with watercolor presents no risk to health. You may wish to wear a face mask as a matter of course, but it is not essential.

Ink drawing with watercolor
In this painting, clean, pure color has been sprayed over ink lines which were drawn with a technical pen.

The line work was drawn in ink, then a subtractive method of spraying was used to create the dark stripes. Only one mask was used to make the image.

GOUACHE

Gouache is very similar in composition to watercolor but is more versatile because it can be used opaquely as well as transparently in thin washes. It dries to a mat, opaque, even finish with a fine surface texture. Like watercolor, gouache is made of very finely ground pigment bound in gum arabic, but with the addition of zinc or china white. The white lends it its distinguishing characteristic of opacity. Gouache is also known as opaque watercolor, body color and designer's color, but is most widely called designer's gouache. Cheaper forms of gouache include poster paint and powder paint, neither of which is suitable for spraying through an airbrush. The main qualities of gouache that make it so popular with airbrush artists, particularly in the fields of graphic art and illustration, are its covering power, the extensive color range of more than 80 colors, and its brilliance.

Because all gouache colors except black contain white, they dry to a lighter color than they appear when wet. Dark colors can be oversprayed with light colours. Each coat should be allowed to dry before another is added to avoid bleeding of overlaid colors. Different colors have different permanence ratings determined by their composition. If permanence is an important consideration, check the ratings of the colors you use. As with watercolors, buy artist's quality' gouache which is more colorfast. There is a special range of photoretouching gouache colors.

Unlike watercolor which relies on the white of the ground shining through for its luminosity, gouache works very effectively on colored grounds.

USING GOUACHE

Gouache is fluid but thick. It comes in tubes and jars and for airbrush use has to be diluted with water to a milky consistency.

White gouache

If you don't use gouache as an airbrush medium, it is still useful to include permanent white gouache in your palette. There are two types of white gouache – zinc or china white for mixing with other gouache colors, and permanent white for adding highlights and finishing touches. Permanent white is often used with transparent inks, dyes and watercolors for highlighting, and in the correcting techniques of blocking out areas that need reworking or alteration.

Mistakes are comparatively easy to correct using gouache. One technique is to spray over the mistake with white, and when this has dried, to complete the correction on top.

Cleaning

Cleaning gouache out of your airbrush is simply a matter of flushing clean water through it after each spraying operation and between color changes. Although gouache is made from very finely ground pigment and should not clog your airbrush, it does have a tendency to build up around the nozzle if it is not regularly cleaned. Dried and hardened gouache can be easily softened and removed by soaking in water.

Acrylizing medium

Acrylizing medium is a resin additive, especially designed for use with gouache, which converts gouache into a water-resistant medium. It can then be sprayed on to acetate.

Fixing

Gouache varnishes are available in bottle or aerosol form. As well as protecting gouache work, the varnish gives it an enamel sheen rather than the mat quality of the gouache itself. The tone values of colors may be diminished by up to 30 per cent by the varnishing process.

Storing mixed gouache

Gouache can be diluted in large quantities which can be successfully stored in airtight jars. It is often useful to mix large quantities to ensure color matching over a long period.

Work environment

Working with gouache, like watercolor, is not a health hazard. Breathing in large quantities of any paint particles over long periods is not to be recommended, however, and a mask should be worn, and ventilation instaled.

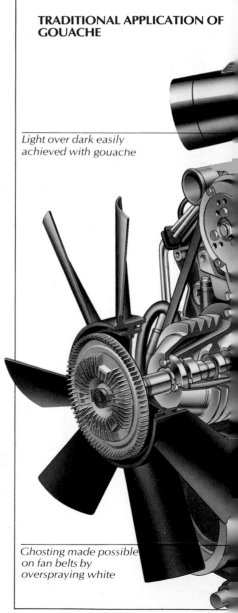

TRADITIONAL APPLICATION OF GOUACHE

Light over dark easily achieved with gouache

Ghosting made possible on fan belts by overspraying white

Using opaque colors

This set of American football helmets is part of a large wallchart. The covering power of gouache was required on this subject for two reasons. Some of the detail on the helmets had to be painted by brush, using light colors over dark ones. This would have been impossible to do using inks.

Secondly, the reference material was suspect and many changes had to be made – using gouache made this easier.

The black line work for the helmets was drawn on a separate overlay and was dropped over the images by the printers – a common technique which is often used in book production.

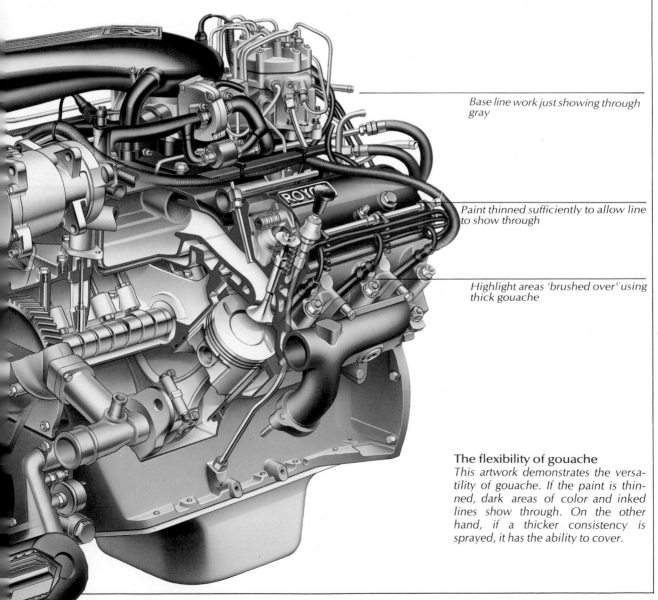

Base line work just showing through gray

Paint thinned sufficiently to allow line to show through

Highlight areas 'brushed over' using thick gouache

The flexibility of gouache

This artwork demonstrates the versatility of gouache. If the paint is thinned, dark areas of color and inked lines show through. On the other hand, if a thicker consistency is sprayed, it has the ability to cover.

INKS

Inks are ideal for illustration, photoretouching and graphic work. Some types have been specially developed for the airbrush and contain no binding agents, so that there is nothing that will clog the inner workings. They are fast-drying, non-toxic, convenient to use, and easy to clean. Inks give rich and vibrant colors that dry to a clean and shiny finish, and are particularly suited to traditional airbrush techniques, such as rendering chrome and technical illustration. They are also a good choice for airbrushing human portraits — the translucency of the color imitates clear skin tones. If you use inks, it is important to note that the properties of different brands vary: what is true of one ink—for example, that it is colorfast — may not be true of another. Check the manufacturer's accompanying literature before you buy.

Drawing inks are very convenient to use. Most makes have a dropper fixed inside the lid of the bottle for transferring the color in accurate quantities either to mixing palette or an airbrush color housing. Formulas for mixed colors can be noted down and reproduced exactly when required. It is well worth forming the habit of noting formulas — it can save on time and effort in the long run.

Inks come in limited color ranges but can be mixed to create an infinitely wide palette. Dia Dye, a German-made range of inks, offer the widest choice of 46 pre-mixed colors. They are not completely colorfast, however, and may fade unless fixed with the recommended fixative.

Contemporary American illustrator, Dave Willardson, has a useful tip for airbrush artists working with inks on artboard: wear cotton gloves. If the natural oils in your hand have come into contact with the artboard, inks will not adhere properly. The contaminated areas will show up as mottled patches through the inks.

As a general rule it is better to work the dark areas of an illustration in inks first. Dark inks can be oversprayed with light inks without their density being affected. Excessive overspray will affect the intensity of any ink, however, and experience may prompt you to mask even black areas.

Both opaque and transparent inks are available. Opaque inks, such as Dr Martin's Permadraft inks, are generally pigmented, giving a deeper, richer color. These can be used on paper, artboard and acetate. Transparent drawing inks can be sprayed on to paper, artboard, cotton canvas and cotton fabric.

USING INKS

Dilution
Inks can be used straight from the bottle or they can be thinned with water. Dilute with distilled water if possible so that the purity of the medium is maintained.

Cleaning
Cleaning procedures depend on the type of ink you are using — follow the manufacturer's instructions on the bottle. Colors which contain no shellac binding agents, such as Dia Dye, can be cleaned by simply spraying a few drops of water through the airbrush, even if the ink has been in the airbrush overnight. It is better not to make a habit of leaving your airbrush with any color in it for too long, however. These inks contain no pigment and will not clog your airbrush. Other inks come with their own cleaning agent which has to be flushed through the airbrush the minute you stop work — if you don't, the ink separates and leaves a solid residue in the airbrush which is difficult to clean out.

Fixing
Whether or not inks need fixing depends on the make. Some inks, such as Royal Sovereign Magic Color are extremely lightfast and waterproof when dry. Other brands are less colorfast and should be coated with the recommended fixative for increased lifespan.

Work environment
Water-based inks are non-toxic, so no special precautions are necessary. Cotton-pad face masks and simple ventilation should give you complete protection. Solvent-based inks, however, may contain toxic constituents. They should be kept away from naked flames and cigarettes, and adequate ventilation should be installed at your work station.

The luminosity of inks
Well observed shadows and highlights, combined with very accurate mask cutting, are obvious in this ink rendered illustration.

The brightness of ink

Inks are usually used straight from the bottle with little dilution or mixing. This means that the colors are unusually bright when they are sprayed. However, this brightness can be lost if the artwork is exposed to bright sunlight for any length of time.

In the illustration (left), the shadows, reflections and highlights have been simplified to exploit the brightness of ink.

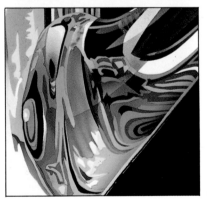

Photorealism and inks

These two examples (above and left) of highly worked product illustration have a photorealistic quality. Artworks like these are often designed to be used on a very large scale and consequently the illustrations themselves usually tend to be big to allow for the level of detail required. Careful planning is essential before mask cutting. The detail (above) illustrates the complexity of the artwork.

ACRYLICS

Acrylic paint is a relatively recent addition to the artist's palette and has proved popular among airbrush artists. It is a plastic paint, originally developed as a weatherproof medium for mural painters. The pigment is suspended in polymer emulsion. Acrylics are water soluble, but once dry they are impervious to water. They are fast drying, unlike oil paints. If for a particular purpose they are too fast drying, they can be mixed with a retarder. They are versatile because they can be worked transparently or opaquely. Acrylic paint will adhere beautifully to most surfaces − canvas, paper, acetate, plastic − and is hard-wearing and durable, and will not yellow with age. Acrylics are available in a wide range of colors − for example, Winsor and Newton Artists' Acrylics come in 33 colors as well as white.

Acrylics can be used on many surfaces and for many purposes − for painting on boards, papers, canvas, for decorating stage scenery and for fine illustration on acetate. Their tough, flexible qualities also make them suitable for fabric spraying, although they are not as reliably colorfast as specially designed fabric colors. Acrylics can be used anywhere where a waterproof finish is required.

USING ACRYLICS

There are two types of acrylic paint − fluid or flow formula or low viscosity, and standard formula or high viscosity. The two types are diluted to airbrush consistency in slightly different ways.

With flow formula, make a 50:50 solution of water and acrylic medium (acrylic medium is available in gloss, mat or glaze − the choice is yours). Mix this in equal volume with flow formula acrylic paint. Acrylic medium adds elasticity to acrylic paint. If you use acrylic diluted only with water and build up an image in fine layers of spray on a flexible surface, the paint may crack.

If you are using standard formula acrylics, make up the same solution as for flow formula above. Add to it one-tenth part acrylic flow improver. This will counteract the flow inhibitor which is included in the composition of standard formula acrylics and which helps to give them their buttery consistency.

Fixing

When your acrylic painting is thoroughly dry, at least 24 hours after the final brushstroke, spray a coat of varnish over the whole surface to protect and preserve it.

Cleaning tips

A little extra care should be taken with acrylic than with other water-based media − the very fast drying quality of acrylic paint and its thicker consistency can clog up the needle and nozzle sections of your airbrush almost while you look at it. A useful tip is to flush out your airbrush between color changes with airbrush or technical pen cleaner, and to wipe the needle between color changes.

Another working method is to work with the back handle of the airbrush removed, giving easy access to the needle, and with a bowl or bucket of water beside you. Immerse the brush in the water between color changes, and flush water back through the airbrush by holding a cloth over the tip and pressing the lever down to let air through. This will dislodge any residue color and flush it back into the color cup or jar.

If acrylic does dry inside the airbrush, leave it to dry fully. Then unscrew the air tip and try to remove the acrylic in one piece with a pair of tweezers.

Remove the needle regularly and check for color residue. Replace the needle and gently work it back and forth.

Storing acrylic

Pre-mixed acrylics can be stored in sealed jars − try the refrigerator. When you come to use it, remove and discard the skin that will have formed on the top, reseal the jar and shake well to mix.

Work environment

Use an extractor fan and wear a mask. Some of the pigments used in the composition of acrylic paints are highly toxic, and you will not benefit from breathing them in.

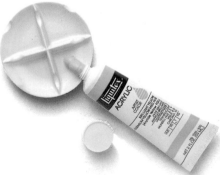

Versatility of acrylics
In this painting (right), acrylics have been both sprayed and brushed. Acrylics paint is a good, general purpose medium.

The painting on the far right was sprayed with a Paasche Turbo and required very little masking. The painting has been built up in layers.

OILS

Many artists hesitate before attempting to spray oil paints through an airbrush. Oils are extremely slow drying, can only be used on certain supports, and are difficult to mix to a proper consistency. After all, acrylics can be used in the manner of oils and are much better suited to the instrument. Oils do, however, come in an enormous color range and there is no match for their durability, permanence, and color intensity.

The great disadvantage of oil paint for the normal working method of airbrush artists is its slow drying quality. There is a long wait between each spraying before you can overspray or mask without danger of smudging existing colors or of the colors mixing on the support. The choice of support is limited with oils — suitably primed canvas or **Masonite** are the only real alternatives.

USING OILS

Dilution
Oil paint is too thick to spray through an airbrush. The best solvent is turpentine, which you should add slowly and mix very thoroughly until a milky consistency is achieved. For the smoothest possible flow of the medium through the airbrush, strain the oil/turpentine mix through a fine-meshed sieve to remove any small lumps of pigment. This will also help you judge the consistency — it should run rather than drip through the sieve. A useful side effect of the addition of

Applications for oil-based paints
Although oil-based paints have some disadvantages like slow drying and the tendency to clog fine airbrushes, they also have several unique advantages which would be hard to achieve with any other medium. Oil paints are particularly useful if you are spraying an object as opposed to a flat artwork.

turpentine is that it cuts down on drying time. Oils also dry to a more mat finish when diluted with turpentine.

Oil paints can alternatively be diluted with linseed oil which will produce a glossier, more translucent finish. The drawback is that linseed oil retards drying. Unless this characteristic fits in with your style of working, you may find acrylic paint an attractive option.

Cleaning
Flush your airbrush out regularly when using oils, either with turpentine or white spirit followed by warm water. Wipe away any oil which appears on the nozzle with tissue or soft cloth soaked in turpentine.

Fixing
A whole range of varnishes is available for oil paints, some of which can be thinned and sprayed through an airbrush. Use a varnish designed for oils and ensure before applying it that the oil paints are completely dry. Depending on the quality of the oils you have used and the thickness of the paint, drying the color can sometimes take weeks.

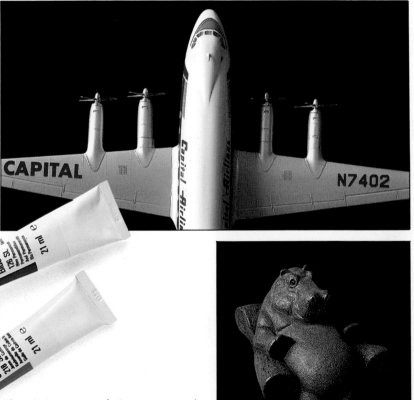

The pig in an armchair was sprayed with enamels which are tough and durable and give a clean, high gloss finish. The airplane (above) was also sprayed with enamels which approximate the finish on real aircraft.

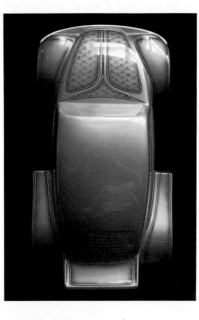

The Volkswagen car (left) was sprayed with many fine coats of high gloss paint. In this particular case, the finish was enhanced by applying a reducing polish which removes superficial irregularities.

Special stoving enamels were used to spray the ceramic piece (left). This type of paint is fixed in an oven and is peculiar to ceramic repairs.

The wheels on the Porsche car (below) were sprayed with metallic gold lacquer to imitate a realistic finish.

FABRIC COLORS

Although some mainstream media such as acrylics can be used for decorating fabrics, textile colors specially developed for the airbrush are available and are certainly worth experimenting with if you do a lot of fabric decoration.

Iron-on synthetic colors designed for heat-bonding on to synthetic fabric only are one type. They are produced in a limited range of colors and can be thinned with water or a colorless extender. These colors are not sprayed directly on to fabric but initially on to a sheet of paper. The paper is then positioned on the fabric, paint-side to fabric, and ironed at the hottest temperature for the fabric. Two good transfers can be made from one light coat of paint in this way. These are permanent colors that will remain flexible for the life of the garment.

One popular brand available is DEKA IronOn Colors.

Colors that can be loaded straight into the airbrush from their plastic bottles and sprayed directly on to the fabric are another option. This type of textile color comes in a wider range of colors including fluorescent and metallic shades, and can be used with either natural or synthetic fabrics — such as polyester, cotton or denim — either light or dark colored. Once these colors have been heat-set by ironing, they are washable and colorfast. They are guaranteed non-bleed and water-proof. Cleaning fluid is also available for removing dried color easily from the airbrush, paintbrush or work surface. Two popular makes of airbrush textile color are Badger Air-Tex and Elbetex color from Lefranc & Bourgeois.

Using fabric dyes
The silk scarves (above and right) bear witness to the richness of color and luminosity of fabric dyes. Spraying fabrics is discussed in detail on pages 224 to 229.

Heat-setting airbrush color on fabric
Most fabric dyes have to be heat-set before the garment they have been sprayed on is worn. Heat setting can be done in two ways. You can either cover the design with clean brown paper and iron over the paper at the setting specified on the washing instruction, or you can put the garment in a tumble dryer at the highest setting for ten minutes. Once the design has been heat-set in either of these ways, the color will stay fast and washable.

PHOTORETOUCHING COLORS

Photoretouching is one of the original airbrush uses and not surprisingly there are specially formulated retouching colors. Black and white, and color sets are both available for positive and negative working. It is not essential to invest in these, however, and many professionals prefer to mix their own palette from gouache, inks and dyes, or watercolors. The nature of the task in hand will determine which of these media is most suitable — gouache for completely obscuring and replacing the original photographic image; watercolors and inks for tinting and adding or changing tone where the image beneath will remain part of the final image.

USING PHOTORETOUCHING COLORS

Mixing Color
For black and white retouching, the basic colors used are white, brown and black. The addition of brown offsets the bluish tinge obtained when black and white alone are mixed.

The photoretoucher needs special skills when it comes to mixing and matching color. The crucial skill is being able to match a tone or color exactly. A very useful exercise for the would—be retoucher is to try creating a value scale by mixing airbrush pigments — say, eight values of gray in even steps. Gouache is a good medium to start with. From there, go on to mix a palette to match the tones of grey on a particular black and white print. Exercise like this will help you to develop an eye for tone.

Work environment
Health precautions depend on the medium you use. The ideal place for the retoucher to work is in a studio illuminated by natural light from a north-facing window — the best light under which to try and match colors. For the times when you cannot work in daylight, use a daylight bulb.

Uses of photoretouching
This compressor (left) was photographed for a brochure. Unfortunately, the original photograph showed up distracting reflections which were subsequently subdued by photoretouching (below).

Highlight on rubber handle cleaned up with photoretouching colors

Leading edges smartened up with brush and ruler work

Ugly reflection killed by spraying neat white color

STUDIO EQUIPMENT

As well as specific airbrush equipment — airbrush, air source, accessories, masking materials — a surface to spray on, and paint media, you will probably find that you need a variety of general studio equipment — for example, protective items such as a spray booth or face mask, cutting and drawing tools, painting accessories, markers for roughs, and a reference library. Some of these you will have already, and others you can buy or acquire as and when you need them. This survey of equipment is not comprehensive and, equally, not everything included is essential. Identify your actual needs before investing in highly-priced graphic tools that sound like a good idea but become no more than clutter on your work station.

It is worthwhile carefully considering protective, health and safety equipment. Your needs will be determined by the scale of your airbrush work and that of others nearby, and the media you are spraying. Atomized paint from an airbrush not only hits your surface, it also fills the air around you. Spraying toxic substances, such as enamels, lacquers and oil-based media, for prolonged periods can produce an unhealthy environment unless there is adequate ventilation. It may also be necessary for the airbrush operator and anyone working close by to wear protective facial masking. The least harmful media are water-based colors, such as watercolors, inks, and dyes.

As a rule of thumb, the area or room where you airbrush should be no less than 4 square yards/3.6 square metres and it should have a window that opens or an extractor fan.

The temperature of your work environment is important — if it is too hot, the high moisture content in the atmosphere will affect the moisture trap attached to your air source and may cause spitting. The ideal temperature is around 70°F/21°C.

Pens, pencils and markers
Illustrated here are just some of the many drawing tools, alongside the sort of marks they make.

0.1
0.2
0.3
0.5
0.7
0.9

DRAWING AIDS AND EQUIPMENT

Technical pens
A set of technical or ruling pens in varying line widths is indispensable for technical, medical, or graphic illustration. Artists very often lay in the outlines and black areas of finished artwork with a technical pen. Some ruling pens can be adjusted to produce lines of varying widths and can be loaded with paint, ink or other free-flowing media — in fact, anything that will go through your airbrush. A ruling pen attachment which can be filled with paint or ink and fitted to a compass is useful for drawing circles in color.

Graphite pencils
Every studio has pencils, but there is an art to selecting the right pencil for the right job. Different manufacturers use different grading systems, but roughly they go from 8H (very hard) to 7B (very soft) with HB as the midway, all-purpose point. For general drawing purposes, use B, 2B and 3B. For technical drawing, the harder H pencils are essential. For some of the techniques for transferring drawings to artboard, a very soft pencil with a broad lead is useful.

Markers/pencils
Thick and thin felt-tip and fiber-tip markers, watercolor pencils, colored pencils — anything that produces instant color — can be used for preparing colored roughs and planning masking sequences, both

important initial stages in any airbrush work, whether a 10 ft/3 m high mural or a birthday card. Felt- and fiber-tipped markers are made with spirit-based inks, so| the color is fugitive. An impressive range of over 120 colors is available.

Rulers

Plastic and steel straight edges or rulers are multi-function tools for the airbrush artist — as well as having obvious drawing and measuring uses, they double up as masks, weights to hold loose masks and guides for hand brush work. Plastic rulers tend to lose their straight edge after a while if they are regularly used to guide a scalpel blade. They are not expensive, however, and can easily be replaced when you have shaved off the edge once too often. Their advantage over steel rules is their transparency — you can check as you are working that you are cutting the right line. Steel rules also have their good points — they cannot be damaged by a scalpel blade, they don't slip as much as plastic ones when you are cutting under pressure and their greater weight comes in useful for holding down loose masks. There are now highly sophisticated cutting and measuring rules designed to overcome these age-old graphic studio problems — plexiglass rules with a steel edge for transparency and durability; aluminum rules with non-slip rubber backing; and two-edged rules which have a deep edge for heavy duty cutters and a shallow edge for scalpels. A 24 in/60 cm ruler is useful for large scale and perspective drawing.

A useful addition is a flexible curve that can be molded into any shape. These are available in different lengths and are generally cased in PVC.

Spray booths

A practical way of containing excess paint spray is by operating your airbrush in a booth. This might be a makeshift compartment fashioned from a large cardboard box or a specially partitioned cubicle. Remember that while you are preventing excess spray falling over a wide area, you are also concentrating the ratio of paint particles to air in the immediate area that you are breathing in. You might, therefore, combine using a spray booth with an effective face mask or instal an extractor fan.

Set squares

For general, technical or precision drawings you will need set squares, which may be elaborate, adjustable models or ordinary plastic, in a range of sizes. A 24 in/60cm size is useful for larger drawings.

Templates and stencils

A vast range of ready-made templates and stencils is available for technical drawing and lettering — lettering guides in various lettering heights, ellipse templates, isometric templates, circle, square and triangle templates, radius templates, as well as specialist templates including engineering, architectural, computing and electronic types. There is also a range of magnetic templates which can be used as drawing aids or actual masks, including ellipses, circles, borders, flashes and corners.

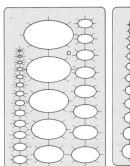

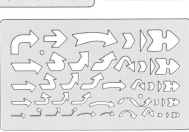

French curves

Like rules, French curves double up as drawing aids, cutting guides and loose masks. They come in a variety of sizes, each with a variety of depths of curve. They are generally made in plastic and are subject to the same advantages and disadvantages as plastic rules

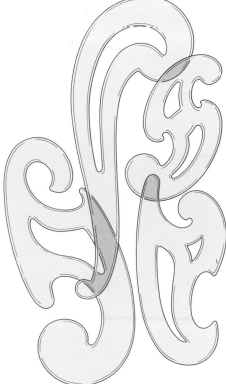

Drawing aids

Among the many different drawing aids are French curves (above), templates and stencils (left) and flexible curves which can be bent to any shape.

Compasses and dividers

A compass with a drawing arm will give you infinite flexibility in describing circles. A circle template is an alternative, but it limits your size options. Unless you have a parallel motion on your drawing board, dividers are useful for scaling up a grid, as well as for technical drawing.

Center wheel dividers

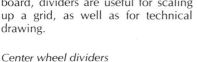

Technical pen attachment

Cutting compass

Pen compass

Pencil compass

Beam compass

CUTTING TOOLS

Scalpels

The most indispensable of the cutting tools is the basic surgical scalpel knife. It is useful to have both a flat-handled and a round-handled scalpel. Keep a supply of blades and replace your cutting blade regularly – even a slightly blunt blade may produce a ragged edge when used to cut masking film. It's not worth sharpening blunt blades – dispose of them carefully when you have finished with them. Like handles, blades come in assorted shapes and sizes, and the different cutting tasks will be best achieved with different blades. A pointed blade, for example, is excellent for cutting along a straight edge, while a curved blade is the best tool for scratching back color to create texture.

A more sophisticated version of the traditional scalpel is the micro swivel knife. A tiny, floating blade is set in a chamber of lubricating gel and follows exactly the direction of the cutting hand, through a full circle of 360 degrees. The angle and height of the blade are adjustable. This knife is particularly useful for cutting intricate masks.

Other cutting tools

For cutting heavyweight materials, such as board, plastic, balsa, thin metal and cloth, use a craft knife. A round-handled swivel knife with replaceable blade is useful for cutting around curves and complicated shapes, although you can do this just as well with an ordinary scalpel knife and a little skill. You might also need a compass fitted with a blade in place of a pencil, circle cutters, parallel cutters and rotary cutters. These specialist items can be accumulated in time.

Scalpel

All-purpose knife

Trimming knife

Swivel knife

Folding knife

Parallel cutters

Cutting tools
Scalpels and craft knives are the most basic cutting tools. Also shown are swivel knives and a pair of parallel cutters.

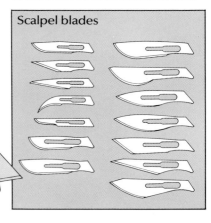

Scalpel blades

Changing a scalpel blade
To remove a blade from a scalpel, first lever up the back section and slip the blade over the lug. Place the new blade over the lug and slide it on until it clips.

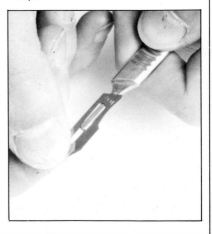

BRUSHES

Most airbrush artists keep to hand a good selection of brushes stored bristle-end up in a brush jar. You will probably want different quality brushes for different purposes — for example, a cheap brush for applying liquid mask, and a top quality sable or synthetic equivalent for mixing paint and charging the airbrush with color, and for adding finishing touches and highlights. It is always worth investing in good quality brushes for these purposes — brushes with seamless ferrules hold their shape better, give you fine, responsive control and last for years. Using inferior quality brushes may result in stray hairs and dust getting into the medium and appearing in the finished work or clogging up the workings of the airbrush. The size and shape of brush you need depends on the medium you use and the scale of the work. If you are not convinced about the need for expensive brushes, test and compare a cheap synthetic brush and a top quality sable or synthetic equivalent — the feel and the results they produce really do not bear comparison.

Choosing brushes can be daunting. Concentrate on one range made by an established manufacturer, such as Winsor & Newton, Daler Rowney or Chartwell Goldline, and choose from within that range. Even so, you may still need advice from the salesperson in the artist's suppliers. Taking the Daler Dalon range as an example — a synthetic alternative to sable of comparable quality — you are faced with: a watercolor brush series in 20 sizes; a long—handled brush series with round cross section for oils and acrylics in 13 sizes; flat rectangular brushes in 10 sizes; long-handled, fan-tail brushes for blending oils and acrylics in 6 sizes; very fine "one-stroke" brushes designed for lettering and ruling in 6 sizes; square-edged, large brushes for laying areas of flat color in 7 sizes (perhaps the airbrush artist can at least discount these); and the Series D22 brushes for laying areas of flat color for washes, with acrylic handles that can be used as palette knives, scrapers or burnishers. This range offers a choice of 65 brushes.

OTHER USEFUL ITEMS

Droppers
Droppers in different sizes are invaluable for transferring inks, dyes and liquid watercolors direct from their containers to the color cup or into a palette, with great accuracy and no mess.

Palettes
A "palette" is essential for mixing color but the definition of a palette can be as loose as you like — a purpose-made ceramic dish divided into quarters, an old white plate, a glass jar, or a plain ceramic tile.

Jars
Large glass jars filled with water or an appropriate solvent contribute to an uninterrupted work pattern — you can quickly and regularly flush out your airbrush between color changes and dip in the head assembly of the airbrush during pauses in spraying.

Q-tips
Along with many other uses in the studio, cotton, Q-tips or pads are ideal for the swift removal of excess or unwanted color either from the sprayed surface or from the color housing on the airbrush.

BRUSH SHAPES AND SIZES

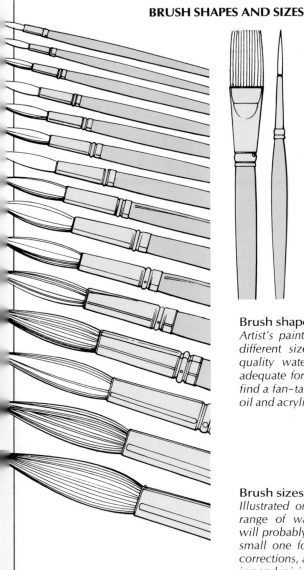

Brush shapes
Artist's paint brushes come in many different sizes and shapes. A good quality watercolor brush should be adequate for most tasks but you may find a fan—tail brush handy for mixing oil and acrylic paints.

Brush sizes
Illustrated on the left is a complete range of watercolor brushes. You will probably need at least two — one small one for adding highlights and corrections, and a larger one for loading and mixing paints.

MASKING MATERIALS

'I can spend a whole day cutting a frisket for one color. The painting is done in 10 minutes!' This is a quote from Robert Anderson, the American artist, in an interview with the airbrushing magazine, *Airbrush Digest*. Mastering the techniques of masking, and acquiring a thorough familiarity with masking materials, are just as crucial to producing airbrush art as learning control of the airbrush.

Flicking through the section on specialist techniques will give you some idea of just how wide a definition the word mask has in airbrush art. It can be a contour mask, which has to follow an uneven surface, as in modeling. This may be achieved with masking tape, film (on some surfaces), adhesive labels or masking fluid. It can mean a flat surface mask. Here the most widely used masking medium is low-tack masking film. Alternatives are loose masks and liquid masking. Masks can be positive or negative − they can expose an area to airbrush spray (positive) or they can conceal one (negative). Experimenting with different masks and materials is the only way to gain experience.

MASKING FILM

Specially developed for airbrush users, masking film enables you to create a hard, precise edge, with no color bleed or smudging. It is a low-tack self-adhesive, transparent film that is sold in rolls and sheets of various sizes in either a gloss or mat finish. The mat finish is a recent development − its advantage over the original gloss finish is that you can draw directly on to it with a graphite pencil and use these lines as cutting guides, eliminating a tracing stage. Roll dimensions include 30cm x 4m, 60 cm x 4 m (A2 and A3 plus overlap), 50cm x 10 m (A4 plus overlap). Sheets of 33 cm x 24 cm come in packs of 10.

The advantages of masking film for the graphic artist, or illustrator in particular, are considerable. Because it is low-tack it will not damage the surface beneath when it is lifted off and it is transparent, so you can see exactly what you are cutting. Some makes also have a translucent backing paper so that you can cut masks on a light box with the backing still in position. It can be laid over a painted surface, as long as the paint is a hundred per cent dry, and it is flexible and will not tear − intricate shapes can be cut crisply and accurately with a sharp scalpel blade. Masking film will not buckle, no matter how many times you spray over the same mask, and a consistent line can be more or less guaranteed. If it is handled carefully so that its shape is not distorted by stretching, a mask cut from film can be reused several times. Always check the fit carefully before spraying, and cut a new mask if the shape is at all! stretched. Masks should be saved on a spare clean piece of backing sheet when not in use − this will prevent dust particles from adhering.

Masking film is suitable for most surfaces, including artboard, watercolor and illustration papers, gessoed surfaces, metal, automotive surfaces, acetate, glass, plexiglass and other plastics, prepared woods, glazed ceramics and photographic papers. It is not recommended for canvas − a combination of paper masks and masking tape work better. Film may damage very soft or textured surfaces, and should be tested first. It should be stored in a cool place away from direct sunlight.

Masking film can also be used to protect finished artwork on artboard temporarily, but should not be left on artwork for prolonged periods.

It may not be necessary to use masking film over an entire piece of work and it is an expensive material to waste − you can use scrap paper held in place with masking tape to protect background areas. Masking tape can be used as a masking material in its own right, particularly for contour masking and to create a precise, but irregular edge. A strip of tape can be torn down the center and the ragged edge stuck firmly in position.

MASKING FLUID

Masking fluid or liquid masking is a rubber compound solution. It is applied with a paintbrush, and dries quickly by evaporation to form a flexible film that will protect the area beneath completely from spray. Once dry, the skin it forms can be cut with a scalpel and sections can be removed, allowing you to spray a sequence of colors or tones with just one application of mask. It is easily removed by rubbing or peeling off with the finger, or with a putty eraser. But beware if you have applied it over a detailed pencil image − it acts like an eraser and will take the graphite with it, perhaps together with hours of detailed drawing work.

Some liquid masks contain a dye, making it easier to see what you are doing as you apply the mask; Colorless masking fluid on a white support can be difficult to see as you apply it. The dye, however, may stain the support, so test it first. Test it also if you are working on paper to see if it damages the surface of the paper as it is peeled off. Don't use a liquid mask if you are spraying with acrylic paint because the paint will glue the mask to the surface, making it impossible to remove. It should not be applied over a painted surface because it tends to lift paint off when it is removed. Its disadvantages make it much less popular among airbrush artists than masking film, although it is particularly suitable for specific tasks, such as masking out tiny areas. You can use the point of a sharpened stick or a very fine paintbrush to pick up a spot of mask and apply it to a pinhead size area. It is useful for masking on photographic papers because it will not stain or damage them.

An interesting mottled texture can be created by first spraying masking fluid through the airbrush, and then spraying color over the top. When the color is completely dry, rub the liquid mask away gently with a finger or putty eraser. Be sure to flush the airbrush after spraying the mask.

LOOSE MASKING

Any object, material or cut shape can be used as a loose mask -- hand-held or weighted between surface and airbrush spray. If your loose mask is of a light material, such as paper or tulle, the pressure of the airbrush spray will cause it to lift at the edges, and a blurry edge will result. Loose masks can be deliberately moved around during spraying to create various effects.

Flat surface masks
You can build up a stock of custom-made templates, cut preferably from acetate for good durability, or stiff paper or card, which you can reuse many times. For a sharp edge, hold or weight a mask against the surface. If you want a blurry edge, raise the mask

above the surface by resting it on an off-cut of card. Although your mask should be stiff and strong, it should also be as thin as possible. Spraying over a piece of thick card will result in either a white line at the edge, or a build-up of color, depending on the angle at which the spray hits the mask.

Flat stencils
For duplicating a design — for example, on a repeat pattern fabric — make a reusable stencil.

Contour stencils
Your work may involve stenciling on ceramics or models. Positive stencils can either be stuck or held in position — say, the shape of a sleeping cat cut from material which is then carefully pasted on the side of a ceramic mug. Using the same image on the same mug, a negative stencil, the reverse of a positive stencil, can be cut from card. Provided the shape isn't too complex, the easiest way of fixing the stencil to the mug is to use double-sided tape. Complicated shapes can be glued in place but this inevitably complicates the job and is best avoided if at all possible. It is worth bearing in mind that stenciling only works well on the outside of the workpiece. For a blurred edge, make a negative stencil from corrugated card in the same way.

Ready-made loose masks
You can buy French curves, ellipse guides and set squares at any good artist's suppliers. These can double up as drawing and cutting aids as well as loose masks. In the same suppliers, you will probably find dry transfers for lettering and for creating textures. These can be used as negative masks. Rub down the transfer gently, and when you are ready to remove it, rub a ball of gum over it to lift it off.

Found objects
Look around you at household and studio objects, and out of the window at organic shapes, and a hundred different things will suggest themselves as masks and templates. Leaves, flower heads, feathers, stones, and twigs can all be used as loose masks. Experiment, record the results, and build up a reference archive of effects.

Fabrics and other materials
As well as spraying around a mask, you may want to spray through it. Texture and pattern may be more successfully rendered by using a piece of material as a mask rather than spending hours cutting an elaborate mask from film, or painting an intricate design with liquid masking. Tulle, burlap, netting, wire mesh, thinly stretched cotton, lace, and rush matting all produce different and interesting results.

Making a reusable stencil

Use a good stiff paper. Manila paper can be treated with oil to make it non-absorbent and to give it a long life. Saturate the paper with a rag dipped in a solution of one part boiled linseed oil and one part turpentine. Wipe off excess oil with a dry rag and hang the stencil paper to dry. Soak the rags in water and dispose of them carefully — they should not be stored for reuse. Cut your design out crisply with a razor sharp scalpel blade. The oiling process makes the paper easier to cut, particularly if your design is very intricate.

Making a tracing mask

Once you have transferred your image to the work surface, an original tracing can be transformed into a mask. Spread a thinned rubber adhesive solution over the back of the tracing and leave it to dry. Once it is dry, you can cut out sections without any danger of the tracing tearing or crumpling.

Using masks — general points
● Always take the airbrush spray over the mask as well as the spray area, otherwise you will be left with a thin, unsprayed line along the edge of the mask.

● Whatever type of mask you are using, if you use it more than once always replace it exactly in its original position before spraying. The slightest overlap will result either in a white line or a double sprayed line, creating the same effect as a printed image out of register.

● As a general rule, wait until the color is dry before removing a hard mask, whether it is film or liquid. With some media, however, such as acrylic and enamel, experience may suggest that the mask be removed when the color is touch dry.

● Never throw masks away before the job is complete. Although remasking is not usually recommended at a late stage, a finishing touch or a missed section is sometimes best sprayed using the original mask.

● Remember that airbrush spray will fall well beyond the area you are aiming directly at. Take care to mask the whole piece of work using scrap paper or newspaper as necessary around the edges. And don't forget to mask the work surface and anything else in the vicinity, particularly if you are not using a water-based color that can be cleaned off afterward.

Double masking (patching technique)

Your image may include areas of flat or graded color where not much is happening, as well as areas of very fine detail. Double masking can be a useful technique to adopt here. Lay a sheet of masking film over the whole area, followed by a second layer of smaller pieces of film cut to fit the detailed sections. Put in the large areas of color first — overspray will obscure the top layer of film but the pieces can be removed to reveal clean film beneath ready for cutting. If you remask these detailed sections once sprayed, use a low-tack film.

TECHNIQUES FOR MAKING AND USING MASKS

● If you want to stiffen a mask to make it more easy to handle, stick it on to tracing paper and slice through both layers when you cut out.

● Before lifting up a mask, check the state of any oversprayed paint on it — wet paint on a mask is easy to smudge and if this goes over the artwork itself, many hours of hard work may be ruined.

● When lifting up a corner of a mask to remove it, be wary of getting any grease from your fingers on the artwork. If grease does get smeared on the work-piece, any water-based medium sprayed over the top won't adhere properly. If you want to reuse a mask, be sure not to handle the tacky side — grease from fingerprints may get transferred on to the artwork.

ART
TECHNIQUES

*"I guess I am an airbrush purist.
I simply don't like paint brushes"*
DAVE WILLARDSON

AIRBRUSHING TECHNIQUES

ESSENTIAL SKILLS

Learning how to wield an airbrush won't make you a great artist, but mastering the instrument itself is a practical skill rather than a creative one. Most people can achieve the dexterity and coordination required with varying amounts of practice. Learning good habits and following a few simple rules right from the start will go a long way to preventing frustration and bad results.

Follow the basic handling rules covered in this section – finger control of both single and double action airbrushes, the golden rule of "air on first, off last", and judging the distance of the nozzle from the surface – and then practice the simple techniques of spraying a flat tone, a graduated tone, a solid circle and a circle outline. Armed with these skills, move on to the basic three-dimensional shapes – the cube, cylinder, sphere and cone – which combine the fundamental handling principles with simple masking techniques.

FINGER CONTROL

All airbrushes are operated in basically the same way – you hold the brush as you would a pen, whether you are left- or right-handed, and use your index finger to control the air and paint on to the surface. The degree of control differs from model to model – the more sophisticated the airbrush, the greater the degree of control.

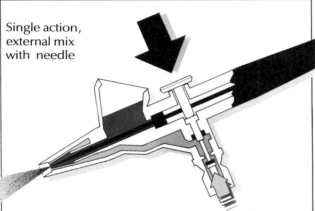

Single action, external mix with needle

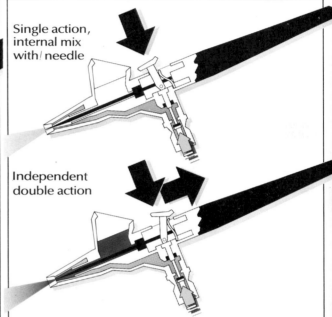

Single action, internal mix with/needle

Independent double action

Single action, external mix with needle

This is the most basic airbrush design. To operate an airbrush of this type, depress the lever with your index finger. As you do so, paint from the color housing and air from the air source are propelled simultaneously but separately through the airbrush and they meet outside the head of the airbrush. Air and paint are either on or off; the lever is either down or up.

Some flexibility exists (the direction of the air jet and the amount of paint delivered by the needle can be adjusted within a limited range) but has to be predetermined – the lever, and therefore your finger, does not control either air or paint separately and they cannot be altered during spraying.

Single action, internal mix with needle

This type is operated in exactly the same way as the external mix type. Depress the lever with your index finger and paint and air are expelled simultaneously in a present ratio.

The greater sophistication of this model, compared to the external mix design, lies in the quality of spray it can produce. Because the air and paint are atomized within the body of the airbrush rather than outside the head, they are more thoroughly diffused when they hit the surface being sprayed. The result is a much finer spray, capable of producing even tones of color.

Independent double action

Finger control of the lever on an independent double action airbrush is the key to its wide range of spray patterns and effects. The principle is again simple – press the lever down with your index finger for air and draw it back with the same finger for paint – but the ratio of air to paint flow is infinite.

To get a feel for the range of spray widths possible, first simply press the lever down with your index finger. Air is expelled. Pull the lever back very slightly. A small amount of paint now atomizes with the air and a very fine spray is expelled. Pull the lever back a little further and the spray broadens. Continue to draw the lever back in steps, each time observing the spray pattern, until the lever is fully back and the spray is at its widest. The better you get to know your airbrush, the greater your sensitivity becomes. With considerable practice you should be able to produce the exact width you want automatically, without having to think how far back you are pulling the lever.

CONTROLLING THE SPRAY

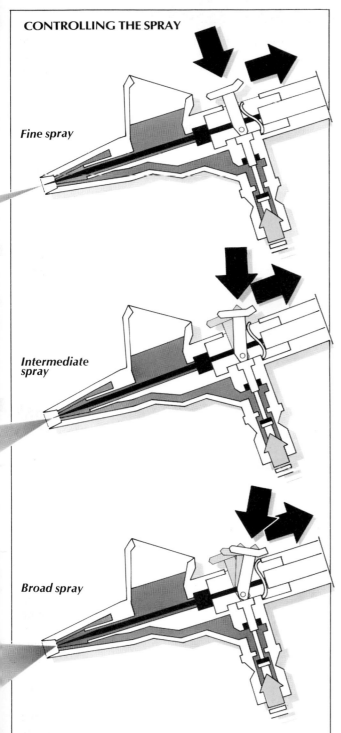

Fine spray

Intermediate spray

Broad spray

Double action control
The lever on a double action airbrush controls both the air and paint flows. It is pressed down to release air and pulled back to release paint. The further the lever is eased backward. the more paint is expelled and the wider the spray pattern becomes.

AIR ON FIRST, AIR OFF LAST

Success with your airbrush is not guaranteed by observing this simple rule, but failure is ensured by ignoring it. A great deal of airbrushing is based on the same movement – sweeping strokes back and forth across the area being sprayed. Begin each stroke with the airbrush beyond the target area. Before the nozzle reaches the target starting point, depress the control lever for air only. As the nozzle reaches the starting point, draw the lever back to introduce the paint. Continue the sweep, maintaining the ratio of paint to air (for a flat tone), until the nozzle reaches the target end-point. Shut the paint off by pushing the lever to its forward position, but keep the air supply on. When the nozzle has passed over the end-point, release the control lever to shut off the air.

The results of not following this procedure are large blobs of paint at the beginning and end of each stroke. Any paint introduced on to the needle before the air supply is opened will splat on to the surface as soon as the compressed air hits it. If the air is turned off before the paint at the end of the stroke, again the paint may splat. If it doesn't, however, the paint will still be sitting on the needle for the beginning of the next stroke, and that initial splat will be inevitable.

Once you've mastered this principle, practice sweeping backward and forward strokes until you achieve an effortless, smooth action. Spray undulating lines and lines of varying widths as well as straight lines.

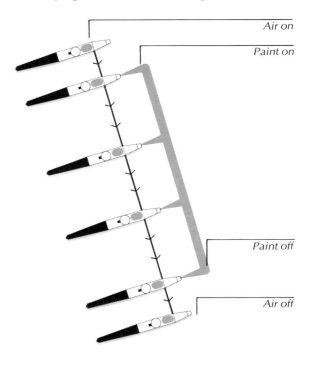

Air on

Paint on

Paint off

Air off

Spraying a line
If you are spraying a line (above), the secret of success is to press the lever down for air before you start spraying.

VARYING LINE WIDTH

Finger control of the nozzle (see page 103) is one way of controlling the width of the spray with a double action model. Another simple but important factor in the width of spray produced with either a single or double action is the distance from which you spray.

The closer the nozzle of the airbrush is held to the surface being sprayed, the sharper and finer the width of spray. The most sophisticated airbrush will produce a hairline of color. As the nozzle is drawn further away from the surface, the line sprayed will broaden, decrease in density, and begin to fuzz at the edges.

The four lines in the example (below) share identical conditions – 0.2mm nozzle, 30 psi/2 bar, water-based dye, same finger control – except for the distance between the nozzle and the surface.

Other factors which influence spray width are the size of nozzle fitted to the airbrush, the air pressure, and the viscosity and composition of the medium.

Varying the width of the line

The width of a sprayed line can be varied by changing the distance between the nozzle and the surface (right). The further the airbrush is held away from the surface, the broader, but less dense, the line will be.

Spraying a line

There are three things to bear in mind when spraying a line: the amount of paint being expelled, the distance of the nozzle from the surface, and the fact that the airbrush must be kept moving. Although this sounds complicated, it comes as second nature with practice.

FIRST MOVES

The best way of getting to know your airbrush and acquiring basic handling skills is by learning and practicing the simple techniques demonstrated below. These strokes – spraying a flat tone, a graduated tone, a circle outline, a solid circle and a semicircle – used in various combinations and variations, are the base strokes on which much of the most sophisticated airbrush art is built.

SPRAYING A FLAT TONE

The airbrush wins hands down over the paintbrush when it comes to creating a flat tone – you can spray a perfectly even block of color which you could never match by hand. The inventor of the airbrush, Charles Burdick, produced his prototype airbrush at the end of the last century for just this reason – to lay down a perfectly even watercolor wash.

Use good quality, hard-surfaced paper or artboard – spraying on an inferior surface may give disappointing results that are nothing to do with your efforts. Cut a 2 in/5 cm square with a scalpel and straight edge from a piece of stiff card to use as a mask. Position the mask on the artboard and weight it down or tape it with masking tape.

1 Mark out the square on a sheet of card, using a pencil and ruler.

2 Cut out the square with a sharp scalpel or craft knife.

Charge your airbrush with a small amount of water-based color such as transparent ink, watercolor or gouache, thinned to the correct consistency (see pp. 86-95). Following the golden rule of air on first, air off last (see page 103), and holding the airbrush about 3 in/7.5 cm above the surface, lightly spray back and forth across the exposed square in broad, even strokes. Start at the top and work down, overlapping the strokes and spacing them evenly. Overspray will fall on the surrounding mask on either side of each stroke.

Allow the paint to dry thoroughly before repeating the procedure, building up a solid block of color in three or four applications. Remove the mask and judge the results. Try the same exercise with different sized masks and different colors, and also try varying the distance between the nozzle and the surface.

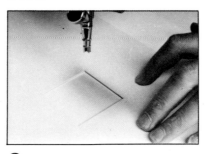

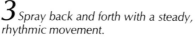

3 Spray back and forth with a steady, rhythmic movement.

4 The finished square should have an even, flat layer of color.

SPRAYING A GRADUATED TONE

Many styles of airbrush art require graduated tones and they have developed because, in skilled hands, the airbrush can produce a perfectly graduated vignette that begins as white and ends as solid color. As with spraying flat tones, the unique capabilities of the airbrush should be exploited.

Assemble the same materials as for a flat tone – a piece of stiff card with a 2 in/5 cm square cut out of it, hard-surfaced paper or artboard, water-based medium and masking tape or a weight.

Position and secure the mask on the artboard and charge the airbrush with color. Mentally divide the square into thirds. Hold the airbrush about 4 in/10 cm from the surface and start to spray from right to left and back again across the bottom third of the square. Overlap the strokes and space them evenly. As you reach the end of the first third, very slightly begin to lift and arc back the nozzle of the airbrush away from the surface. Continue to lift and arc back through the middle third and then release the paint flow and the air flow. As you work your way up the square, the overspray travels ahead of your strokes and produces a graduated effect as it falls. The final third of the square should be colored only by overspray with the very top of the final third remaining uncolored.

A vignetted square with solid color that gradually gives way to pure white.

SPRAYING A CIRCLE

This third technique of basic control involves a continuous circular movement and is a useful confidence building exercise. The objective is to produce a circle of color within the square keeping both the inside of the circle and the four corners of the square outside the circle as free from color as possible.

Assemble the same materials as for the flat tone and graduated tone. Secure the card mask in position and charge your airbrush with medium. Hold the airbrush about 2 in/5 cm above the surface and try to maintain this distance throughout. Introducing the air only, begin a circular movement following a pencil guide, and gradually introduce the paint. Continue the movement until the circle is the density you want – perhaps four or five complete rotations – matching each rotation as exactly as possible to the one before to avoid excessive overspray falling in the corners and center of the circle. The movement should be slow, but not so slow that you get a spidering effect or your hand wobbles from its course, and it should be continuous. Release the paint flow slowly and then the air flow, continuing the movement until both paint and air are off. A skilled airbrush artist will be able to produce a perfect circle with almost white corners; a beginner's first attempt might be an almost solid square of color. This is a difficult handling exercise which will take time to master.

When spraying a circle, keep the airbrush moving in a continuous circular movement.

SPRAYING A SOLID CIRCLE FREEHAND

This freehand technique is again an exercise in basic control – the end result is a solid circle with an ill-defined fuzzy edge. It doesn't involve a mask. All you need is artboard or paper, water-based color and the airbrush. You may want to draw a pencil guide for the first few attempts.

Charge your airbrush with color and hold the nozzle about 3 in/7.5 cm above the surface, maintaining this distance throughout. Introducing air only first and then slowly introducing the paint, spray into the centre of the circle. Keeping the movement continuous, build up the color in the center and gradually spiral out into a slightly wider circular movement – the movement should not reach your pencil guide which is the outer edge of the circle and made up with overspray. Releasing first the paint flow and then the air flow, finish spraying. The application of the spray shouldn't be interrupted at any point or the uniformity and evenness of the sphere may be affected.

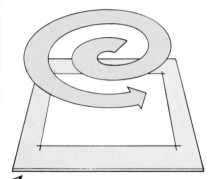

1 For a solid circle, build up color by moving in a spiral motion.

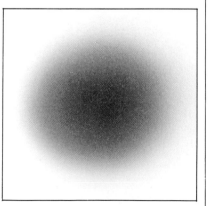

2 The finished circle should have an even covering of paint with no blotches.

SPRAYING A SEMICIRCLE FREEHAND

This technique combines the sweeping strokes of the flat tone and the circular movement of the circle. You don't need a mask but a pencil guide might be useful for the first few attempts. Use artboard or art paper and water-based color. Load your airbrush with color. Hold the airbrush nozzle about 2 in/5 cm above the surface and maintain it at that distance. Following the golden rule (see page 103) to avoid a build-up of paint or blobs at either end of the semicircle, begin spraying in sweeping semicircular strokes. Four or five strokes matched each one over the one before should produce a solid semicircle with fuzzy edges caused by the overspray.

Practice this freehand technique, which is widely used for highlighting in three-dimensional work (see the sphere on page 110), in different sizes and densities.

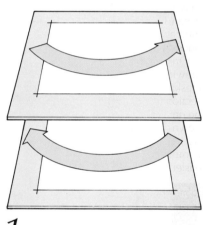

1 Spraying a semi-circle requires a combination of both sweeping and circular strokes.

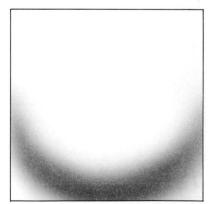

2 The finished semi-circle should have fuzzy edges caused by the overspray.

THE BASIC FORMS

Most complicated and simple forms can be reduced to a combination of any or all of four distinct three-dimensional forms – the cube, cylinder, sphere and cone. Courses in airbrush art techniques traditionally start with these objects. Learning to render these shapes provides a solid grounding in basic representational art techniques, as well as giving practice in elementary airbrush techniques such as planning a masking sequence and airbrushing a graded tone.

The airbrush is widely used to render objects with photographic precision and realism, where the individual strokes produced by a paintbrush could never achieve the desired result and where the eye of the camera is too unselective and all embracing. Part of this precision is the accurate observation and depiction of light and shadow falling on an object which give it its

form. Practice in airbrushing the basic forms lit from different directions and different heights is also practice in how to create form with light and shadow.

The techniques of rendering these basic forms shown on the next few pages combine the first moves of spraying a flat tone, vignetting or spraying a graduated tone, and freehand circular spraying shown on pages 105 to 106. The sharp contrast of light and shade in these examples suggests objects made of a highly reflective material, such as metal. The method of masking can be used to determine the texture of an object, as well as the air: paint ratio expelled by the airbrush, the distance at which you spray from the surface, and the texture of the surface itself. Masking film is used to render a metallic finish. Try the same exercises with a loose mask, such as a handheld card mask, to create a mat finish texture.

USING MASKING FILM

The mask is almost as crucial as the airbrush in even the most basic techniques. Low-tack masking film is the masking material most commonly used. It can be cut to any shape, however intricate, and if properly laid will produce a perfect line.

Once you have transferred your drawing on to artboard, cut a piece of masking film slightly larger than the section of the drawing you are working on on all sides. Don't tape the artboard down on the work surface – you want to be free to turn it around as you cut complicated edges as this makes the task easier.

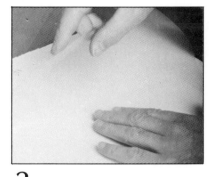

2 Position a corner of the film and lay down the piece, smoothing out any air bubbles as you go. Gently burnish the film all over with your fingers to ensure one hundred per cent adhesion.

1 Nick up one corner of the piece of masking film and carefully peel off the backing sheet. Try to keep the tacky side of the film free from fingerprints and specks of dust.

3 With a sharp scalpel blade and a cutting edge such as a ruler, cut around the section you are going to spray. Avoid pressing down on the scalpel or you may scratch the surface beneath the film. Nick up one corner of the film and peel off to expose the area for spraying.

Creating a cube by subtractive masking
First draw the outline of a cube. Then lay on a sheet of masking film.

Cut out what will be the darkest face of the cube and spray a flat even tone over the exposed face. Follow this by cutting out what will be the second darkest face. Spray a flat even tone.

Finally cut out what will be the lightest face. Spray a flat even tone.

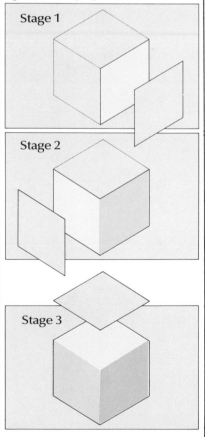

Stage 1

Stage 2

Stage 3

BASIC FORMS: THE CUBE
Stage one

The cube is the simplest of all three-dimensional forms. The masking procedure has three stages — one for each face of the cube. Decide which direction the light is coming from and work out the tonal value of each face. Use an actual card cube and an adjustable lamp to experiment with different distributions of light and shadow. Do a color rough using felt tip markers.

Once the drawing has been made, lay a sheet of masking film over the whole area of the cube. Mask out the surrounding area with scrap paper.

1 Select the darkest face of the cube. With a sharp scalpel blade and a straight edge, cut around the darkest face. Remove the film.

2 Lay in a graduated tone, starting at the darkest corner. Make this face fairly dark to provide enough contrast with the other two faces.

Stage two

You can either use the same sheet of masking film for the whole cube, removing one face at a time as in the subtractive method of masking (see page 107) or discard the used film and lay a new sheet at each stage. The film surrounding the face being sprayed gets covered in overspray and it can be difficult to follow the lines of the drawing beneath.

Cut around the second face of the cube and remove the film to expose the second face. Compare the first face with your color rough and adjust the density of the color if necessary.

Remove the film and lay in a graduated tone. If you are not using a new piece of masking film, overspray will fall on to the first face, darkening it further.

Cut out the film to reveal the second face of the cube and spray in a graduated tone. Allow overspray to fall on the first face, darkening it further.

Stage three

If you are using a new mask at each stage, discard the old mask and lay down a new sheet. Cut around the remaining face and remove the film to expose it.

1 First check with your color rough and then spray in the lightest face starting at the darkest corner. Spray lightly, pulling the head of the airbrush back a quarter of the way across the face and shutting off the paint flow altogether by the halfway point. Overspray will lightly colour the rest of the face.

2 Finally remove the masking film and the surrounding paper mask to reveal the perfectly rendered three-dimensional form of a cube.

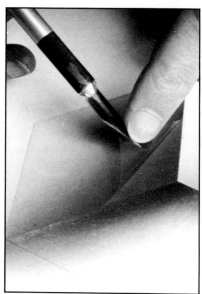

BASIC FORMS: THE CYLINDER
Stage one

Airbrushing a cylinder is more complicated than a cube, involving additional techniques and loose masks. The planning again falls into three stages. Do a series of roughs with markers to help you work out the masking sequence.

Once the drawing is on the artboard lay a sheet of masking film over the whole cylinder. Use the ellipse template you used for the drawing as a cutting guide for the curved end. Use a ruler as a cutting guide for the straight sides. Don't try cutting freehand – every tiny imperfection in your cutting will be blindingly obvious. Remove the film from the body of the cylinder and set it aside to be reused at the third stage, leaving the end masked.

Cut a paper or card mask to cover the strip of white highlight where the light hits the cylinder directly, and either hold it with your hand or weight it in position. This will give a softer edge than the sharp lines representing the boundaries of the body of the cylinder.

Spray a light flat tone over the exposed sections of the cylinder.

Stage two

As well as the light hitting the cylinder directly and the planes of lower tonal value falling away from the light, the shadow areas will reflect light. The darkest area of the shadow is slightly away from the edge.

1 Loose masks are used to create the thin strips of dark shadow. A sheet of paper forms one edge of the strip on the left side of the cylinder and a plastic ruler the other. Spray along the edge of the ruler, giving a hard edge against the ruler and a soft edge as the paper mask flaps slightly under the impact of the spray.

2 Two rulers are used as masks for the dark strip of shadow on the right side of the cylinder, giving two hard edges. The shadow is sprayed through the two rulers laid in position, held there by their own weight.

Stage three

The body of the cylinder is now complete, leaving only the end section. To protect the completed part of the work, replace the masking film cut out for the first stage.

Spray on a graduated tone, starting at the point where the end section meets the lightest point of the body – the white highlight strip – and pull back the airbrush about one-third of the way across, to complete the cylinder.

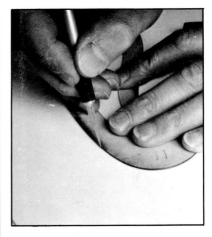

Match the film exactly with the drawing around the curve or you will be left with either a white ring at the edge of the curve or an ugly overlapped ring of spray.

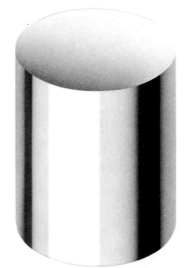

BASIC FORMS: THE SPHERE
Stage one

Airbrushing a sphere is easy in terms of masking because only one mask is involved, but difficult to master because most of the spraying is freehand. Do some color roughs with markers, experimenting with densities and contrasts of light and dark.

Use a compass to draw a circle on the artboard. Cover the circle with a sheet of masking film about 2 in/5 cm wider in diameter. Mask the surrounding surface with scrap paper. With a circle cutter, or a compass fitted with a blade, cut round the edge of the circle. Remove the film to expose the sphere.

Identify in your mind's eye, or by referring to your rough, where the lightest and darkest points will be. Start spraying at the darkest point. Spray in regular semicircular sweeps back and forth.

Stage two

The sequence of spraying falls less obviously into stages for the sphere than for the other forms. The first stage is identifying the darkest areas. The second stage is laying in the darkest shadows and the mid-tones.

1 The darkest part of the shadow falls slightly inside the edge of the circle – the underside of the sphere, although in shadow, reflects light from the surface it is sitting on. The next step is to darken up the shadow. Use the same freehand spraying technique – semicircular, back and forth – but with much shorter strokes, concentrating the color on the darkest arc of shadow.

2 Working around the edge of the circle, lay in the mid-tone shadows, leaving the soft-edged white highlight directly opposite the darkest area of shadow. The form of the sphere now begins to emerge.

Stage three

This final stage is very much a matter of individual judgment. For the form to appear to be entirely spherical, you may need to darken the edges further. You may not be happy with the whiteness of the highlight – in this case, blast some white gouache into the center of the highlight letting the overspray merge with the soft edge.

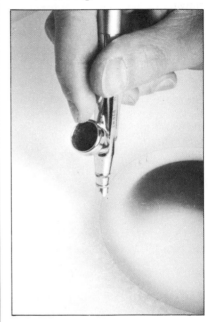

Overspray on the masking film will have obscured the outer edge of the circle. Nick up a corner of the mask and peel it back a little way to judge the density of the spray against the background. Replace the mask exactly if you decide to adjust your work.

BASIC FORMS: THE CONE
Stage one

Rendering a cone is similar to rendering a cylinder, although the cone involves flaring the spray from the point of the cone to the base. Do some color roughs to experiment with the different densities of shadow.

Lay a sheet of masking film over the drawing of the cone. Use an ellipse template to guide your scalpel blade around the curved base of the cone — don't attempt to cut freehand. Use straight edges to cut the sides. Remove the film to expose the whole shape.

Cut a paper mask to cover the white highlight down the centre of the cone and weight it in position. Spray an even tone over the exposed sections of the cone.

Stage two

Loose masks are used to lay in the shadows. Some of the shadows have hard edges and some soft — spray along rulers for the hard edges and loosely weighted paper masks for the soft edges.

1 *If you use a ruler, try lifting one end to vary the quality of the edge — the higher you raise it, the softer the line will be.*

2 *For the shadows hard-edged on both sides, spray between two rulers crossed at the point of the cone and wider apart at the base.*

Stage three

The third stage is to add the finishing touches freehand. Darken up the shadows to heighten the contrast, or lighten the highlight by spraying white gouache into the center of it. The overspray will merge with the soft edges.

Widen the spray towards the base of the cone. Check the darkness of the shadows and alter them if needs be to get a convincing image.

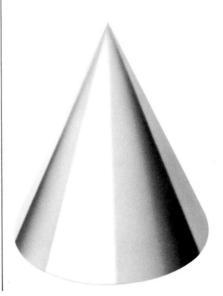

USING CUTTING EDGES

This sequence demonstrates the use of French curves and straight edges as drawing, masking, and cutting guides. Choose simple shapes to practice on rather than a more complex image where there are distractions of color and composition. Concentrate on accurate, precise drawing and cutting until it becomes second nature.

1 Lay a sheet of masking film on to a piece of artboard. Draw directly on to the masking film with a finely sharpened HB graphite pencil, using the French curve to make a shape. Maintain the point of the pencil at the same angle throughout the sweep of the curve at an angle that feels natural and that you can reproduce when you come to cut out the mask. Draw a rectangular shape in the same way using a ruler.

2 Reposition the French curve or ruler on the drawing and use it as a cutting guide. Use a scalpel with a razor-sharp blade. Many people find that a round-handled scalpel knife is more comfortable to hold and easier to manipulate than a flat-handled one.

Hold the scalpel as you held the pencil, and cut slowly but confidently following the sweep of the curve in one movement.

Just the weight of your hand on the blade is probably sufficient pressure to cut cleanly through the masking film without damaging the surface of the board.

3 Knowing exactly how much pressure to exert comes with practice. If you score too deeply into the board, medium will collect in the cuts and show through the final image as dark outlines.

Take care when cutting not to shave the edge off the French curve. Prolonged use of plastic cutting edges almost inevitably produces misshapen edges.

4 When you have cut round all the edges of the drawn outline, check the corners – if they are not cut cleanly through, the masking film may tear as you peel it away.

Use the point of the scalpel blade to nick up the corner of the cut mask, making sure you don't stretch it if you are going to use it again.

5 Bend back the edge you have caught with the blade and peel the piece of film away.

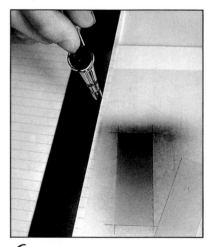

6 Hold the temporary mask in place with a steel rule or something similar and start spraying, using a small amount of transparent ink.

7 Remove the mask and check the precision of the edges. Look particularly for clean corners and strong lines with no sudden undulations. Practice this exercise as many times as you can.

CUTTING A PERFECT CIRCLE

This short sequence of photographs demonstrates how to cut, mask and spray a perfect circle. The airbrush is the ideal tool for rendering perfect geometric shapes, both in two and three dimensions — the same crispness of line and evenness of tone would be very difficult to achieve with a paintbrush. Spraying circles and other shapes helps you to get the feel of your airbrush and enables you to tune in to its characteristics and idiosyn-cracies. The accuracy of the mask determines its effectiveness — it's best to use a circle cutter.

What you need
White, hard-surfaced artboard, a drawing compass and pencil, layout paper, low-tack masking film, a circle cutter or scalpel blade, a scalpel knife and violet transparent ink.

MAKING THE MASK

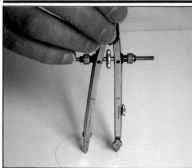

1 Draw a circle on the artboard with a pencil and drawing compass. Use a hard pencil – 4H to 6H.

2 Lay a piece of scrap layout paper – preferably transparent – over the artboard and tape it down. Roughly draw around the pencil circle.

3 Allowing a generous margin all round, cut a circle from the layout paper with a scalpel, exposing the finely drawn circle beneath. This outer mask will protect the artboard from overspray.

4 Cut a square of masking film large enough to cover the whole exposed area. Peel off the backing paper, taking care to protect the adhesive side of the masking film from dust particles or from grease.

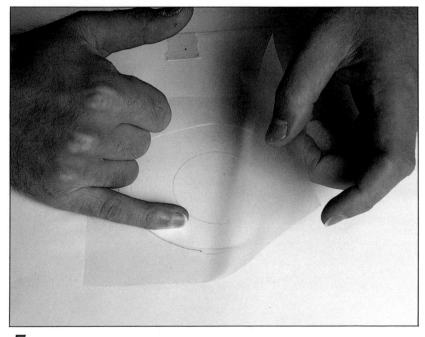

5 Lay the masking film in position, smoothing it down with your fingers or a burnishing tool, to eliminate any air bubbles.

If you are working on a fluffier surface than artboard, de-tack the film before laying it down by touching it on to a sheet of tracing paper, or the surface may pull away with the film when you remove it.

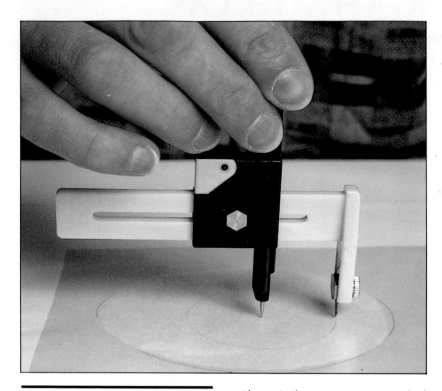

2 *Lift out the circle of masking film with the point of a scalpel blade, taking care not to nick the surface of the artboard. Airbrush spray will accentuate the slightest blemish.*

Cutting the circle

1 *The pencil circle and center point made with the compass will be visible through the mask. Position the point of the circle cutter, which is like a compass but has a knife point instead of a lead, on the compass point and cut around the pencil line.*

Alternatively you can use a scalpel blade fixed in a compass, but it is difficult to produce a true circle in this way, mainly because you have to improvise a way of fixing the blade.

A third option is a circle template, but these have two disadvantages. They are difficult to cut round while keeping the scalpel blade at the same angle, and they come in predetermined sizes.

Spraying the circle

1 *Charge the airbrush with a small amount of violet ink. Holding the nozzle of the airbrush at a distance of approximately 2 in/5 cm from the surface, spray an even, flat tone over the exposed circle.*

Avoiding point holes

When using a circle cutter as shown above, or when drawing a circle with a compass, there is a useful trick for avoiding point holes in the artwork surface. Cut a tiny square of artboard and stick it to the center point of the circle using either double-sided tape or ordinary adhesive tape. The point of the compass can be inserted into this, preventing any damage to the surface of the artwork.

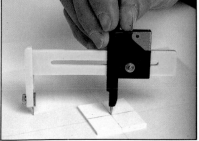

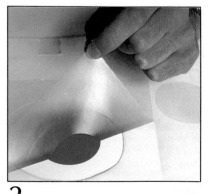

2 *Allow the ink to dry – a matter of minutes. Lift off the masking film – low-tack masking film will not affect the surface of the artboard.*

USING A SPATTER CAP

In this three-dimensional image of a black snooker ball, the airbrush work is limited to laying in the textured background, the shadow cast by the ball and the white highlights which bring the picture to life. The three techniques employed − spattering, masking in a drop shadow, and/highlighting − produce a unique effect that could not be achieved with a paintbrush.

This image actually forms part of a larger artwork (see page 119) and demonstrates how an apparently complex piece can be broken down into a series of relatively simple sequences.

The textured background is produced using a combination of techniques. The very large blobs are achieved by dropping the air pressure on the air source until it is very low. The finer spatter is produced by raising the pressure slightly. Two contrasting colors are used − blue and red − to create a lively effect. It takes a certain amount of time to master the use of scrap paper before you start in earnest.

What you need
Hard-surfaced, white artboard (CS10 or Schoelleshammer), graphite pencil, technical pen, jet black technical pen ink, drawing instruments (set square, ruler, inking compass or circle template and a compass cutter) transparent inks in lemon yellow, violet and magenta, designer's white gouache, masking film, tracing paper, spatter cap, tissue or rag, and a fine paintbrush.

STARTING THE IMAGE

1 With a compass or circle template and pencil, draw a circle directly on to the artboard. With a set square and ruler, draw in the outer square. Ink in the square, and block in the circle with a technical pen and jet black ink.

Once the black ink is dry − a matter of moments − oversprayed transparent inks will not show up and there is no need to mask out the circle.

Mask out the background area along the edges of the square. Load your airbrush with pale yellow transparent ink and spray an even tone over the image.

3 With magenta ink spray along the edge of the ball, allowing the overspray to form the soft outer edge of the shadow. This soft edge creates a more convincing shadow than a hard edge.

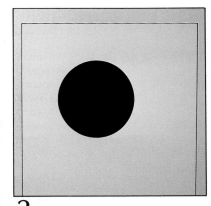

2 Spraying in a soft-edged drop shadow will raise the ball off the surface. Lay a square of tracing paper reinforced with masking film over the image. Secure it in place with tape and cut exactly around the edge of the black circle. Remove the circle to expose the ball. Decide on the direction in which the light is falling, and pull the mask over a fraction on the opposite side, exposing a crescent shaped area of yellow background tone. Weight the mask in position.

The drop shadow
After checking the strength of color *with the background, peel away the mask to reveal the drop shadow.*

Fitting a spatter cap

The diagram below shows how to remove the air and needle caps from the body of the airbrush prior to fitting the spatter cap itself.

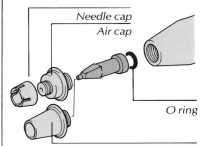

Needle cap
Air cap

O ring

Spatter cap

1 Unscrew the handle of the airbrush and expose the needle chuck assembly. The spatter cap is also shown in the photograph.

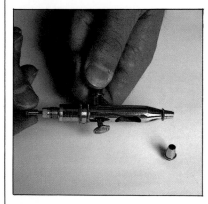

2 Loosen the needle clamp screw on the needle chuck and withdraw the needle by about ¼ in/5 mm or so. This will prevent you from damaging the delicate needle when you fit the spatter cap. Remember not to force any parts of the airbrush while you fit the spatter cap.

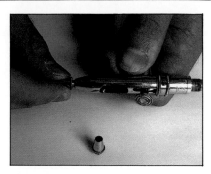

3 Unscrew the air cap and needle cap from the body of the airbrush. Do this over a table so that the pieces won't be able to roll away.

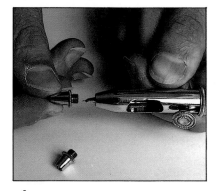

4 Carefully position the spatter cap over the end of the exposed nozzle set.

Using a spatter cap

1 Lower the pressure of your air source from 30 psi/2 bar to 10 psi/0·7 bar. With the spatter cap fitted, the airbrush charged with magenta ink · and the original mask around the square still in position, start to spatter over the whole image. Hold the airbrush approximately 18 in /45 cm above the surface and let the spatter fall on to the image.

You can vary the texture by holding the airbrush at different distances from the surface. The further away it is, the looser the pattern and the less control you have over it.

2 As you work, paint will build up inside the spatter cap and eventually drip off the end. Have a piece of tissue or rag handy to wipe the end regularly and to keep the paint build-up under control.

The spatter background
The spatter effect is emphasized by using two colors. Note how the spatter has been taken over the shadow.

3 *Leave the magenta to dry and then repeat the operation with violet ink. It is particularly important to allow each color to dry thoroughly if your spatter pattern is made up of large blobs of color.*

The textured background is now complete.

Cleaning the spatter cap

First unscrew the handle of the airbrush and remove the needle (see Section 1, pages 52–55). Carefully unscrew and remove the spatter cap. Clean it gently with a Q - tip dipped in water, or an appropriate solvent if you are using a spirit- or oil-based medium. Screw the air cap back in position then finally replace and refix the needle and handle.

Adding the white highlights

Visualize where the highlights will fall on the ball, perhaps sketching them in roughly on a piece of tracing paper laid over the ball.

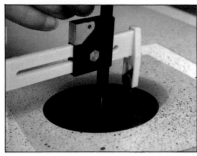

1 *Lay a new sheet of masking film over the circle. With a compass cutter positioned on the center point of the ball, cut two parallel lines. Cut the outer line, which describes the outer edge of the highlight, just inside the edge of the ball along about a third of the circumference and parallel to the drop shadow. Cut the inner line just beyond where the area of spray should end – the inner edge of the highlight is formed by overspray. To remove the mask, lift the strip of film in the center and gently tear away both ends leaving a ragged edge.*

2 *Spray a line of thinned white gouache along the outer edge of the highlight, allowing the overspray to form the top edge and ends.*

3 *Remove the mask. Once the white is dry, blow a little magenta ink to reflect back the color of the shadow and to add warmth to the highlight.*

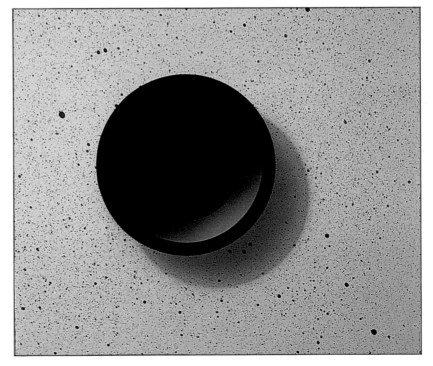

Fringe highlights
Highlighting not only adds an illusion of dimension but it also emphasizes the texture of the ball.

5 *A large spot of white gouache applied to the center of the highlight provides the final flourish.*

4 *Spray the spot highlight freehand, a technique which takes practice. Start with the airbrush about 2 in/5 cm above the surface and spray the solid center of the dot. Pull the airbrush back, spraying the outer halo of white as you go.*

6 *Remove the outer mask that has stayed in position throughout the exercise, exposing a clean white edge to offset the finished artwork.*

Point highlights
The point highlight adds "shine" to the ball and completes the illusion. The *illustration on the opposite page shows how this image was incorporated into a larger one.*

Other techniques for spheres

Airbrushing spheres provides the artist with a challenge because there are two things to convey – the texture of the material and the illusion of dimension. The four examples below demonstrate four different techniques. The more reflective a surface is, the more detailed the highlights ought to be – "chrome-effect" being the ultimate.

shadow and highlights added

detailed reflections added

full color reflections

chrome-effect

The complete painting
Spatter has been used to create three different effects. Whereas it has been used as a general background on the table top, it plays a different role in the jacket and the speaker. Here it has been used to imitate the texture of cloth and gauze.

Large spatters made by splashing on masking fluid with a brush before the background was sprayed. The fluid acted as a resist. A similar effect could have been achieved by using white gouache. However, the danger with this method is that if the splash goes wrong, the artwork background is damaged and may require repair. The advantage of using liquid masking is that if the splashes were not quite right, they can be rubbed off by hand. Liquid masking can be sprayed through an airbrush for a more subtle effect.

White gouache spots were spattered on to the jacket at a final stage so that they would not be polluted by other colors. The spots are most visible on darker areas like the shoulders.

PLANNING A MASKING SEQUENCE

Skillful masking is just as important as practiced handling of the airbrush — many illustrators, graphic artists, and photoretouchers spend more time cutting masks than actually spraying through them. Success with even the simplest of masking techniques comes down to planning.

Look at your image carefully and identify the colors and tones involved in it. Rough out a visual using Magic Markers or colored pencils. Work out how many separate masking operations will be involved and the order in which you should put down the different colors. You can quickly sketch each stage using a different colored marker or pencil. If you are using transparent inks, as in the image below, you should spray from dark to light, starting with the black. If you are using an opaque medium, such as gouache, you can work in any order.

Missing out this vital planning stage, particularly if your image involves more than two masks, usually results in using more masks than you need. And the more masks you use, the more cuts you make over the same lines on the artwork. This can have two negative results — it may cause the surface of the artboard to lift, or, if the cuts are too deep, they will show through the paint surface and blemish the finish.

Once you have got the hang of laying and lifting cut masks, you can start reusing the same masks. This reduces the number of cuts made on the surface of the artwork to a minimum. Lay a sheet of film over the whole image and cut all the lines before you start spraying. Carefully remove each section of film, replacing it on the backing sheet. Transfer sections of cut film to the artwork as you need them, returning them to their original position on the backing sheet after use. Take care to keep the mask free from dirt and moisture. Dirt is particularly easy to transfer to the artwork, and often the only way of disguising it is by respraying the area. Remove each piece of mask with the tip of a scalpel blade and one finger. Avoid touching the tacky side of the masking film with your finger.

CREATING A STYLIZED FACE WITH FOUR MASKS

This simple but striking graphic image demonstrates how to plan and build up an image through four masking stages using three colored inks. For each stage of the image we isolate the color being sprayed, show the actual mask used, and finally combine the new color with previous colors, as the image would be built up in reality — color on color.

Materials and equipment

Airbrush, hard surfaced, white artboard, transparent water-based inks (black, red and blue), low-tack airbrush masking film, scrap paper for masking, a scalpel holder and sharp blade, a technical pen (optional for putting down the black|color), cutting edges (French curves and a ruler, depending on your image), and tissue.

The first mask — flat black

If you are using transparent inks, put the black down first. The great advantage of these inks is that you can overspray dark colors with another color or without affecting the color beneath. Lay masking film over the whole image. Mask off surrounding areas of artboard with scrap paper. Cut around the areas to be sprayed black, taking particular care with the very small, thin sections. Lift off the cut pieces and begin spraying. A flat tone is easy to achieve with black. Have some tissue handy around the areas you are spraying for mopping up any beads of ink sitting on the mask-

ing film. This ink will not dry because masking film is non-absorbent, and you may smudge the artboard as you lift off the film when this stage is completed. Another advantage of transparent inks is that they dry on artboard very quickly. Check that you have sprayed all the black areas — it is easy to miss one, particularly if you have very tiny sections as in this image. When the ink is dry, lift off the mask.

You may wish to achieve this first stage with a technical pen. The final result will not be very different, but the quality of the edges may suffer unless you are practiced at using a pen.

A solid line achieved with a hard film mask.

A soft line achieved with a soft paper mask.

Order of spraying spatter effect

Cut around the triangle, the petal shape and the thin strip. Lift the triangle first and spatter from dark to light. Lift the petal shape next and spatter. Finally lift the thin strip and spatter. Take care not to spray the darkest areas too dark – as you spray the lighter areas with the darker areas exposed, the color will build up on the darker areas.

The second mask – spatter effect

In this artwork, spatter effect is used sparingly and contributes to the strength of the image. Resist the temptation to use spatter effect for the sake of it or the impact of the final artwork may be lost. Lay a second piece of masking film over the image and cut around the areas to be sprayed, but this time don't lift them off. You will of course have the black area sprayed in Stage I beneath. Go back to your visual and identify the darkest areas. Lift off the mask from the darkest area first, and work from dark to light.

In order to produce a spatter effect you have to drop the air pressure. If you have a compressor with a regulator, you can control the flow of air easily. Reduce the pressure of 30 psi/2 bar to 10 psi/0.7 bar. If you use aerosol cans rather than a compressor, you can achieve the same effect with a can which is almost empty. Many professionals use this second method. It is more a case of trial and error, however, so practice on a spare piece of paper first. You can build up a supply of almost empty cans for this purpose.

The softer line around the edge of the hair can be achieved with a paper mask. Lay a piece of tracing paper over the area and draw round the soft edge (the inner edge of the hair in this case). Cut out the mask, attach it loosely to mask off the inner edge, and spray through it. As you finish an area, say the chin and neck, cover it with a scrap paper mask to avoid spatter from the next section falling on it.

The third mask – scarlet vermilion

Lay a third sheet of masking film over the image. Cut around the areas to be sprayed with the third color, in this case, red. Use cutting edges, particularly for the fine, thin sections. Don't try cutting freehand until you are fairly proficient. Be careful when using plastic cutting edges not to cut through the plastic. Masking film is transparent so you can see the image clearly through the film. Take care not to mark the artboard with the scalpel — learning the correct amount of pressure to apply will come with practice.

The red is solid color, so spray a flat, even tone. When the ink is completely dry, remove the mask. Low-tack masking film will not lift off the colors already on the board when it is removed. If you are using a thick pigmented paint, such as thick gouache, however, some of the paint will be removed with the mask.

The highlight areas in this image are represented by the white of the artboard. Remember to leave these areas masked at each masking stage.

The fourth mask – Prussian blue

Fading tones are introduced into the image at this stage. Work out the spraying order carefully – thorough initial planning rears its head again – and work from dark to light. Lay on the fourth piece of mask and cut around the areas to be sprayed. Lift the mask off the first area to be sprayed and fade the color from dark to light. Again, remember to leave the white highlight areas masked. When the ink is completely dry, remove the mask. Now you have your final image.

The blue mask overlaps the gray already sprayed to give a blue-gray

Accurate cutting is required to get subtle forms such as the narrowing shadow area on top of the nose

Checking the final image

When you have removed the fourth mask, check the final illustration for any missed areas. If you have missed anything, don't remask at this stage, but complete with brushwork.

MASKING WITH TORN PAPER

The airbrush has long been used by artists to create atmospheric sky backgrounds — gently graduated tones, wispy clouds, and melting sunsets exploit fully the capabilities of airbrushed spray. Starting with a graduated night sky ranging from deep black to bright orange, this sequence of pictures demonstrates the techniques of rendering soft, thin cloud and adding a half-obscured rising moon. The artist wants to convey atmosphere and drama in this image, rather than realism either of color or form. The techniques used here could be equally well used for dawn, daytime or twilight skies, and for the sun rather than the moon. Color plays an obviously large role in any artwork—choose yours carefully.

What you need
Tracing or layout paper, scalpel, circle template, masking tape, red and orange transparent inks, and white designer's gouache.

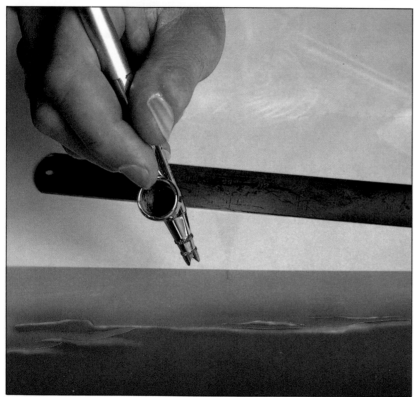

3 Lay another piece of tracing or layout paper over the area where you want to add the moon. Draw a slightly elongated circle around the immediate area of the moon on the tracing paper; bright highlights will reflect from the clouds immediately above and below it. In order to obscure the moon slightly behind a thin wisp of cloud, draw a thin line across the center of the circle, where you plan to put the moon in.

STARTING THE IMAGE

1 The first task is to introduce low-lying thin cloud lit up by a rising moon and the last rays of a dramatic sunset. Roughly tear a long edge of a piece of tracing or layout paper wider than the area of sky. This is used as a mask for the cloud. Weight the tracing paper in position on the orange sky.

Holding the airbrush about 2 in/5 cm away, spray light red ink loosely along the edge of the mask, allowing the mask to flap up and down under the impact of the spray. Let the overspray merge with the black of the higher sky. This will produce a soft-edged impression.

Move the mask down and spray along the same edge again, creating a second layer of cloud. Lift up the mask from time to time to evaluate the effects.

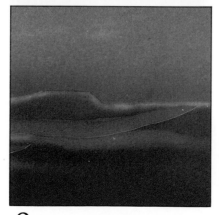

2 This close-up shows the tracing paper edge flapping under the air pressure from the spray. This enhances the overall effect by producing an inconsistency in the edge of the sprayed area.

4 Cut the two semicircles that make up the mask with a scalpel. Don't cut too precise a line or you will get a hard instead of a soft edge when you spray in the moon. Tape the tracing paper mask in position.

Using a circle template as a mask

1 Choose an appropriate size circle on a circle template to represent the moon and position it over the tracing mask, ensuring that the thin bridge of the tracing mask runs through the center of the moon. Use masking tape to block out the surrounding circles.

With thinly mixed white gouache, spray into the center of the exposed area, letting the overspray form a soft outer edge. Remove the template mask.

2 With the tracing mask still in position, lightly spray freehand with white around the area of the moon to loosen up the effect.

3 Remove the tracing mask. Add some freehand highlights with white gouache along the underside of the cloud to suggest moonlight reflections.

The sky has now been transformed from a fading orange sunset on a clear night into a slightly ominous cloudy sky with a late moon rising just above the horizon.

The sky formed the backdrop to a rather gory image of a gravedigger returning from a night's work with a bloodied spade. The image was used for a book jacket.

The finished sky
When all the masks are removed, the soft edges of the sky contrast sharply with the stark silhouette.

OPAQUE SOFT PAPER MASKS

The previous sequence used masks of tracing paper, a material which cuts or tears in a particular way. Experience shows that different types of paper create subtly different effects when used as torn masks, because of the range of weight, density and fiber quality. In the steps shown below, ordinary lined writing paper is used to create a mist effect.

1 *Tear the paper to create the edge quality required. It may take two or three attempts to get it right.*

Detail of soft edges

2 *Position the mask on the artwork and spray along the torn edge with white. Hold it far enough back to leave the torn edge free to flap under the spray, softening the color. Repeat with white over blue-gray to build up the misty effect of fine clouds.*

REINFORCING TRACING PAPER

Tracing paper is flexible and tends to be pressed down on the artwork by the airbrush spray. To make the starburst effect shown below, a stiffer texture is required. You can make a stiff mask from card or heavy paper, but in this case its positioning is crucial, so the mask must

1 *Mark the starburst positions on tracing paper. Apply adhesive masking film.*

be semi-transparent. However, a loose mask is required; adhesive masking film will not do. To solve the problem, the tracing paper is reinforced with a layer of masking film and this combination provides the quality needed. You cannot draw in pencil once the film is in place, so mark the tracing paper before applying film.

2 *Smooth the low-tack masking film over the tracing, making sure that you avoid creases.*

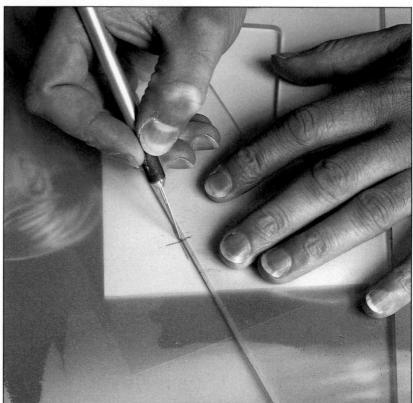

3 *Attach the mask to the top of the artwork to register the positions of the starbursts. Insert a piece of plain card* underneath the mask to protect the artwork. Cut small star shapes in the mask.

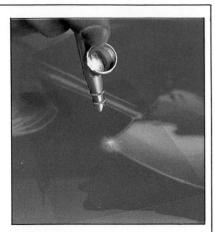

USING A FRENCH CURVE AS A MASK

Minor adjustments may be needed at the last stage of a piece of airbrushed artwork.

The highlight area on the shovel needs a little more contrast. This was originally executed with a cut film mask, but to avoid possible damage to completed surface detail, a plastic French curve is used to remask the shape.

4 *Remove the protective card and spray a burst of white into each cut.*

5 *Peel back the tracing paper carefully to reveal the airbrushed shapes.*

6 *To heighten the effect of the star-bursts, spray a white dot freehand into the centre of each.*

The finished image
The major highlight on the shovel falls *in one line with the moon for a touch of realism.*

OTHER MASKING TECHNIQUES

This simple technique, using dry transfer lettering as an instant mask, produces a quick but slick result and is widely used by professionals to render colored lettering in presentation quality roughs. It is also a useful technique if you are producing posters by hand. And you are not restricted to lettering. As well as a vast selection of typefaces in different weights and sizes, manufacturers of dry transfers include in their catalogs a comprehensive collection of symbols and pictograms — for example, decorative frames, borders and corners, musical symbols and architectural pictograms (vehicles, human figures, plants and furniture). For texture and pattern, there are dotted screens, lined screens of varying density, graduated screens and miscellaneous patterns, including representational effects such as brick, tiling and paving. Other effects such as hatching, mesh, reflections on water and wood grain are also available. These sheets can be cut to the exact size needed for your illustration and they can be used as masks in the same way as lettering.

At the end of the process demonstrated here, the transfer itself is discarded. In mixed media work, you might want to incorporate the transfer as part of the finished image.

What you need
Hard-surfaced white artboard, straight edges for rendering the square panel, masking film, dry transfers, burnisher (this can be the wrong end of a pencil), Indian red and light yellow transparent inks, scalpel and tape.

USING DRY TRANSFERS

1 The dry transfer acts as a negative mask – you lay it down, spray over it and remove the transfer to expose its white image beneath. Draw the square panel on to the artboard. Lay a piece of masking film over the area you are working on. Mask out background areas with layout or scrap paper. Cut the square panel in which the lettering is set out of the masking film and remove.

Position the dry transfer in the exposed square and burnish it down. A spatula designed for the job is used here, but the blunt end of a scalpel knife or pencil would do just as well. Any tears or wrinkles in the transfer will be doubly obvious in its airbrushed outline – if you have damaged the transfer, use a piece of tape to lift it carefully from the surface.

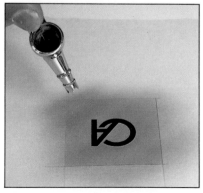

2 Spray an even tone over the exposed square. If you plan to spray the actual lettering in a second color and you are using a transparent medium such as watercolor or ink, use a darker color for the background. You will then avoid having to remask.

3 When the color is completely dry, lay a piece of tape over the dry transfer and lift it off. It should come away cleanly. Use a second piece to pick up any bits missed the first time.

This trick can be used on most hard-surfaced artboards without the tape damaging either the surface itself or the color you have sprayed on. Nevertheless, do an initial test with a piece of tape on a corner of the surface you are working on.

You could use the point of a scalpel blade to scrape off the transfer, but you risk damaging the surface of the artboard.

4 *This may be as far as you want to go — crisp white lettering set in a square of flat red tone.*

For colored lettering, overspray the whole square lightly with the second color — here, light yellow. If you spray only over the area of the lettering itself, the overspray will deepen the immediate background red and give an uneven overall result.

5 *Remove the mask. Include a dry transfer catalog on your studio bookshelf — it is an invaluable source of reference.*

The finished image

Left hand side of small gold script darkened with a fine spray of darker yellow

Because of the size of the illustration, the larger lettering and drop shadows were masked with cut film

The larger colored letters were hand painted in gouache over transfers that were laid over the base yellow

Complex lettering

This image contains some very complex examples of lettering, including type with serif and script faces. The curved surface of the bottle makes the job of mask-cutting even more difficult.

The size of the original artwork makes the cutting easier but very careful construction of letters is required to make complicated type styles appear to go around corners.

SPRAYING A REPEAT PATTERN

Alternative method

A cheaper alternative to acetate is a piece of stiff card. Draw and cut out the image and spray through it in exactly the same way. If you are using a loose mask made in this way for a repeat pattern, make registration marks on the edge of the card.

Acetate, or cel as it is sometimes called, is an excellent material for making a stencil for a repeat pattern. It is durable and has the great advantage of being transparent so that you can see exactly what you are doing. Any overspray can be wiped off between sprays to preserve its transparency.

Draw the image directly on to the acetate.

Cut out the image with a sharp scalpel on a cutting mat. If you are using it for a repeat pattern, draw registration marks on to the acetate. These marks can be lined up with faint pencil rules on the spraying surface.

CREATING PATTERN AND TEXTURE

The section on masking materials describes a range of objects, materials and cut shapes that can be used as loose masks. These photographs illustrate just a few.

Thinking of ways to render a particular texture or pattern may involve some lateral thinking — for example, a piece of wire mesh may not be the first object that springs to mind when you are looking for a mask for a checkered tablecloth. Equally you might not associate pale green reeds standing out against a dark murky pond with a handful of dried spaghetti. Observing other people's work closely, and storing up ideas for future reference, will help you build up an imaginative repertoire of solutions to masking problems.

Paper doilies

Paper doilies provide ready-stencilled patterns which you might use to suggest the edge of a piece of fabric, or just to spray a pretty pattern on the top of a birthday cake.

The doily is simply hand held on the surface, producing a soft-edged pattern.

Once you have cut out the mask, can use it to create a repeat pattern simply by moving it along a step and respraying through it.

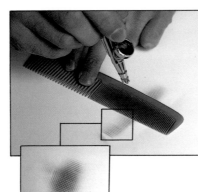

USING REPEAT PATTERNS

Simple repeat pattern cut from acetate and reused to create a frieze.

The movement lines on this part of the illustration were sprayed against a mask cut for the purpose from acetate. The mask imitated the shape of the rock drill. It is often a good idea to keep masks like these for later use.

Applying reusable masks
The lines used to convey the impression of pulsating movement in the drill and hand were sprayed through a reusable mask. Similarly, a single mask was sprayed through five times to create the motif along the top.

Cotton
Spraying against cotton produces a soft if somewhat random edge. Cotton can be molded into whatever shape you want to suggest, whether for wispy clouds, or a mottled pattern, such as the black-brown surface of bamboo, or sunlight falling through cloud. It can be used in a thick wad or stretched thinly so you can actually spray through it as well as round it provided the fibers are teased first.

Organic materials
Organic materials should not be overlooked in the search for loose masks. This ivy branch, loosely held against the surface, becomes a simple but effective mask. A lot of pattern variation can be achieved with just one mask, perhaps by moving the mask a fraction after spraying the first color and then lightly overspraying a second color.

Combs
A comb is a good example of an ordinary household object that can be transformed into a loose mask. By spraying through the teeth first one way and then a second time with the comb laid at right angles to its original position, you can produce this faded out grid effect, with its suggestion of vibration. The size of a comb limits its uses, but it can be used very effectively in small areas — for example, to put texture into the finish of a piece of cloth.

USING AN ERASER

Erasers have several uses in the airbrush artist's studio apart from the most obvious one of obliterating errors. They can be used to add highlights, create texture and sharpen soft edges. Different types of eraser are suitable for different purposes.

The pencil eraser is ideal for deleting details and for cleaning up a hard edge. It can be sharpened to a fine, pristine point giving you maximum control over what is erased.

The soft rubber or kneadable putty eraser is less useful for removing errors but excellent for producing soft edged highlights. To create a spot highlight, for example, rub hard in a tight circle at the center of the highlight and a fluffy, fading outer circle will appear automatically. A putty rubber is also useful for correcting pencil drawings on artboard because unlike a hard eraser it won't damage the surface of the artboard. A scuffed surface will show through a thin-medium such as drawing ink or water-color.

If you use liquid masking in your airbrush work, a putty eraser is a good way of removing the dried mask—simply rub the eraser over the mask and it will pick it up and peel it away.

Jumping from the commonplace desk eraser to a sophisticated piece of equipment, there is the air eraser. The air eraser works in the same way as an airbrush. Erasing powder is propelled through it to blast off the surface of the artwork. However, used in this limited way it is rather like taking a sledgehammer to crack a nut, unless you work on a very large scale. One of the air eraser's specialized uses is in glass etching, where the powder is used to skim off the surface of the glass.

Creating soft highlights

To achieve a soft highlight with a bright center as on the rounded surfaces of these ripening apples, you need a pencil eraser, a fine paintbrush, white designer's gouache, and a scalpel knife.

1 Rub in the center of the highlight area with the pencil eraser. The soft, fading outer edge will appear as you rub. This method produces a softer, grainier texture than airbrush spray and is more appropriate to the subject in this case.

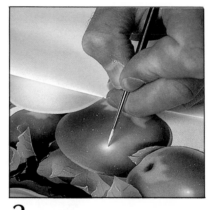

2 Load the fine paintbrush with a tiny amount of thickly mixed white gouache and apply a dot of paint in the center of the highlight to strengthen it.

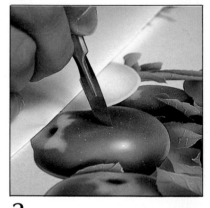

3 A rounded scalpel blade is used here to scratch back spots of the red color on the apple skins, adding a touch of character to the image.

Diffused edge of highlights obtained by using a pencil eraser in a circular motion

Edge of red in apple softened by rubbing with an eraser

Softening edges

This illustration looks as if it was done with a paint brush using pale water-color washes, but it was, in fact, executed with an airbrush. If you look at it carefully, you can spot the tell-tale signs. It would be impossible to get such flat washes using a paint brush. Much of the softening of the edges and the highlighting was done with an ordinary pencil eraser.

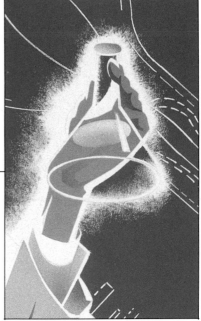

The aura or haze around the hand of the scientist was made using a hard pencil eraser. These eraser. allow greater accuracy and can be used like a pencil

The broken edge of the cloud formation was made with a hard eraser

TRACING AND SCALING AN IMAGE

Once you have attained a certain level of manual dexterity, and have mastered the basic techniques that are so essential to certain types of successful airbrushing, you will inevitably want to move on to the next stage where you want to incorporate a specific image in an artwork. In essence, you have two options; either you create the image from scratch, using a critical observer's eye, or you hunt around for a suitable reference drawing or photograph that you can plunder for your own uses. If you are to succeed in the first approach, you have to enter the realms of "fine art" where nothing is certain and interpretation becomes something of a tightrope where you either win or lose. Most illustrators and graphic artists choose to skirt around elements of doubt, and for this reason, they find an existing image which suits their needs and they then translate this image on to the artwork they are creating.

CONSTRUCTION AND SCALING

Assuming you have opted for the latter method of integrating an image into an artwork, you will either be lucky or unlucky. If fortune is with you, you will be able to trace the image directly on to the artwork, but, and this happens most of the time, you will probably find that the size of the found image is wrong, or the angle is wrong, or it doesn't tell you everything you want to know. If this is the case, you will have to reconstruct the image, using mechanical or geometric means. At the most base level, you will have to enlarge or reduce the image, but you may also have to alter viewpoint angles, or amalgamate information from two or more images into one – these are techniques which are largely gained from experience; they would take a veritable tome to explain, and even then they wouldn't necessarily be very successful or particularly suitable.

PUSHING THROUGH

The most basic method of transferring an image, and it doesn't require any special equipment, is called "pushing through". It can be done using a variety of surfaces but tracing or layout paper suits the technique best.

Tape the image securely to your work surface and lay the sheet of tracing paper over the top. Anchor the tracing paper so that it can't slip.

Using a hard pencil – an H or a 2H – trace out an outline of the image; unless you are absolutely sure of what you are doing, it's best to refrain from adding fine details at this stage.

When you have completed the outline, remove the tracing paper and turn it over. Shade over the outline you have made with a softer pencil – an HB is best as anything softer will smudge the artwork surface at the next stage.

Tape the artwork surface to your drawing board and lay the sheet of tracing paper, right side up, on top. Position the tracing exactly where you want it on the artwork, and tape it down.

Trace over your original outline with a hard pencil – a 5H or 6H – and you will find that the softer graphite on the underside transfers the image to the artwork surface.

Reversing the image

If you want a reversed or flopped image for your final artwork, you can miss out a stage of the pushing through sequence.

When you draft the original outline, use an HB pencil. Then, to transfer a reversed image, turn over the sheet of tracing paper and run over your outline with a burnishing tool or the end of a pencil.

Using manufactured alternatives

When transferring an image, you can use carbon paper. However, using carbon paper tends to be messy, because imprints of hands or any other pressure points are transferred as well as the outline you want.

The manufacturers of graphic art materials have come up with a solution to the problems caused by the smudge marks of normal carbon paper, and several now make a finer version which is usually termed tracing down paper Many professional illustrators find tracing down paper an invaluable aid and something they would sorely miss if it wasn't available.

If you are the buccaneering sort, you can make up a substitute tracing down paper yourself by applying traditional grate polish (Zebrite) to the reverse of ordinary tracing paper.

REFERENCE SOURCES

If you are lucky enough to be commissioned to produce a highly detailed artwork for something like a prototype for a certain manufacturer, you will almost certainly be given something to go on. In other words, you will be given engineer's drawings which you will be expected to interpret. Alas, if you are a novice, you needn't expect a commission of this caliber because they are extremely difficult to execute successfully unless you have much experience.

However, assuming you aren't an expert, but have been asked to produce an artwork containing certain images – you will be presented with a problem; where do you find reference material?

The old adage that "the local library will suffice", seldom succeeds when your commission begs something totally original. For this reason it is worthwhile building up your own reference file which might include magazines, books, postcards, sketches and catalogs.

SCALING IMAGES USING A GRID

In 99% of cases, the size of the image you have to hand won't match the size of the image you have in mind. The cheapest, but most laborious, way of converting the image to suit your design is to use the grid system . Although this method is reviled by students, and despised by aficionados, it remains fundamental to many aspects of graphic design and is well worth appreciating.

The essence of the "gridding" procedure is as follows. Lay a grid tracing paper over the original, and scribe the outline using a hard (H or 2H) pencil.

Using your tracing as a guide, reduce (or enlarge) the image on to another sheet of grid paper. If you want to reduce the size of the image, use a smaller scale grid; if you want to enlarge, use a larger grid. To transfer a key point, first determine where it lies on the grid by counting up and across. Then reverse the procedure to plot the point on the second grid. When you have plotted all of the key points, draw in the detail lines.

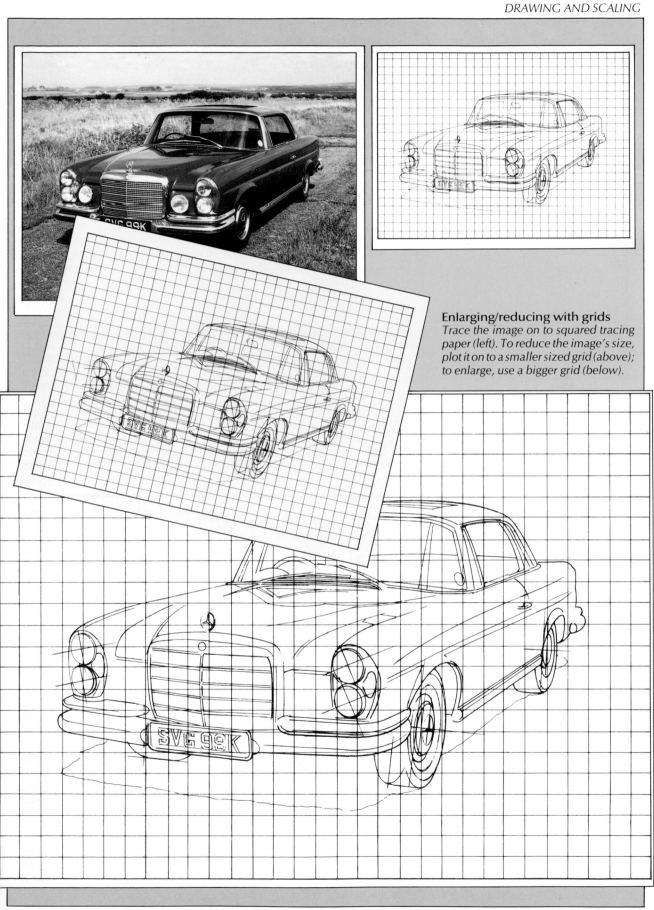

Enlarging/reducing with grids
Trace the image on to squared tracing paper (left). To reduce the image's size, plot it on to a smaller sized grid (above); to enlarge, use a bigger grid (below).

REDUCING/ENLARGING EQUIPMENT

There are several types of machines which are specially designed for enlarging or reducing the scale of an image. They can save a great deal of time and trouble but they are usually very expensive.

Visualizers

Visualizers project an image from either a photograph, a transparency or a printed page from an adjustable bed on to a glass screen which is often housed under a fabric hood. The image is either enlarged or reduced by cranking the bed up or down. The image that is projected on to the viewing screen can be traced off directly.

Visualizers are expensive machines but they are invaluable if you have a lot of tracing up to do. Some visualisers have a facility for add-on accessories which can convert them into simple line print cameras, known as PMT machines.

Vertical art projectors

These machines are essentially sophisticated slide projectors that are purpose-built with designers in mind. They have to be operated in subdued lighting, but they are small enough to sit on a desk top. They can be used to enlarge images from transparencies or small prints up to about three times the original size.

Working from transparencies

An ordinary slide projector can be pressed into service if you want to take a tracing from a transparency. If you aim the projector at a flat, pale wall, the amount of enlargement can be altered by varying the distance between the projector and the wall. Although tracing an image off a wall is not particularly comfortable, the method does work quite well. If you do use a slide projector, make certain that it is positioned square to the wall or else you will get a distorted image.

Photocopiers

Many recently manufactured photocopiers have an enlarging/reducing facility. On some machines the ratios are preset, but on the more sophisticated models, you can decide your own ratios within a fairly limited range. Photocopiers can be used to reduce or enlarge flat images like photographs, and the copy can then be transferred to the work surface.

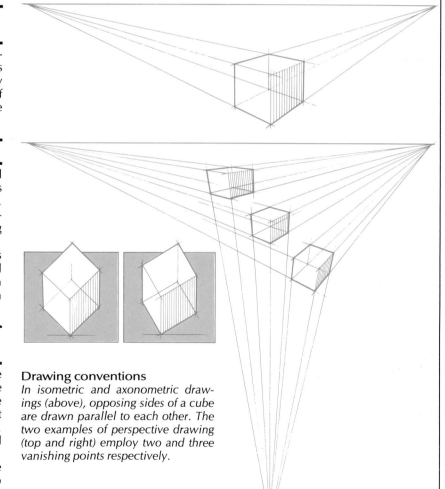

THREE-DIMENSIONAL CONSTRUCTIONS

Simple, three–dimensional constructions of the basic geometrical forms featured on pages 102 to 111 are easily achieved. And, with the exception of the cube, all the constructions can be built up without using perspective.

Using ellipse templates

A relatively expensive but very useful piece of equipment for any serious construction is a set of ellipse templates. An ellipse is simply a circle in perspective and the templates come in varying sizes and in varying degrees of flatness.

Ellipse templates are invaluable aids when it comes to drawing cylinders and cones. It is worth experimenting with the shapes before you use them in earnest.

DRAWING IN PERSPECTIVE

In the cube that is used to demonstrate techniques and effects in this book, the construction is simple: the sides are parallel and the edges of the image that recede from the eye do not converge. This type of construction is called isometric drawing.

Convergence, or perspective, can be constructed by taking the lines back to their "vanishing points". One, two or three vanishing points can be used.

Drawing conventions
In isometric and axonometric drawings (above), opposing sides of a cube are drawn parallel to each other. The two examples of perspective drawing (top and right) employ two and three vanishing points respectively.

Perspective grids
Pre-drawn perspective grids assume three vanishing points. The grid pattern is sub-divided, and complex volumes can be plotted and constructed along the three axes.

APPLYING BASIC FORMS

The technique of breaking down complex forms into basic elements has been used by artists and illustrators for generations. The theory is that even the most sophisticated shape can be constructed using combinations of the four basic forms — the sphere, cylinder, square, and cone. Once a shape has been simplified into its elements, it becomes easier to draw and understand.

One of the most difficult subjects to draw effectively is the human form and by implication, robot forms which are surprisingly difficult to make convincing. Even the most accurately traced image of the human form will require subtle alterations in order to make it look convincing. Making a body appear to have bones relies upon an understanding of anatomy and the way in which everything fits together. One way of understanding a body's shape is to construct an image using the "combination of basic forms" theory.

Construction of a robot hand
The image of the robot hand (left) was carefully constructed from scratch using sections of the four elementary shapes — the cone, square, sphere, and cylinder. Ellipse guides were valuable drawing aids.

CASTING SHADOWS

Shadow areas are fundamental to many artworks as they add depth and reality to a drawing. Cast shadows not only improve the sense of reality of an image but they also serve to "ground" an object on the surface on which it is sitting. Similarly, shadows can be used to establish the position of an image which is apparently suspended in space.

As with perspective constructions, there are geometrical methods of plotting the fall of a shadow but it is a complicated procedure and a grasp of the essential principles is sufficient for most people.

Shadows from sunlight

The angle and intensity of shadows cast by the sun vary from the beginning to the end of the day. Knowing this, an illustrator can convey an idea of the time of day in an artwork and also the type of climate. Rays of sunlight are assumed to be parallel for the sake of convenience and in the diagrams below, the varying directions of light are shown with their respective shadow patterns.

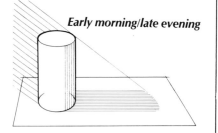

Early morning/late evening

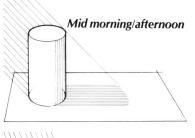

Mid morning/afternoon

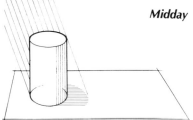

Midday

Shadows from artificial light

Rays of light travel in straight lines and they cannot change direction unless a reflector of some sort is introduced. However, whereas the rays from the sun are considered parallel, the rays from an artificial light are not because they come from a single point (of course, fluorescent lighting is different again but it complicates the issue and is not discussed here). Because, for the sake of argument, artificial light comes from a point source, the shadows it creates are different from those cast by sunlight. In the first place, they are different in shape and, secondly, they are larger.

Constructing shadows cast by artificial light is relatively straightforward and is best described by a diagram (below). The important point to remember is that the further the light rays are from the source, the more they diverge, and the wider the shadow becomes.

Of course, few artworks consist solely of a cube in a desertscape, but even if you are drawing a complicated scene, the principles of shadow construction remain the same and add realism.

Geometric construction of shadows

Simple shadows cast by a single point source can be constructed using ruled lines as shown in the diagram (below).

The four basic forms and their shadows cast from a single point source of light (below).

Using shadows

Shadows can add intense drama to some types of artwork. In the surreal image (above), long, evening shadows help to convey an aura of mystery.

The ant (above centre) has been "grounded" on the surface by the shadow. This technique is useful where

you want to clarify the position of an object in the context of its surroundings.

The shadows on the prisoner (above right) come from a curious angle which adds to the dramatic image, even if they are totally unrealistic.

The shadows for the film poster (below) serve several purposes. In the first place the smoke shadow has been manipulated to form the profile of a

snake – a simple device which helps to give an idea of what the film is about. Secondly, the harshness of the shadows helps to give the impression of strong, hot sunlight.

LETTERING TECHNIQUES

This complex logo incorporates three-dimensional lettering sunk into a reflective panel. It is set against a textured and shiny background and the whole image is raised off the surface by a drop shadow. It demonstrates several classic techniques of lettering.

Rendering reflective or chrome surfaces and lettering are standard airbrush applications. The familiar style of chrome lettering reflects a desertscape of blue or pink sky above a black horizon line fading into yellow sand – a style dating back to the emergence of hyper-realistic American illustration that coincided with the production of heavily chromed automobiles in the late fifties and early sixties.

A wealth of reference material is available – look at illustration annuals, illustration manuals, graphics magazines, album covers and books like this one. Or set up your own reference. You can reflect anything you like into a shiny surface – a city skyline or a country scene. Experiment by reflecting different pictures into a piece of silvered paper or foil. An urban environment offers lots of inspiration. Look for mirror-faced buildings or reflective **store**-front lettering and take photographs of them. The images and atmosphere reflected will alter throughout the day as the light changes, and from season to season. With all these sources you can quickly build up a comprehensive reference file.

What you need

Tracing paper, cutting edges (rulers, ellipse guides, circle guides and set squares), lettering reference (for example, a dry transfer catalog), a grid for scaling up (or enlarging equipment), white hard-surfaced artboard, tracing down paper, masking tape, hard graphite pencils (4H – 6H), technical pen and jet black ink, mat masking film, scalpel and blades, scrap paper, spatter cap, transparent inks in black, gray blue, carmesine, red Indian ink, white designer's gouache, a weight (anything to hand), and a fine paintbrush.

DRAWING OUT THE IMAGE LINE MARK

1 Once the artist has worked out the design of the logo in his head or in pencil roughs, he starts to draw it up on tracing paper. For a precisely rendered drawing like this, you will need a variety of drawing aids, including a ruler, a set square, a circle guide and an ellipse guide.

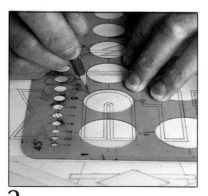

2 Here, the artist is using an ellipse guide to draw in the curved base of the U.

3 You will also need reference for the lettering, and one of the best places to find this is in a dry transfer lettering catalog. Trying to create your own lettering tends to be unsuccessful unless you are very skilled. Scale the lettering up to the required size, using either a grid or enlarging equipment (see page 136).

The final pencil trace should be done with great care and precision. Check it over thoroughly when you have finished for any missed lines. Note that the horizon line along the center of the reflective panel is not drawn in at this stage, but is drawn directly on to the mask later on – it does not form part of the outlined framework.

4 The next step is to transfer the tracing to the artboard, using whatever method you prefer (see page 134). Here, the artist uses tracing down paper. Position the tracing on the board and tape it down securely, ensuring there are no wrinkles in the paper. Slide the tracing down paper between the tracing and the board and tape it in position. Trace over the image with a hard graphite pencil (4H, 5H or 6H are suitable), again using straight edges and templates as guides.

5 The artist has made life easier for himself by making thick and thin black lines an integral part of the logo. It is infinitely easier to cut masks and to achieve clean lines with a line framework, than if each line or edge has to be created by sprayed color. He has also chosen to use transparent inks, so overspray falling on the black lines will not be visible.

Ink in the whole image using a technical pen, jet black technical pen ink, and drawing instruments to achieve exact lines.

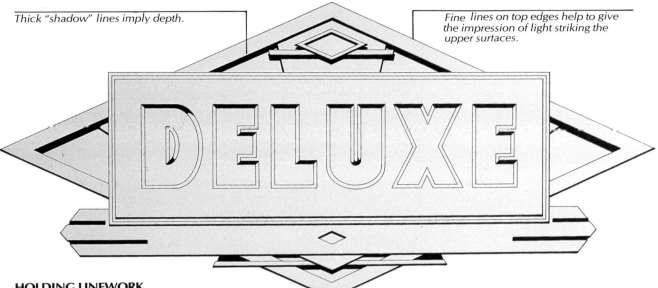

Thick "shadow" lines imply depth.

Fine lines on top edges help to give the impression of light striking the upper surfaces.

HOLDING LINEWORK

6 *Also block in lines and any solid areas of black in the same way. Professionals often use this technique of an inked framework to save time at the mask cutting stage.*

7 *Check over the finished black line work for any missed sections and for any corners that may need tidying up.*

PROJECT PLANNING

At this stage sit back and plan the airbrushing and masking sequence (see page 120). As you develop your own system of working, for example whether you make new masks for each color or use one master mask, a working plan will form in your head almost automatically as you are drawing up the image. It cannot be stressed often enough that considered planning at this point will save a great deal of time at later stages.

For this image, which requires intricate masking, a new piece of masking film is used for each color. Smaller pieces of mask can easily be mislaid or overlooked, particularly once they become obscured by overspray.

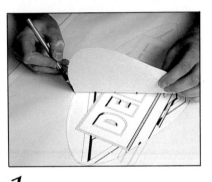

1 *Mask out background areas of artboard with scrap paper, or layout paper as here, to protect against overspray and to cut down on the amount of masking film needed for each mask. Accuracy is not essential in this case.*

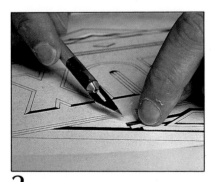

2 *The artist has identified the dark background areas as the first section to be sprayed. Lay a sheet of masking film over the whole image. Using a sharp scalpel blade and cutting edges as necessary, cut around the sections to be sprayed and gently remove the cut pieces of mask.*

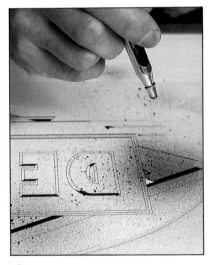

3 *The artist has decided to introduce some texture into the background using a spatter cap. With jet black ink and a low pressure of 10 psi/0·7 bar, spatter over the exposed areas. Flush out the airbrush with water and reload with grey blue ink. At normal operating pressure lay in a grey tone over the black spatter to give it depth. Recharge the airbrush a third time with pink carmesine ink and gently spray over an even tone. The addition of pink, although hardly noticeable, warms up the image and prevents it becoming too harsh.*

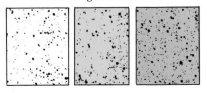

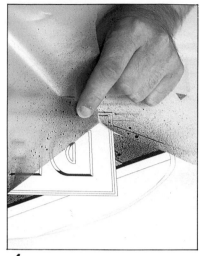

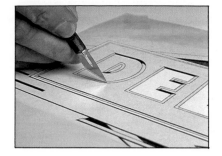

4 As you build up this background color with gray and pink, occasionally peel back a corner of the mask in order to check the color you are creating against the white background. You generally find that the color appears stronger against white than you imagined, and you may want to correct this. Always smooth the mask down carefully before starting to spray again.

Remove and discard the mask.

5 The next color to go in is the Indian red, and a second sheet of masking film is laid over the whole image. Identify the red areas, which include the lettering, the two diamonds, and the border of the reflective panel. Cut out and remove these sections.

7 Spray a flat even tone of Indian red over the whole image. Again check the strength of the color by lifting back a corner of the mask. Deepen the hue evenly if necessary. Remove and discard the mask. Think through the rest of your planned sequence at this stage – you may decide to introduce new colors or textures.

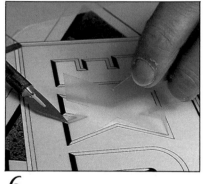

6 After cutting around a letter carefully, lift a corner of the mask section you want to remove. Take care not to nick the surface of the board.

8 The most complex area – the reflective panel behind the word 'Deluxe' – comes next. Although interrupted by the letters, the color and spray must be consistent across the panel.

THE PANEL

Lighter section left where light catches

Outside rim of panel sprayed at the same time as the letters

DRAWING ON TO FILM

1 It is important for this stage to use mat film/so that you can draw directly on to the mask with a soft graphite pencil. Draw in the central line of the reflection – the horizon line. Cut around the letters and along the central line.

2 Remove the bottom half of the mask, leaving the letters covered. Spray a thin line of jet black ink along the edge of the mask.

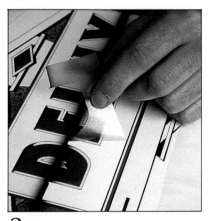

3 Replace the bottom half of the mask, but move it down a fraction. Spray over the new line of the mask to create a lower hard edge. Remove the mask.

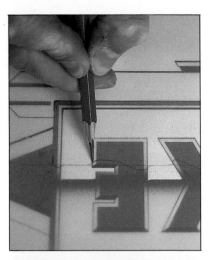

4 To create a third, softer line, lay a piece of tracing paper over the panel and draw a freehand line to represent the lower, softer edge of the horizon with a hard pencil.

5 Cut out the tracing mask and weight it in position. The top half of the panel mask should be in place at this point. Expose a strip about twice as wide as the black line. With gray blue ink, spray along the tracing mask – the pressure of the spray will lift the mask at the edge, leaving a softly defined line.

Remove the tracing mask and load your airbrush with pink carmesine. Overlapping with the gray blue line, spray on an even tone of pink, fading out as you move towards the bottom of the panel. The bottom edge of the panel should be left reasonably white to help create an overall feeling of solidity. This completes the bottom section of the panel.

7 Remove the top half of the mask, leaving the letters still covered, to expose the completely white top half of the panel.

8 With blue ink, spray evenly along the top edge of the panel and down towards the center. Fade out fairly quickly, leaving a large expanse of white between the blue and the horizon line.

9 Carefully remove the masking film from the lettering and the surrounding panel. Be careful not to get grease from fingertips on to the sticky side of the film.

Creating the horizon line
The light blue has been faded out to give the impression of sky, whereas the pink has been rendered evenly.

ADDING DIMENSION TO THE LETTERING

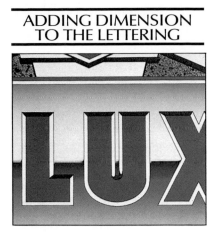

1 Remask the whole image. Cut along the parallel fine lines around the edge of each letter to expose the thin line which gives form to the lettering. In this case the word 'Deluxe' appears to be sunk into the panel, but you might choose instead to raise it out of the background – the actual drawing would be the same for both effects. This decision should be made at the initial planning stage when you work out the direction from which the light is striking the image. Spray in the different tones, consulting your reference or colored roughs to check how the light falls. Use a ruler as a loose mask at the corners.

2 Lay over a new sheet of masking film and cut out the areas of the background diamond still to be sprayed. Picking up the colors already used, tone in these sections fairly lightly.

THE COMPLETED LETTERING
The lettering and reflective panel are now complete but they still look comparatively dull and flat. The best way to bring them to life is to add subtle highlights to enhance the illusion of metallic gloss.

Darkening of borders at junctions where sections of the image meet.

Strip running round central image, improving contrast and adding depth.

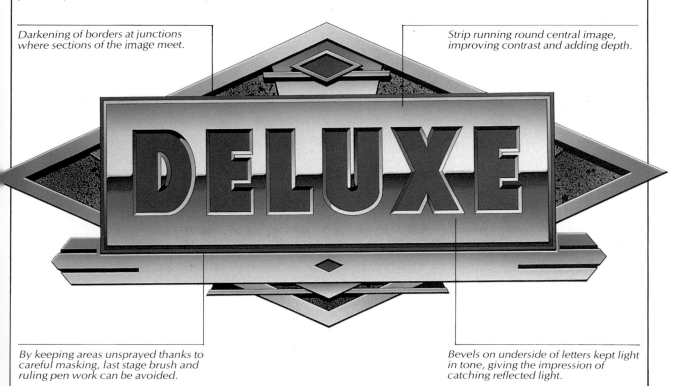

By keeping areas unsprayed thanks to careful masking, last stage brush and ruling pen work can be avoided.

Bevels on underside of letters kept light in tone, giving the impression of catching reflected light.

INSERTING A DROP SHADOW

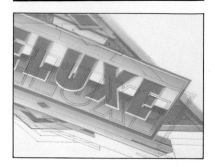

1 The basic spraying is now complete. At this stage, you can bring the logo more to life by raising it off the paper with a drop shadow.

Lay your original tracing over the image, but pull it slightly down and to the right, judging by eye the correct amount of shadow to put in.

2 Trace the line of the shadow on to the board as before, using tracing down paper inserted between tracing paper and board. Lay a piece of masking film over the whole image and cut along both edges of the drop shadow. There is no black outline to this shadow, so the edges appear softer. Spray a light gray even tone over the exposed areas. Lift a corner of the mask to check the color isn't too dark or too light. Remove the mask. Only the highlights now remain to be added.

ADDING HIGHLIGHTS
Line Highlights

1 Use a ruling pen filled with white gouache, and a ruler. Draw in white highlights around the edge of the panel to give it a three-dimensional feel. Draw in highlights on the letters in the same way, along the edges that would be hit hard by strong light.

BEFORE

2 Paint out small areas of underspray with a fine paint brush and white gouache. Underspray can be caused by a mask not sticking to a section properly, or by the air pressure from the airbrush lifting the film. Fine blobs of color can also creep under masks when the paint is allowed to get too wet. A steady hand is called for when touching up with a brush and it is a good idea to use a hand rest to protect the underlying artwork.

Before and after highlighting

AFTER

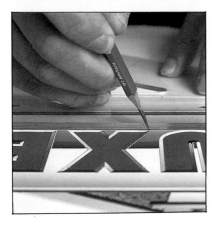

Cleaning up with a pencil line

Slight imperfections in brush or ruling pen work can be corrected and straightened by restrained lining using a graphite pencil. Make sure the pencil is pin-point sharp.

Points of Light

1 Apply a dot of white gouache with the end of a paintbrush to indicate a point of light – at corners and on curves. Allow the gouache to dry as a hard white dot, then load your airbrush with a small amount of thinned white gouache.

2 Hold the tip about 3 in/8 cm from the dot, expel a small amount of paint to flare out the dot, and pull the airbrush back from the surface. If the dot of gouache is not dry, the spray from the airbrush will blast the paint everywhere.

Star sparkle

1 A star sparkle is added at the top of the diamond. Lay a piece of tracing paper over the diamond and draw in a star Reinforce the area with masking tape.

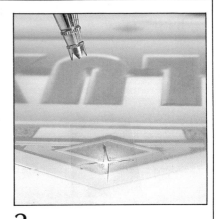

2 Carefully cut around the shape of the star and lift it out. The adhesive or making tape film helps to keep the tracing keep its shape – otherwise the pressure of the spray would cause it to lift and flap.

3 With thinned, white gouache, spray right into the center of the star, letting the overspray form the points of the star. If you spray into the points, you will get a hard edge and lose the sparkling effect. Remove the mask, and as a final touch, flare out the center of the paint.

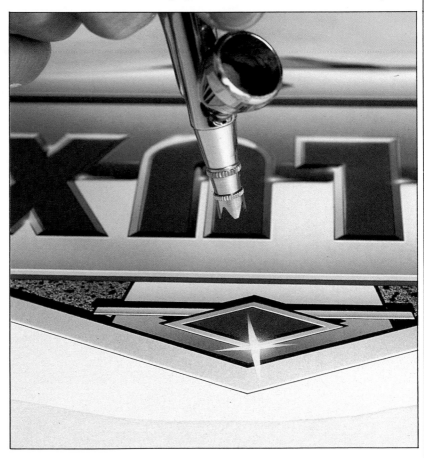

THE FINISHED IMAGE

Remove the clean scrap paper mask to reveal a clean, sharp, and precise image against a pristine white background.

Background color can have a dramatic influence on the visual impact of an image of this kind. With a white background, the warmth of the purples is much more evident, picking up the warmth of the red. A backdrop is a good idea as it helps the color balance and prevents the whole image from appearing too cold.

Background color
A black background will effect the impact of the image. It is best to stick to a white, black   lightly tinted background, otherwise it may detract from the overall effect.

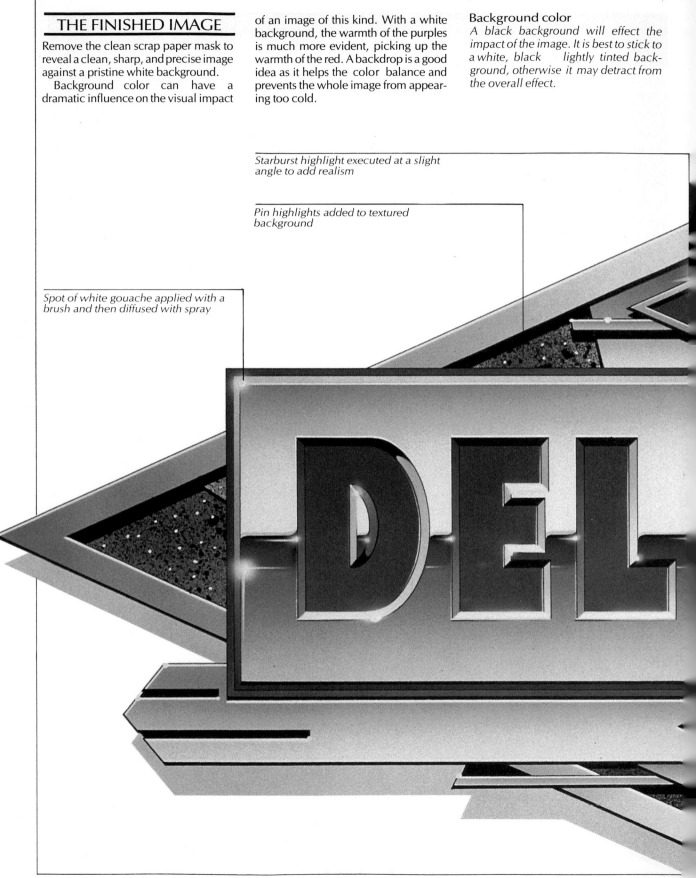

Starburst highlight executed at a slight angle to add realism

Pin highlights added to textured background

Spot of white gouache applied with a brush and then diffused with spray

Line highlight applied with a ruling pen held against a straight edge

Ruled highlight on upper edge of molded fins

CREATING CHROME EFFECTS

Classic technique

This example of "chroming" displays all the classic techniques that were partly responsible for giving airbrush art its reputation. The color-tinted reflections, highlights, and vignetted background, all go to enhance the image.

Sci-fi images
The artist who painted this image hasn't fallen into the common trap of overusing "chroming" techniques. This helps to make the image more acceptable. The illusion of speed was created using very simple masks.

Photorealism
The "chroming" in this artwork (left) is more subdued and subtle, but horizon lines make the reflections all the more realistic.

COMBINED TECHNIQUES: CONSTRUCTION

Certain types of technical illustration present such a detailed and complex effect in the finished image that to less experienced artists it may seem impossible to work out how they have been done. However, even the most complicated construction can usually be broken down into a series of elements treated individually with relatively simple airbrushing techniques. The success of the final piece depends on how well these elements are combined to create a coherent overall image.

To demonstrate this principle, the different stages in drawing and painting of a highly sophisticated illustration are detailed in the following pages. They show the structure of an oil rig described by various conventions of technical illustration and given an impressive, highly finished quality with airbrush rendering and careful brushwork. The illustration is both technically descrip-

tive, and attractively presented – an excellent sample of the best traditions of this type of work.

The projected image is drawn from engineers' orthographic plans and constructed on a pre-drawn 3-point perspective grid – although where the illustration relates to an existing structure, it is possible to scale up the projection from aerial photographs. The first stage is seen below in the inked perspective drawing; the successive stages of coloring the image, with airbrushing and hand-painted detail, are seen in sequence over the following six pages.

What you need
Technical drawing pen, ink and gouache colors, scalpel, masking film, ruling pen, fine sable brushes, loose masking materials.

Inked perspective drawing
The drawing was executed with technical pen black ink. Although the drawing looks intense at this stage, much of the inkwork will be sprayed over and this reduces the severity of the lines.

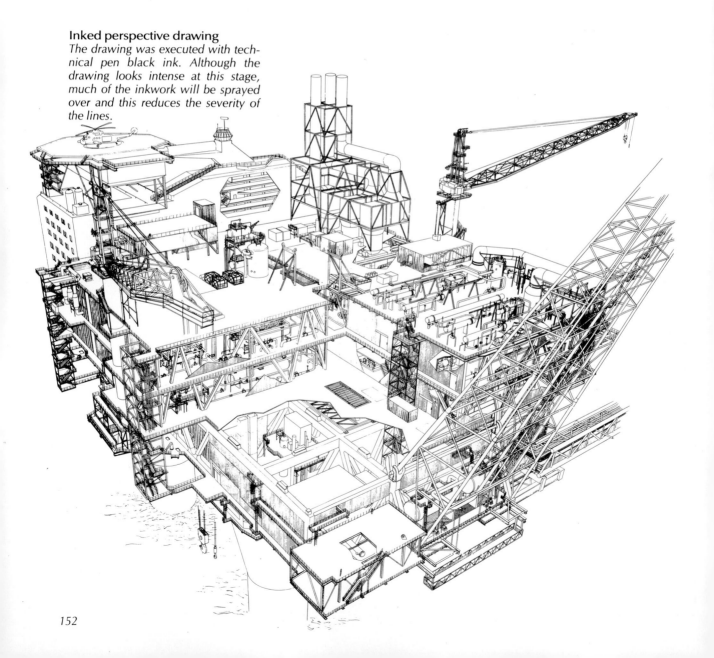

ADDING BASIC DETAILS

Once broad areas of color have been blocked in using simple film masks, the first details can be added.

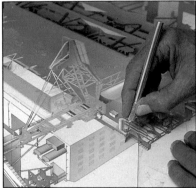

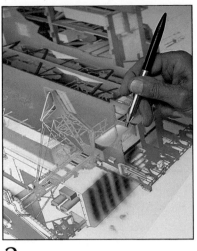

1 After spraying the background, the windows are cut out of masking film.

2 Each window piece is lifted out on the blade of a scalpel. The windows are then sprayed through the masking film.

3 The mask is lifted to reveal the basic window shapes.

First steps
Major areas of color are sprayed on before detailed work begins.

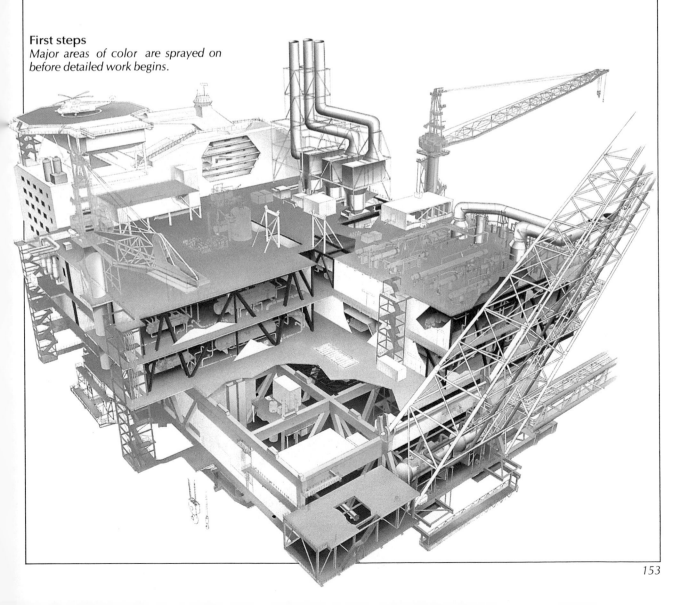

Adding detail

This view of the construction shows the artwork with some detail added. The insets highlight areas where fine detailing has been completed.

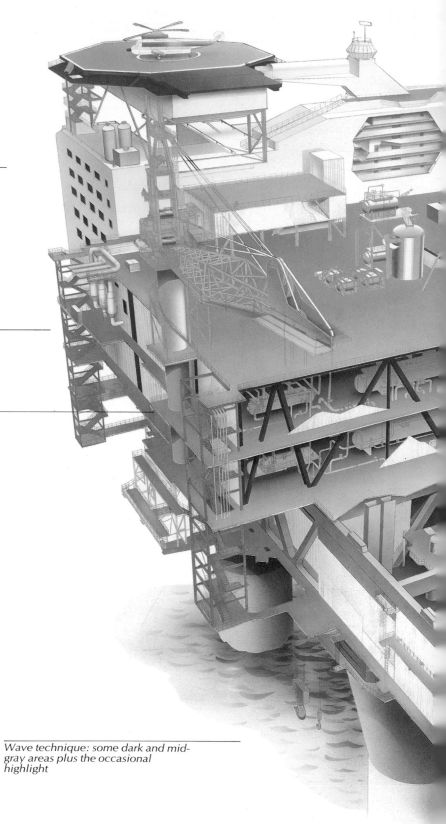

Upper surfaces left white to keep maximum contrast

Basic linework still showing through to give corrugated look

Items in shadow areas left a lighter tone

Drawing over color

The fine linear rail construction of the jib is drawn with a ruling pen over the airbrushed color.

Wave technique: some dark and mid-gray areas plus the occasional highlight

STAGE 3

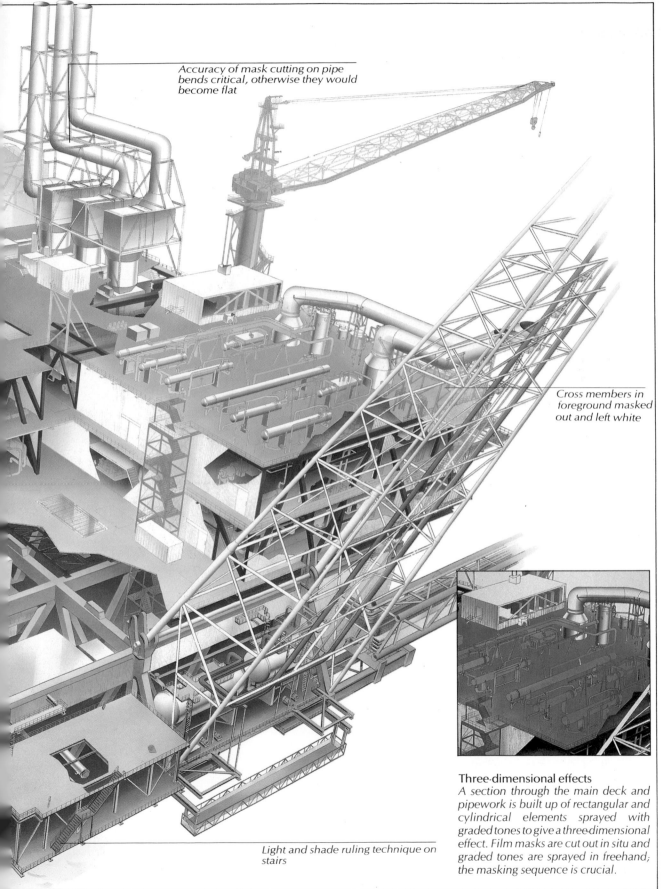

Accuracy of mask cutting on pipe bends critical, otherwise they would become flat

Cross members in foreground masked out and left white

Light and shade ruling technique on stairs

Three-dimensional effects
A section through the main deck and pipework is built up of rectangular and cylindrical elements sprayed with graded tones to give a three-dimensional effect. Film masks are cut out in situ and graded tones are sprayed in freehand; the masking sequence is crucial.

THE FINAL IMAGE

This is a highly sophisticated illustration containing a wide range of information conveyed by the full vocabulary of technical illustration – vertical sections and cut-aways, subtle coloring of broad areas to suggest relief and distance and careful linework.

Horizontal planes

The cool blue-gray horizontal surfaces are very subtly gradated by freehand spraying in a darker tone to create an impression of distance. Differences in construction materials are suggested by different ways of gradating the tone. With the reflective surfaces, for example, masks are used to separate the areas of tone more distinctly, although in some places the tone is afterward softened by freehand spraying. It also hints at the difference between opaque and reflective surfaces, thus indicating the variety of materials used on the construction.

Vertical planes

Vertical surfaces are clearly distinguished from horizontal surfaces by use of a warm, neutral tone, and line detail which adds to the vertical emphasis.

Cylindrical components

Highlighting (with a masked white stripe) and shading of curved surfaces enhances the three-dimensional effect and gives coherence to similar structures, such as the three angled pipes rising vertically, and the sequence of large and small pipes spanning the width of the roof area to the right.

Cut-aways

Through-views within the basic structure are complemented by irregular sections cut out of the vertical walls to reveal inner components. The large horizontal cut-away (center front) creates a downward perspective and draws the eye into the image.

Wave effect

Discreet use of a stylized wave effect balances the base of the illustration and locates the image within a particular context.

Helicopter grounded on pad by application of soft cast shadow

Leading edge of staircase brought forward by ruled white line.

Parts of original base linework show through areas thinly sprayed.

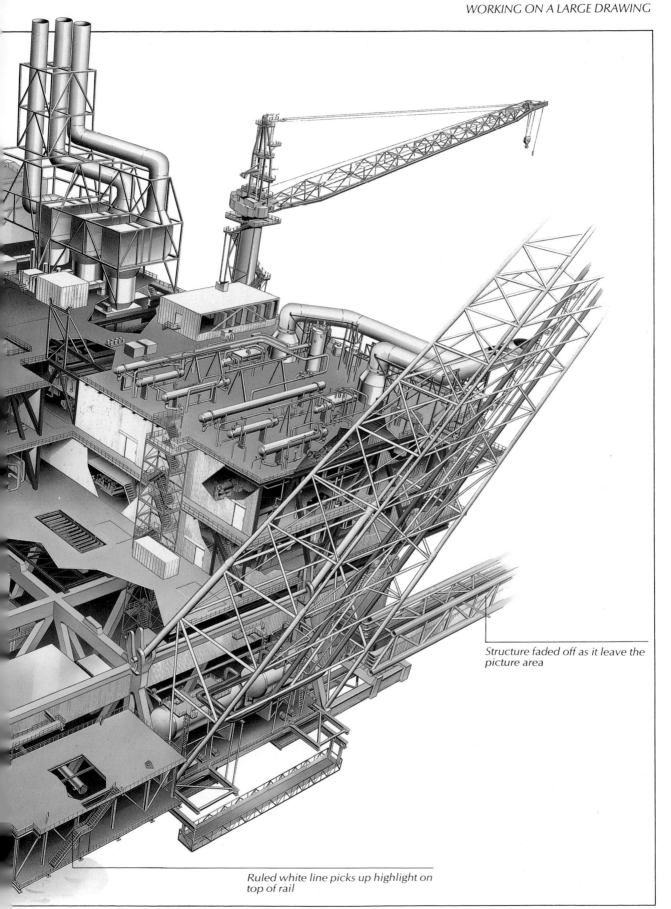

Structure faded off as it leave the
picture area

Ruled white line picks up highlight on
top of rail

CORRECTING TECHNIQUES

You may want to correct or alter a piece of artwork for any number of reasons. Perhaps a blot falls from the spatter cap attached to your airbrush exactly where you don't want it; or, as you move your ruler across the artwork, the line of paint along its edge smears along with it. Similarly, you may find that an earlier choice of color is wrong when taken in context with the rest of the image, or perhaps an uneven surface has allowed paint to creep under a section of mask, causing a furry edge. Another common reason for correcting an artwork is if you have used a scalpel blade once too often and you find that you have a jagged edge instead of a clean, sharp one.

There are several techniques for making good. It is important to choose the most appropriate method for the type of job, or you may find yourself wasting laborious time producing an unconvincing and highly visible correction. In severe cases, you should be prepared to scrap the whole piece of work and start afresh. It will probably be worth it in the end. Remember, if you do have to start again, that you are not going right back to the beginning. The drawing simply needs transferring; the masking sequence has been worked out and the color choice has been made. As you revise some original decisions, you may end up with a more satisfactory result.

CORRECTING A FURRY EDGE

If you discover a furry edge where there should be a sharp edge, first identify the cause to prevent it happening again. Masking film used on an uneven surface such as heavily toothed watercolor board or cartridge paper often results in furry edges as color creeps under the edge of the mask. The only sure prevention technique here is to use a smoother surface for work that involves precise lines. On smooth surfaces a furry edge may be the result of spraying too wet, using a blunt scalpel blade, not burnishing the mask down thoroughly, or not cutting cleanly.

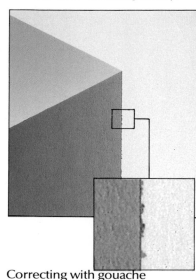

Correcting with gouache
This furry edged along one side of a cube is fairly straightforward to correct because it falls against a white ground. Two techniques are possible. One is simply to rule a line of thick white gouache along the edge, using a ruler and a fine paintbrush or a technical pen. If the work is to be reproduced, this correction will be invisible.

Using a scalpel
The second and more standard technique uses a straight edge and scalpel blade, and should only be used on hard-surfaced artboard. A softer surface such as a watercolor board will be irreparably damaged by this method. Use a curved scalpel blade which gives you an edge rather than a point. Lay the straight edge against the line, exposing the white of the ground, and draw the blade along it, scraping away a thin layer from the hard board.

REMOVING A BLOT

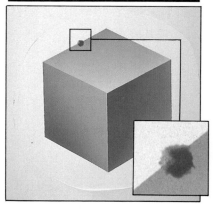

In this instance a blot of blue transparent ink has fallen half on and half off the edge of a cube rendered on hard-surfaced white artboard. Different techniques are used to deal with the two halves.

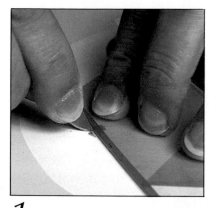

1 The same technique is used to deal with the blot that has fallen on the white ground as was used to make good the furry edge (see above). Lay a straight edge along the side of the cube, exposing the white ground, and gently scrape along the affected area with a curved scalpel blade.

2 The half on the cube itself now remains. The materials you need for this technique of masking and respraying are a scalpel with a curved blade, masking film, white gouache, and the blue dye used in the original.

3 Lay a sheet of masking film over the whole cube. Cut along the edges of the affected face of the cube and remove the masking film. Be careful when lifting and handling the film.

4 The color of the blot is relatively dark and in this case it is first necessary to reduce the density with a scalpel. Using a curved scalpel blade, which is easier to control and doesn't dig into the surface as much as a pointed scalpel, nick the surface of the damaged area.

5 Charge your airbrush with a small amount of thinned white gouache and spray lightly over the affected area, letting the overspray fall naturally on to the surface, until the blot becomes invisible.

6 Allow the white to dry thoroughly and then begin spraying back in the blue dye, matching the tone carefully against the rest of the face and the other sides of the cube. Don't allow blue overspray to fall on the original blue, because it will increase the denisty and the whole face will look wrong. A practised eye will know when to stop. This is a skill which takes time to master — your judgment will improve with experience.

7 Allow the blue ink to dry, remove the mask, and the cube should be restored to its original appearance.

This correction technique is used time and again by most airbrush artists.

PATCHING

This time the artist's ruler has picked up a splatter of white paint and spread it all over the place — something that is very easy to do. The whole face of the cube needs respraying. Two alternative techniques can be used.

You could white out the whole face with a coat of gouache and respray over the top. This technique is never really satisfactory, however, because the thick coat of gouache is easy to damage or scrape, and because the ink sprayed on the gouache will be dull and muddy compared to the ink sprayed directly on the artboard.

The recommended technique here is patching. The materials you need are art paper (to match your artboard), a scalpel with a pointed blade, masking film, tracing paper and tracing down paper, a fine paintbrush, spray adhesive, and blue ink.

1 Using your original tracing, or a new tracing taken from the cube artwork with tracing down paper, transfer the face of the cube to art paper.

2 Mask the image to expose the face to be resprayed. Spray the face, matching exactly what you did the first time around. Keep the original cube beside you for reference as you spray (but protect it from overspray or further damage). Remove the masking film.

3 With a very sharp scalpel blade, cut out the patch. Cut the two edges which join the original cube very precisely — there is no room for error here. Allow roughly (¼ in/5 mm) excess white paper along the other two edges. Always cut a patch slightly larger than the original where possible.

4 Although art paper (in this case CS10 paper) is very thin, the white edges of the patch will be visible when it is fixed in position. If the work is for reproduction, these edges may catch the light and show up in the printed image.

To counteract this and to dull the stark whiteness, paint the edges with a watered down version of the surface colour (if it is a light color) and a fine paintbrush. If it is a dark color, match it. Leave any edges that fall against a white background.

5 Spray a very light coat of spray adhesive over the back of the patch. If you use too much it will seep out of the sides when you press it in position.

6 Position the patch with great care and press it down lightly. Cover with a piece of scrap paper and smooth it down firmly.

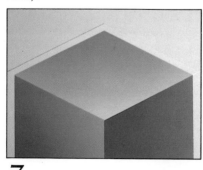

7 The repaired cube with its new patch which should not be visible to a camera.

In this case, the damage was not too difficult to repair. If too much needs altering, however, start again rather than waste hours producing a less than perfect end result.

LETTING IN A PATCH

The damage to this artwork is serious but not impossible to correct. Fortunately, only one face of the cube is affected. If the damage extended on to a second face or on to the surrounding white, it would probably be just as quick to start again rather than try and salvage the original work.

1 *Spilled coffee dabbed off with a piece of tissue caused this stain. The surface of the artboard itself has been damaged.*

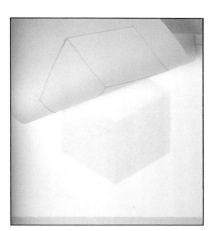

3 *Keeping the trace taped in place, lift it and position a sheet of CS10 art paper beneath it. Tape down the art paper securely.*

4 *Trace down the outline of the cube on to the art paper. It is essential to keep the art paper in the same position throughout the operation. Fold back the trace, leaving it taped in position.*

5 *Respray the new section through the masking film cut to fit.*

6 *When the new section is dry, lay the trace back over the top. Using the trace as a guide, cut through all three surfaces – the trace, the art paper and the top layer of the artboard.*

7 *Remove the trace and the art paper from the artboard. Pick up one corner of the damaged face and peel back the cut section of artboard, making sure you are taking only the top layer.*

8 *Spray glue on the back of the patch and carefully let it in to the surface of the artboard. The fit should be perfect. Lay a piece of paper over the top and smooth it down.*

9 *The corrected image. This is quite a tricky operation and there should be no tell-tale edges showing around the patch. It gives a smoother finish, however, than patching over the top of the artwork.*

ALTERING THE DIMENSIONS OF ARTWORK

Somebody somewhere made a mistake. A perfectly executed commission is returned by the art director with a seemingly impossible request – to increase the depth of the sky by the amount indicated on the rough overlay. As with all corrections to finished work, the first step is to assess how long repair work will take, how complicated it will be and whether it will look right or botched. It may be quicker to start from scratch – after all, the planning is done, the original trace is probably still around, and if not a new one can be quickly made from the original artwork.

The extent of this particular problem is not as bad as it

appears. An extra piece of artboard will have to be patched on and the top half of the sky resprayed to hide the join. The crucial component of the repair is clear acetate.

What you need
A piece of artboard of the type used for the original illustration, masking tape, a sheet of clear acetate large enough to cover the entire artwork, matt masking film, scalpel, HB pencil, white designer's gouache, and blue ink as used in the original illustration.

PREPARING THE BOARD

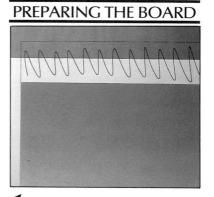

1 A rough scribble on a piece of layout paper indicates how much the illustration needs to be extended.

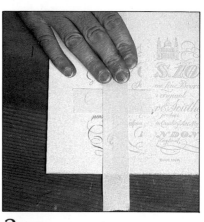

3 Working on the reverse side, tape the two pieces together with masking tape.

4 To prevent the join buckling, tape over it temporarily on each side of the board.

2 The first task is to extend the artboard. Cut a piece of board to the same width as the existing artwork and to the depth of the correction plus a top border.

5 Lay a sheet of clear acetate over the entire artwork, even though only the top third needs correcting. Fix the acetate in position with masking tape. This is the surface on which the correction is made. If the repair work is unsuccessful, therefore, it can be done again on a fresh sheet of acetate or the whole attempt can be abandoned and the original artwork rescued unscathed.

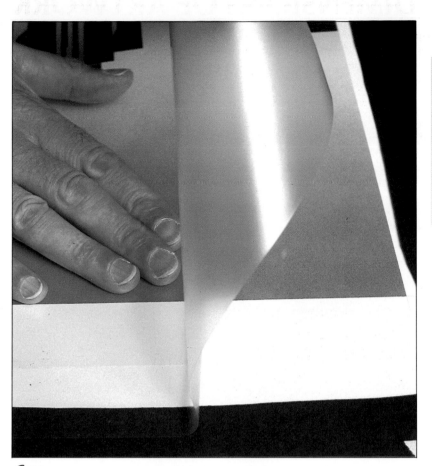

6 *Identify the area to be resprayed and cut a sheet of mat masking film large enough to cover the area with a margin* all around. Lay the masking film over the acetate, smoothing out bubbles and wrinkles as you go.

7 *Draw around the area to be re-sprayed, including the extension, directly on to the masking film with a sharp pencil.*

With a scalpel and using a ruler as a cutting guide, cut along your pencil line.

8 *Remove the whole section of mask.*

SPRAYING WHITE

Tips for spraying on acetate

Before spraying on acetate, clean it thoroughly. The best way of getting rid of grease marks is to wipe over the acetate with a paper towel dipped in lighter fuel. After cleaning, be wary of handling the acetate as this will leave behind oily finger marks.

Be particularly careful when cutting acetate — the slightest nick or wayward cut will show up if the piece is to be photographed.

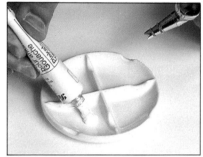

1 *Mix a quantity of white designer's gouache to a thick consistency. Here, tube gouache is diluted with water sprayed in small amounts from the airbrush.*

2 *Using a stiff good-quality paintbrush that will not lose its hairs in the bowl of the airbrush, load the cup with gouache.*

continued . . .

3 Start from the top edge and spray white over the blue, fading down as you reach the halfway point of the original sky.

4 Gradually build up a thick coat with sweeping strokes back and forth across the acetate. Above all, spray evenly.

5 Continue spraying until the join between the two pieces of artboard and the hard top line of the illustration are disguised.

6 Stand back and check the work at this stage. The original blue is still slightly visible through the white, but because the blue is fairly dark it will merge with the new color in the later stages. If you are unsure whether the cover-up is effective enough at this point, carry on spraying white until it is almost solid.

7 Load the color cup with the same color and make of blue ink used for the sky the first time around. If the original blue was mixed, the importance of noting down the formula of any mixed color now becomes apparent.

ADDING COLOR

1 Start to tone in the blue of the sky, spraying lightly from side to side from the top of the masked area to the midway point.

2 Start from the top again, building up the color until you get the density you want and an overall even tone.

3 To get an even tone that matches the original, you may have to apply more color.

4 Keep spraying color until you are satisfied with its tone and depth. Standing back from the artwork often helps.

5 Lift a corner of the mask in order to judge the blue against the white of the artboard surround. If you are satisfied, remove the mask altogether.

The completed change
The join might still be visible under a microscope, but for reproduction purposes the artwork is as good as new.

THE COMMISSION: WORKING TO A BRIEF

This full scale sequence shows an actual job commissioned from a top airbrush artist by a leading international magazine. It demonstrates several airbrush techniques and some implications of working to a professional brief.

At the three points of the commission triangle are the artist, the artist's agent and the art director. The artist's work in this case is widely used in international magazines and had caught the eye of the art director, who felt the style was appropriate to the tone of a magazine feature he wanted illustrating. The feature was about a School for Butlers in London. He didn't want to tie the artist's hands with a detailed brief and simply gave him the gist of the text – that the perfect butler appears to live behind a mask but is always poised to obey commands.

Time was a crucial factor – one week from acceptance of the commission to finished artwork on the art director's desk (which happened to be in Germany, hundreds of miles away from the artist's drawing board). There was no time for roughs to be done; the art director had to trust the artist. Top magazines generally use top artists and give them freedom to interpret the brief, but they don't necessarily use the artwork. Work is often rejected, not because it is bad artwork, but because the art director feels it conveys the wrong concept. From the artist's point of view, the commission had to be slotted in with an already busy schedule. He estimated that the job would take two full days and shuffled existing work within that week to accommodate it.

MAKING THE FIRST SET OF MASKS

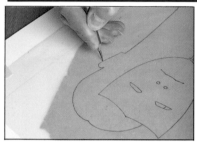

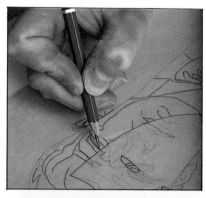

1 An outline trace was drawn, using reference for some of the details. The artists also prepared color roughs with markers for his own benefit. The outline of the image was then transferred on to artboard.

3 As with all complex airbrush pieces, the masking sequence needs to be worked out at this initial stage. The artist first concentrates on the face, shirt and glove. A new trace is taken from the artwork and the details are lightly transferred.

4 Red is used to distinguish the chrome areas which will be treated separately. Although part of the face is hidden in the final image, the whole face is drawn in to ensure the proportions are correct.

2 The first stage is to lay in the black background. The outline of the image and the external border are masked out, and a flat tone sprayed into the exposed area, using jet black drawing ink.

The face masks

The masking sequence for the face is first black (below and right), then dark brown (bottom and below right), and lastly the skin tones.

A paper mask is first taped over the whole image and the area of the face then roughly cut out. Masking film is laid over the exposed area and the face and neck cut out.

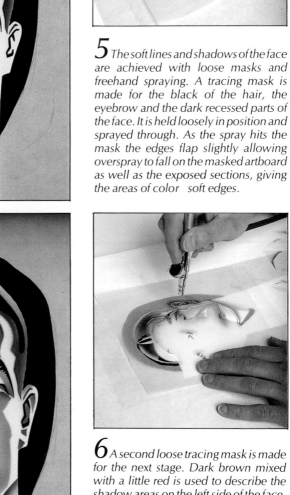

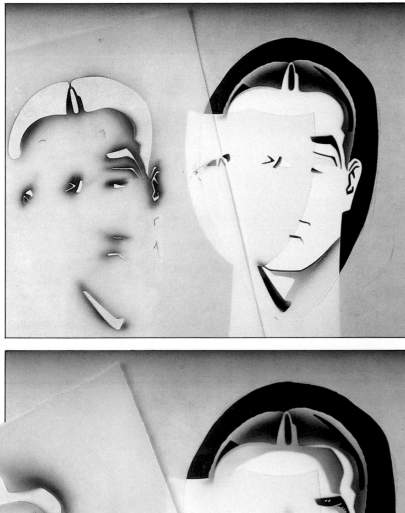

5 The soft lines and shadows of the face are achieved with loose masks and freehand spraying. A tracing mask is made for the black of the hair, the eyebrow and the dark recessed parts of the face. It is held loosely in position and sprayed through. As the spray hits the mask the edges flap slightly allowing overspray to fall on the masked artboard as well as the exposed sections, giving the areas of color   soft edges.

6 A second loose tracing mask is made for the next stage. Dark brown mixed with a little red is used to describe the shadow areas on the left side of the face. The basic form as well as the details of the face and neck gradually emerge. The loose masking technique is the same as that used for the black.

SCRATCHING OUT HIGHLIGHTS

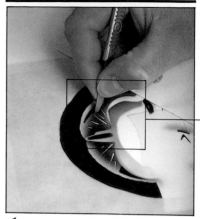

3 The face and neck are now complete and the mask is peeled off the butler's chrome mask.

With this mask removed the artist can check the work so far and reassess the next stage if necessary.

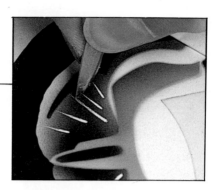

1 White highlights are usually added as finishing touches at the end of a project. In this case however, the artist wanted overspray from the skin tones to tint highlights in the hair.

With the point of a sharp scalpel blade tapering lines radiating from the center of the forehead are scratched into the black, creating the feel of a glossy and well groomed head of hair.

2 Skin tones are sprayed in freehand to complete the face and neck. The whole area is exposed, except for the left eye which remains masked. With a mixture of raw sienna, burnt sienna, red and yellow, the artist uses his experience rather than pencil guidelines to color and sculpt the contours of the face.

Skin tones
The main skin tones to the butler's face have now been done along with fine details to the ears.

ADDING DETAILS

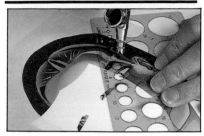

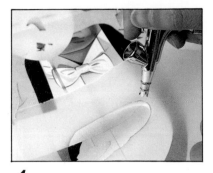

1 The butler's left eye, still white, is treated before going on to the shirt and glove. It is left until this stage to ensure that the white of the eye remains pure. The area around the eye is masked with low-tack masking film. A circle template is used as a loose mask for the eyeball.

To prevent the eye standing out too starkly against the face, a gentle tone is sprayed into the corner of the eye.

4 The shirt and dicky bow go in next. To save time, a single sheet of masking film is laid over the area and the details drawn directly on to the film. The darker areas are sprayed first, and then the lighter areas.

5 The shirt is masked out with a paper mask and a new film mask made for the glove.

Three tracing masks are used to lay in the soft pink, green and brown tones of the glove.

2 The mask is removed to expose the face with the eye now completed.

3 Again the artist stands back and checks the work so far. Taking time to reassess after each section is completed gives you the flexibility to adjust and develop your original ideas.

The butler's features
The face, shirt front and gloved hand are now virtually complete, leaving the chrome mask and tray to do.

ADDING CHROME EFFECTS

The artist now changes gear as he moves on to the chromework of the mask and tray. He worked out how the light would be reflected at the initial planning stage, taking licence with reality for the sake of visual impact.

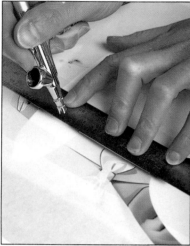

1 The stem of the mask is tackled first. The background is masked out and the stem exposed. The lines suggesting the light and shadow reflected in the shiny surface of the chrome are sprayed using a straight edge as a hand held loose mask.

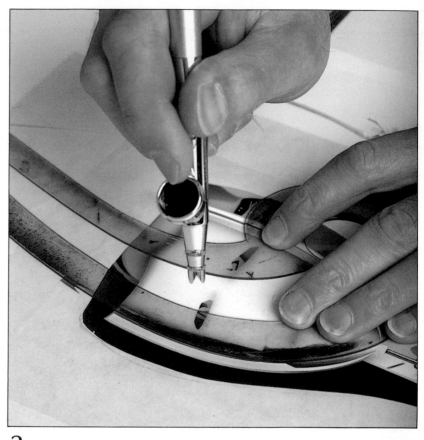

3 Cobalt blue and scarlet are used at the sides of the mask to suggest a reflective finish. The curve of the shadow must be perfect if it is to be at all convincing and the ideal mask is an appropriately sized French curve.

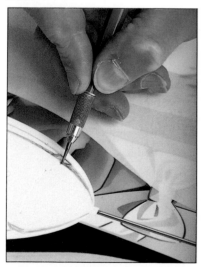

2 A sheet of masking film is laid over the main part of the mask. Again, to save time, the details of the light and shadow are outlined using a sharp hard pencil directly onto the masking film. The hard-edged darker areas are sprayed first.

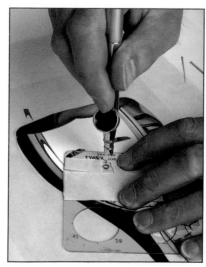

4 A small hole on a circle template acts as a mask for the nostrils. The other holes on the template are masked with masking tape to prevent overspray falling through them on to the artwork. The nostrils are sprayed in grey tinged with scarlet.

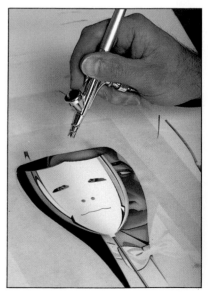

5 The final touch on the mask is to lay in a freehand tone to soften the hard blue and scarlet shadows, and to suggest the curve of the mask, leaving a strong white area in the center.

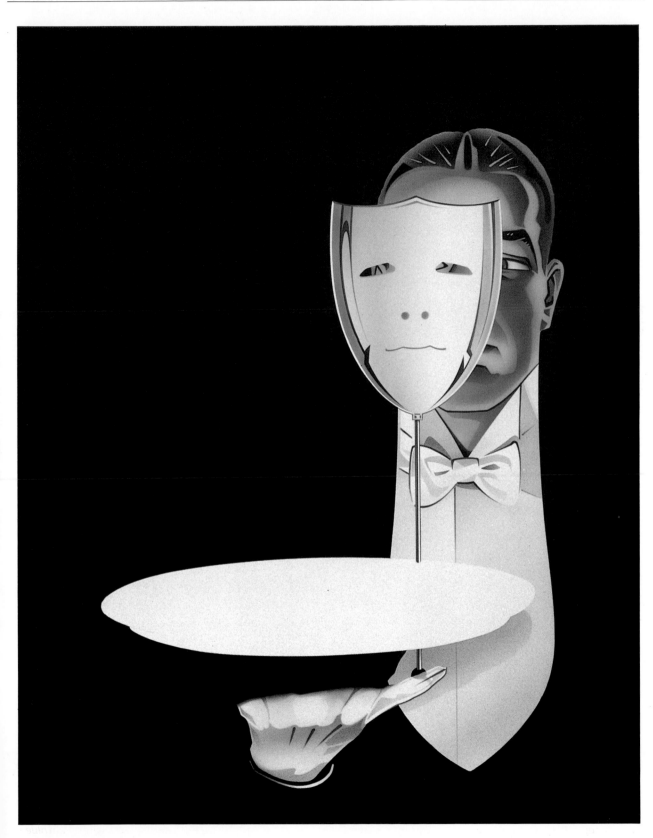

The finished mask
It is important to remember that chrome reflects all light. In this artwork, color reflections are hard-edged and dark.

THE TRAY SEQUENCE

By now the artist has invested a lot of time in the artwork and he is anxious to make the tray work. It is a complicated section and he plans a four-stage sequence, leaving the crucial cast shadow of the mask and stem until last. A new mask is made for each stage. The colors used repeat those in the mask and pick up the colors of the glove, providing a visual link between the chrome and butler.

1 A sheet of tracing paper is used to mask the background and the area of the tray is cut out.

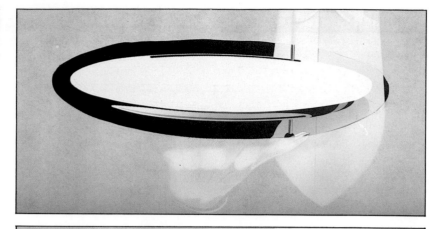

The darker tone on the inner rim leads the eye around the edge.

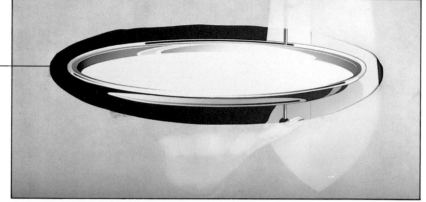

2 The inner rim is laid in next to provide an edge for doing the surface of the tray. The brilliant white of the artboard will represent the brightest light, catching the inner rim as well as the surface.

A thin dark line around the base of the rim emphasizes the curve and depth of the tray.

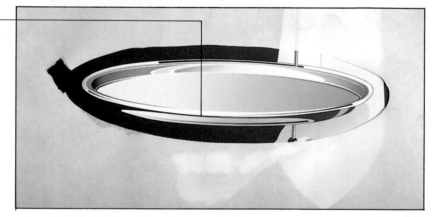

3 The soft scarlet tone on the surface goes in next, facing gently from the right edge to give depth and substance to the tray. The section is simple but crucial, and easily overdone.

4 Finally the key shadow of the mask and stem goes in. The artist uses licence here to create a visually credible result which is in reality an impossibility. The shadow diffuses as it reaches the furthest edge of the tray.

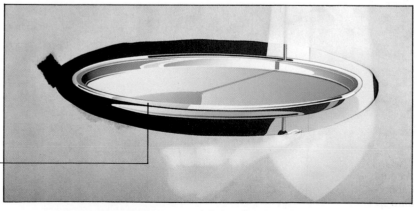

The cast shadow of the mask at its weakest point steps over the rim of the tray.

FINISHING TOUCHES

Professional airbrush artists often spend a considerable time at the end of a project refining and correcting tiny details and adding highlights. Whereas subtle highlights can make a project, overuse of white gouache can make the image appear unconvincing and unacceptable.

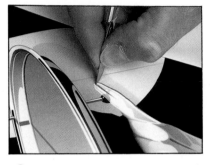

2 A paintbrush and jet black ink are used where the correction is black – here correcting a dent in the reflection on the underside of the tray.

1 A scalpel is used to correct minor masking errors where the correction is white – here scratching out the white around the brim of the tray.

3 A highlight is scratched into the thumb of the glove. A scalpel is quicker to use than a paintbrush and the results reproduce well.

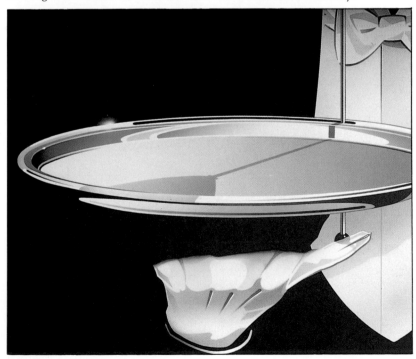

The tray highlights
A couple of spots of white gouache are dabbed on the rim of the tray, and a third spot on the outer edge of the rim is flared with the airbrush. The highlights should be subtle rather than overstated or else the whole image will be ruined.

4 White highlights are added to the mask. White gouache is brushed in freehand above the mouth, nostrils, and eyes. These could alternatively be done with a scalpel.

continued. . .

ADDING THE FACIAL HIGHLIGHTS

The brightness of the mask and tray at this stage rather overpower the figure of the butler. He is intended to be almost shadowy in the background but is now in danger of becoming invisible. White highlights on his face and hair bring him back into the picture.

A mark of professionalism often shows up in the composition of an artwork. Balancing an artwork to give the right emphasis is a skill that is partly intuitive, partly gained through experience. One of the advantages of using an airbrush is that it is ideal for retouching images to provide the correct balance.

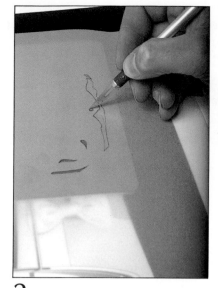

2 A cutting mat is inserted between the tracing and the artwork. A thick piece of card would do just as well. The shapes of the highlights are carefully cut out with a sharp scalpel.

3 The artist blows in strong white gouache which will cover the inks beneath. The spray of the airbrush is concentrated on the central point of each highlight section, allowing the overspray to form softer edges and blend with the skin and hair tones.

1 A large sheet of tracing paper is taped in position over the image. The highlights are drawn on to the tracing with a hard pencil.

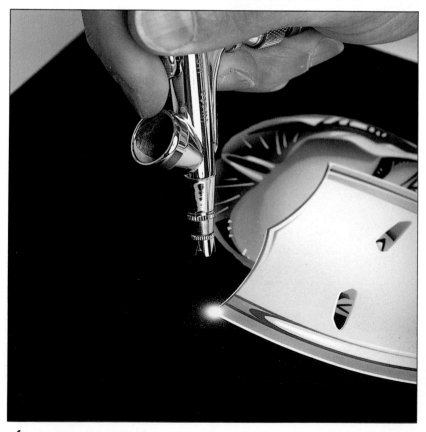

4 The artist decides on a final flourish — a highlight to bring the corner of the mask out of the black shadow. A blob of white gouache is dabbed on with a paintbrush. Air is then blown through the airbrush into the center of the white gouache spot to flare it while the paint is still wet.

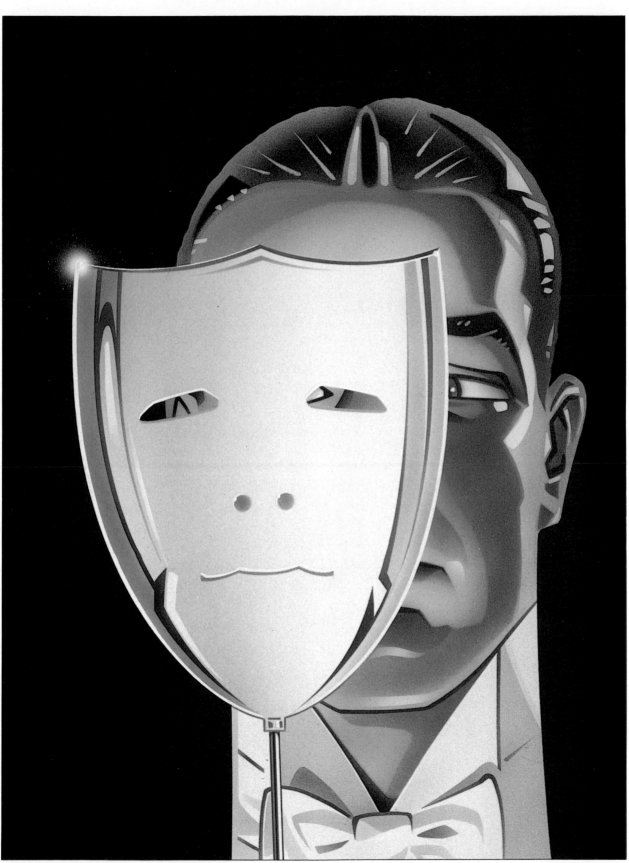

The completed face and mask

WORKING FOR PRINT

Modern color reproduction methods have removed a lot of the old restrictions that existed on artwork intended for print. Any color that the artist can produce can be reproduced on the printed page, although it is always worth checking with the client what method of color reproduction is being used.

SURFACE

The most common method of color|origination is scanning. This involves the artwork being wrapped around the drum of the scanner and the surface therefore needs to be flexible. It is best to ensure that your surface can be bent rather than leave it to the printer. For the airbrush artist this does present a problem. Nothing can match the shiny hard white surface of artboard for airbrush work, but it is too stiff for the scanner. The top layer of the artboard – which is actually a piece of art paper-stuck on a pulp base – has to be stripped off. This is always an agonizing moment. You nick up a corner of the top paper surface, put a ruler behind the edge and use the ruler to rip the surface off. Your precious artwork should survive intact, but practice on spare pieces of artboard before attempting this for the first time.

To avoid this problem you can work on art paper, spray mounting it on to a piece of board while you work to minimize buckling. There will probably still be some buckling, however, which is why many artists prefer to work on artboard and go through with the heart stopping process of stripping it.

PROTECTING ARTWORK

Always protect finished artwork with an acetate or tracing overlay taped in position. If the artwork has to go in the mail, wrap it with great care between pieces of thick board that render it unbendable. You're protecting the time you've invested in the work as well as the work itself.

CLIENT RESPONSE

Be prepared for the artwork to reappear with alterations requested, or even a total rejection. Top artists frequently have commissions rejected, because the concept or style is wrong or the original idea does not work. Very often the client simply does not like it. There is very little you can do in this case except accept the rejection fee gracefully – usually 50% of the fee.

THE FINAL CHECK

Take a rest from the finished work and then come back to it. You'll probably want to make a few changes. It is worth looking at the artwork at the size it will appear on the printed page, using an enlarging projector or a reducing glass – you might want to compensate for something that disappears when it is reduced.

The history of a magazine artwork
Some of the stages in the life of a piece of magazine artwork – the original pencil trace, a color rough rendered with markers, a page proof of the magazine spread, and the finished artwork.

The finished artwork
This is how the artwork looked before it was sent away to the publisher. In this particular case, the work was accepted and nothing more had to be done to it. However, artists are often asked to amend or correct work in order to satisfy the publisher.

AIRBRUSH
APPLICATIONS

*"My very first airbrush painting
was done with a truck tire"*

ROGER HUYSSEEN

AIRBRUSH USES

What place do cake sculpture, punk pigs or textile design have in a book on airbrushing? Well, alongside the less surprising areas of medical illustration, model aircraft, animation, and ceramic restoration, they all involve professional use of the airbrush. In some of the areas covered in this section the airbrush is regarded as simply another implement in a well stocked toolbox; in others it is an extension of the artist's hand. Some artists view it with suspicion; others would never be without it.

This section is more a walk through a gallery of specialized airbrush uses than an exhaustive presentation of each one. In each case specialized techniques are focused on rather than more mainstream airbrush techniques already covered in the general sections of this book. Each area has its own problems and its own solutions – for example, how to achieve a convincing camouflage pattern on model aircraft or how to "antique"

a fresh glaze on a restored china plate. Experts in each field have demonstrated their working practices and shared some of their secrets and tips. If you are interested in, say, fabric spraying or technical illustration, you will find here a thorough introduction to the methods of working and materials involved – an introduction which may help you decide whether to pursue your interest further.

Even more esoteric uses than the ones covered here exist, for example taxidermy. The rainbow colors which delicately ripple across the scales of a live fish begin to fade from the moment it is caught – sadly ephemeral, except that they can be permanently recreated with an airbrush. Who would have thought of it – until one day a taxidermist came across an airbrush? As the airbrush and its capabilities become more widely known, it will no doubt come to be found in more and more places.

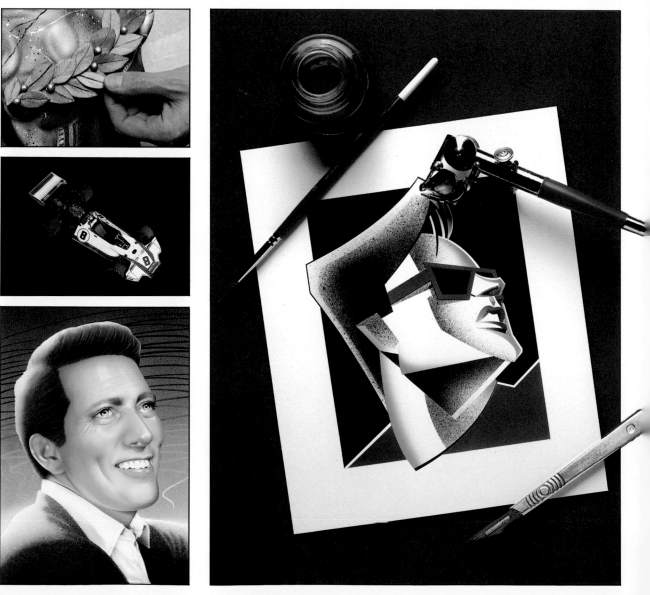

AIRBRUSHING ON A GIANT SCALE

A giant dust sheet goes up over the London Pavilion in Piccadilly Circus. It hides scaffolding and portrays accurately and in detail the new-look Pavilion slowly taking shape behind. As well as being one of the largest dust sheets around, the artwork is also one of the largest pieces of airbrush art ever attempted. The artwork is not painted by hand-operated airbrushes, however, but by robotic spray guns. These form part of a complete color imaging system designed by Eye Media and called Aerosonic Print System.

Giant murals are created by spraying on fabric sections. They can be any size and shape, can hang inside or outside, and are easy to transport and construct on site. The colors are light-fast and waterproof and the whole lot can go in the washing machine. The results can be breathtaking.

HOW THE SYSTEM WORKS

The client supplies an image, which may be color or monochrome, a drawing or photograph. A computer digitizes the information in the picture and stores it on tape.

An image processor receives the information and can manipulate tone and line if required. The approved result is stored on tape for transmission to the color synthesizer.

The color synthesizer is a sophisticated matrix printer. It electronically mixes the required print colors from a theoretical base of more than sixteen million different colors and grays. It feeds the taped information to an array of up to five robotic guns, which fire a measured amount of pigment of the correct mix of colors on to the fabric. All colors print simultaneously.

The spraying nozzles of the guns do not come into contact with the work, so the system can print accurately and in full color on rough textured as well as smooth surfaces. The mood of the image can be dictated by the choice of fabric. The broader the weave of the chosen fabric, the more the color diffuses as it penetrates the fibers, and the softer the edges become.

Work in progress
The giant fabric mural goes up in sections across the facade of the London Pavilion in Piccadilly Circus showing how the revamped building beneath will eventually look.

Installing the artwork
The scale of the artwork is so vast that elaborate installation procedures are needed.

The finished artwork
The Aerosonic Print System is fully automated and the artwork is actually painted with robotic spray guns which are controlled by a computer.

This system makes use of the latest technology to offer full color reproductions, producing high quality prints on papers and vinyls as well as fabrics

SPRAYING 3-D CARICATURES

"SPITTING IMAGE"

At Limehouse Studios in London's Docklands, caricaturists, modelers, technicians, wardrobe specialists and artists work together to produce latex replicas of the faces that populate our daily newspapers and television screens – these are the "Spitting Image" puppets. The faces are painted and the finishing touches added in a small room cluttered with disembodied heads, wigs, large jars of gouache, cans of hair spray, and airbrushes. The length of one wall is taken up by an enormous extractor fan – two airbrushes going full time expel a lot of paint particles into the air. The models being worked on are mounted on metal supports and can easily be rotated through 360 degrees.

MODELING MATERIALS

The puppets are cast in flesh-colored latex or foam rubber, which gives them their characteristic flexibility. Initially, however, this caused problems for the paint studio – paint sprayed directly on to latex used to crack as the puppets were manipulated – so a suitable medium that would coat the latex and receive the paint had to be found. First they tried an aerosol adhesive, which worked fairly well. But even better proved to be prosetic adhesive, a substance used in the theater to attach masks, beards and so on to human skin.

A first coat of half prosetic adhesive and half pink gouache is applied with a brush, taking care not to clog up the creases in the face or to stick together the lips or eyelids.

PAINT MIXTURES

The studio gets through an enormous amount of paint, and the most frequently used gouache colors are premixed in large quantities in an old food mixer. The proportions are roughly 1/3 pint/200 ml gouache to 2 pints/1.2 litres water, producing a consistency similar to single cream. The diluted gouache is then strained through a piece of gauze to filter out particles of pigment which would clog the airbrush, and stored in rubber sealed jars. It keeps well for a few weeks, but will go off after a while.

Gouache is a good airbrush medium, but regular cleaning is still essential – water should be flushed through the airbrush between each color and at least once an hour if it is in constant use. In the "Spitting Image" studio they find that their airbrushes stand up well to regular daily use, as long as they are properly looked after and well maintained. A useful tip when flushing out your airbrush is to hold your finger or – safer

– a piece of cloth over the end of the air jet and let the water bubble back through.

For white skin, a second coat of pink gouache is sprayed over the whole head using a Badger single action airbrush. Pink can appear too red and it tends to flare under camera lighting. It often needs to be taken back by dusting down with a mixture of olive green lightened with base white acrylic paint. Dusting down involves increasing the paint flow and spraying from a distance of, say, 12 in/30 cm.

The same mixture of olive green and base white acrylic is used to catch the reflective flesh-on-flesh shadow cast on human skin.

Using photographic reference to help judge the amount and intensity of color, red is sprayed directly on to the mouth, nose and cheeks. A large area of red is used to highlight fat cheeks, and sharp points of color are used on small cheeks, as here in the case of Mick Jagger.

Raw umber is used to represent a sun tan. A mixture of burnt umber and cyclamen is used both for a swarthy complexion and to quieten the black color inside the mouth, otherwise the contrast between the black and the surrounding pink skin would be too stark.

Black skin is built up in layers of color. A base coat of pink is followed by a dusting of raw umber. After this comes green to represent the flesh shadows in the recesses of the face, a coat of burnt umber all over, and a dusting of black. Yellow is used instead of black for a mid-tone color.

The teeth are painted in with a brush and an off-white, mixed from white, a touch of black, and Naples yellow.

Fine detail is often added with a double action airbrush, rather than the single action model used for the base colors and flesh highlights. Very thick eyebrows, for example, are painted on with a fine brush and then feathered over with the double action airbrush. For feathering, the airbrush is preset to a fine spray and a low ratio of paint, and the color is built up in layers, fading the brushstrokes in with the basic color.

FINISHING TOUCHES

Unusual masking materials are used in this studio – the artist's hand is often used to block out areas of the face, such as the skin around the mouth, and plastic wrap is used to cover the eyeballs and teeth. The plastic wrap is held in place either by tucking it under the eyelids or spraying the model first with spray adhesive and then attaching the plastic wrap.

"SPITTING IMAGE" PUPPETS

Modeling color sprayed on then touched up with brushwork

Shadow areas sprayed

Moles applied with a brush; some blotted wet for a particular effect

Medium pink on browns

Green flesh tones on upper eye lids

Medium pink paint sprayed over browns

Green flesh tones sprayed into shadow areas

Highlight areas left the lighter skin tones

Building up the image

This puppet (left) of politician Douglas Hurd was first sprayed with prosetic adhesive mixed with gouache. This forms a stable foundation for subsequent layers of paint. Photographs are used as reference to ensure that the colors are accurate.

Puppets for television

Certain colors, especially pink, can flare underneath television spotlights so they are toned down as can be seen in the photograph below of three politicians.

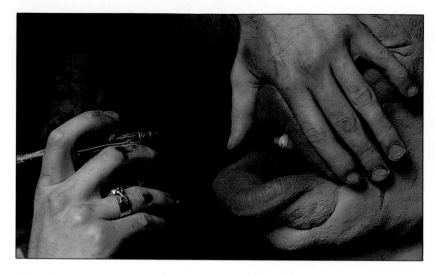

Masking the eyes
Plastic wrap is used to mask the eyes before spraying the lids. The film is tucked under the eyelids with an ordinary sewing pin.

Mouthparts
Before spraying the lips and mouth, the pressure is dropped to less than 40 psi/2.7 bar. This is so that particles of paint won't penetrate the skin of the hand which is used as a mask.

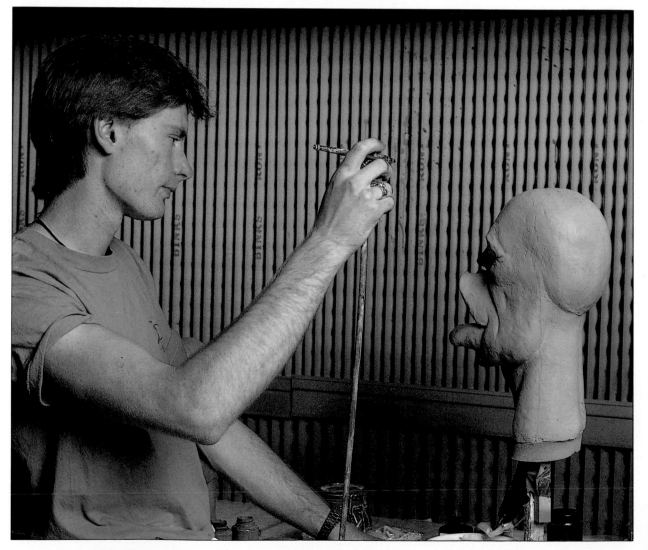

Using a hand as a mask

Masking isn't easy using traditional methods, especially if they are flexible. Using a spare hand as a mask is both practical and satisfactory, but care must be taken to drop the air pressure and to use non-toxic paint.

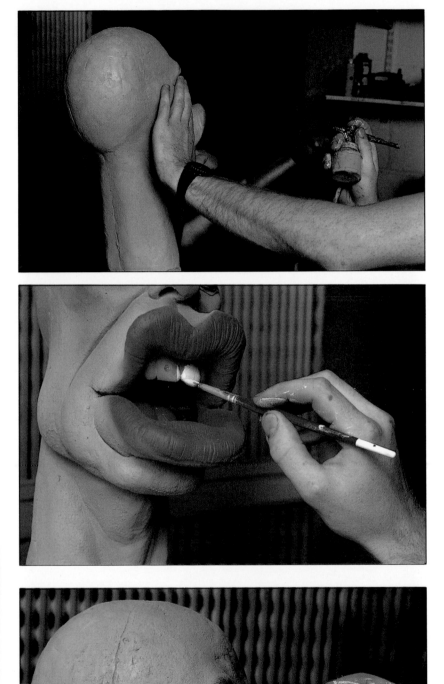

Painting the teeth

The teeth are painted using a paint brush and white acrylic tinged with black ink and yellow gouache.

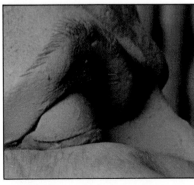

Spraying dark shadows

Dark areas, such as eyelids, are sprayed from a distance of only 2-3 in/5-6 cm.

Spraying skin tones

Green flesh tones are sprayed on at different angles to catch the varying planes of flesh. Shadow areas are sprayed from a distance of roughly 10 in/25 cm (see left).

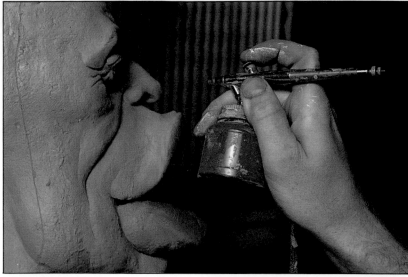

Red highlights
Red highlights are sprayed on last. A large area of red is sprayed on fat cheeks, and small points are used on other areas.

The finishing touch
The last addition is the wig when the puppet springs to life, ready for the television cameras.

Hand painted eyebrows

Sprayed shadow area

Inside of mouth hand painted black

As they appear on television
Puppet images of Mick Jagger and Keith Richard all ready to be filmed in a life-size television set.

SPRAYING FIBERGLASS MODELS

Not all modelmakers produce racing cars and airplanes. The models on these pages fit into a category all of their own — punk crocodiles, pigs you wouldn't like to meet on a dark night, and three-dimensional seaside postcard characters.

Each of these models starts out as a master model in ceramic clay. Once this is complete and dry, it is sealed with polyurethane to give it a protective film. The next stage is to make a cold-cure rubber casting mold. Five layers of cold-cure rubber are applied, which, when cured, become a flexible skin that is an almost perfect replica of the original. A support mold is a good idea, made in two parts from plaster of paris. Next, each individual model is cast in resin by painting in layers of resin to build up a shell. Three to four layers of resin make a shell ¼-½ in/5mm—1cm thick. If the model is to have a dominant overall color, as a hippopotamus might

have a purple-brown hue, the resin can be tinted before making the model. Once the resin is dry, first the support mold and then the rubber casting mold are removed, and the base of the model is sealed with cardboard or plaster. For small models, the resin can simply be poured in and cast solid rather than as a shell.

If you make plaster models, it is essential that the water in the plaster mix has completely evaporated. Any remaining moisture will cause the paint to come away. Plaster models should be left to dry in sunlight or in a warm place, such as on a radiator, for a couple of days. Seal the plaster with a coat of polyurethane before beginning to paint.

The first step is to identify and spray on the overall local color. The airbrush is ideal for this purpose — if you can avoid touching the model with a paintbrush at this stage, you can get a perfect overall flat color.

High gloss with enamels
These seaside characters — three-dimensional interpretations of seaside postcards — were sprayed with high gloss enamels which somehow seem eminently suitable for the cheerful faces.

Metal flake paint has been used on one of the swimming costumes to add texture.

Simple masking techniques
The hippo and elephant on the sofa (right) required surprisingly little masking. The polka dot effect was arrived at by using round adhesive labels as masks (see page 190).

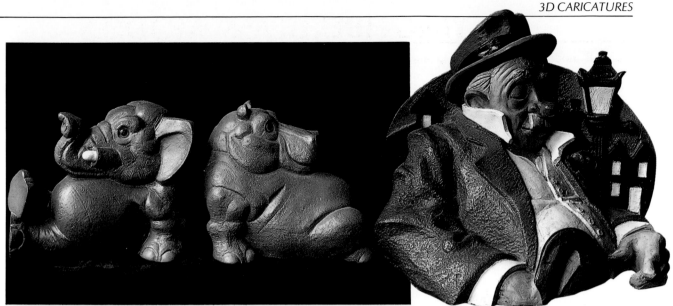

Textured models
The model of a man (above) has several textures: the vest and jacket are coarser than the skin and hat. These textures have been emphasized by spraying them with either mat or gloss paints.

Mat enamels
The hippo and elephant (top left) were sprayed with a matting agent to deaden the effects of the high gloss enamels.

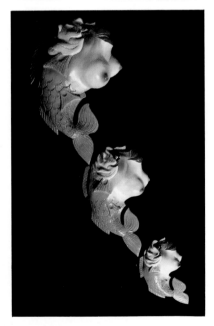

Finishing off by hand
The eyes on the mermaids (above) were painted in using a brush. Very little masking was used to spray these models.

SPRAYING ENAMELS

Enamel paints, in both high gloss and matt finish are used to color resin models. A satin finish can be achieved by mixing matt and gloss enamels together. For a completely matt finish, you can add a matting agent, such as matt white. The airbrush then needs constantly flushing out to avoid blockages building up. Thin the enamel with an equal volume of turpentine to achieve the correct consistency. If it is too thin, it will separate out when it is sprayed, because there will not be enough paint to key into the surface – a 50:50 ratio seems to be reliable. Enamels are completely opaque, and can be used one color on top of another. In between color changes, blast turpentine through the airbrush to prevent it becoming gummed up with color residue and to prevent the previous color contaminating the new.

CLEANING ENAMELS

If you work with enamels, your airbrush has to be cleaned with extra care. You can soak the nozzle attachment of your airbrush, minus its perishable rubber washer if it is a de Vilbiss, overnight in cellulose thinner, a very strong solution rather like paint stripper.

Spraying skin tones
These models were first sprayed with a gloss enamel in skin color, then a pinker mix was added over the parts of the body which catch the sun.

ADHESIVE LABELS AS MASKS

Adhesive labels are an original idea for masks. Stationer's adhesive spots were stuck down all over the sofa in this model after an initial layer of purple had been applied. The green was then sprayed over, the spots removed, and a fabric pattern created. Adhesive labels come in all shapes and sizes, but remember to check that they will not damage the surface beneath when you remove them.

Glitter effect
To achieve a glitter effect on a model, choose a glitter powder close in colour to the local colour you want to achieve, and apply it inside the mould before the coats of resin.

Combining techniques
A variety of effects are found in the Punk Crocodile although very little masking was used. After an initial coat of green enamel, the darker hues were added – the reds going on last of all. Because of the heavily textured surface, there wasn't much need for texturing the paint, although this can be achieved with enamels by spraying from a distance; if you spray from a distance, the droplets of paint tend to solidify by the time they strike the surface, creating a matt texture.

The creator of the Punk Crocodile, and all the models featured on these pages, Terry Webster, is also in the photograph.

SPRAYING "PIGMAN"

If you use a spray gun for a large area, wear a face mask and cover everything within 10 yards/9 metres of the object that you don't want dusted with a film of fine paint particles.

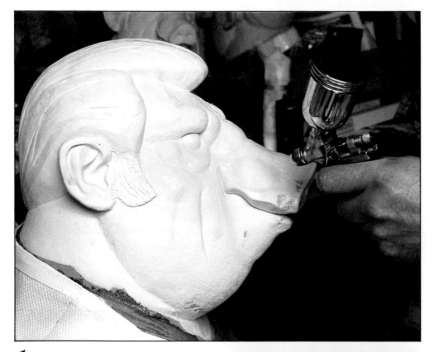

1 The first coat on "pigman" is applied with a spray gun.

2 Uneven freehand spraying gives the required effect of flesh texture on the face. The colors need to be subtle to produce a realistic result, and it can take years of practice to get this right. The flesh tones are built up on the foundation pink with yellows and greens in this case. In the case of the crocodile, it would be blues and greens.

3 The pig man's hair is done by hand. First apply a coat of light orange all over. Then lay on a coat of burnt umber, and wipe off with a cloth when still wet. A streaked effect is created as the darker burnt umber remains in the recesses scratched into the surface of the model's hair. The colors could just as easily be applied with an airbrush, but there is no real advantage.

4 Models present awkward masking problems, particularly models with such odd curves and bulges as these pigs. For masking off a local area, liquid rubber masking fluid is ideal. It is applied with a paintbrush, which will take the masking fluid around the most difficult contours. You can rub the mask off afterwards with your fingers, or seal in a strip of paper when you apply the mask to act as a handle for pulling it off. Masking fluid won't affect the color or surface beneath. Use an old or cheap paintbrush for applying the mask, and clean the brush afterwards with thinner. Masking fluid shouldn't be left for more than three days or it will become difficult to remove. For masking off a large area roughly, scrap paper, paper towel or rag fixed with masking tape are perfectly adequate.

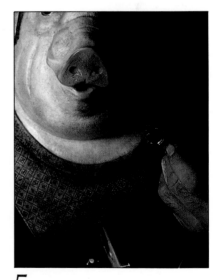

5 Much of the spraying is done freehand with little or no masking. This calls for a steady hand although some overspray can add texture.

continued . . .

MOTION PICTURE SPECIAL EFFECTS

Airbrushing plays an important role in several different areas of film production. Perhaps the most obvious is the coloring of models and puppets which are increasingly being used in science fiction movies. Major production companies budget for a certain amount of model making research, and sculptors, painter and designers work together to produce convincing and realistic images. The models themselves are usually constructed from a prosetic rubber and the outside is sprayed with a variety of media including oil and acrylic paints; some studios create their own paints from secret formulae.

A less obvious, but nevertheless very important part played by the airbrush artist, is in the creation of story boards. These are immensely detailed so that the director and scene managers can plan the scene sequences to perfection.

Design visuals are also spray painted and are used to give the set builders an idea of what they are aiming at before they start on expensive construction work.

Promotional posters are often airbrushed so that different scenes of a film can be combined to give an immediate impression of what the film is about.

Airbrushing and motion pictures
The veins on the ghoulish mask (above) are being touched up seconds before the model goes in front of the camera.

Airbrushing artists play a vital role in promoting films by producing publicity posters (top opposite). They also play a large part in creating detailed story boards and design visuals (below opposite).

6 *Final details of the eyes are applied with a brush.*

This bizarre and frightening image relies for much of its impact on effects created with the airbrush that could not *be simulated with a paintbrush – effects such as the luminosity of the pink tones, which suggest the density of pig flesh combined with the softness of human skin.*

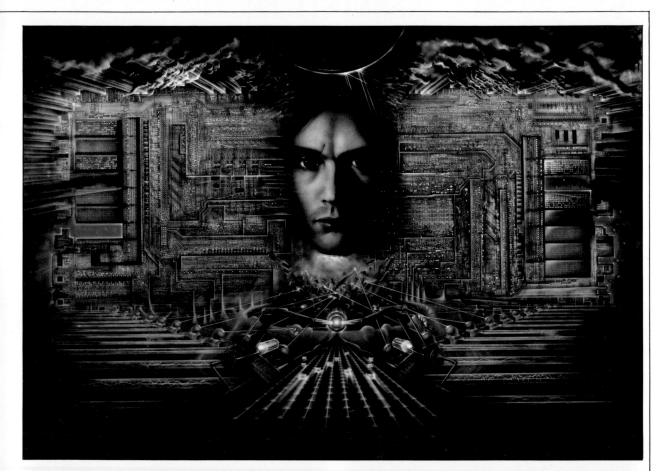

ANIMATION

Airbrushing has a long association with animation work—at one time in the Walt Disney studios, the airbrush team working on a single feature film consisted of twenty people. Despite increasingly sophisticated camera techniques, and the advent of computer animation, airbrushing maintains a unique role in animation for certain effects which cannot be achieved in any other way.

As with artwork for print, one important asset of airbrushing for animation is its ability to make flat images look solidly three-dimensional. It provides the rounded quality and sleekness of finish which makes a cartoon character, or an advertised product, lively and convincing.

Airbrushing is generally used for background color and shadowing, and for special effects of various kinds: distinctive lighting in an image, for example, or a smoke trail or "scent" wafting across the screen. This sort of effect can be done on clear acetate overlays or by means of "mats" which allow an airbrushed element to be superimposed on other action in a film.

Character animation is a separate art, and most character artwork is hand-brush-painted. However, an inventive airbrush artist can often find solutions to specific problems which it would take unnecessary time and expense to deal with in other ways. To a degree, though, the scope of this work is up to the skill and involvement of the individual artist.

One important difference between the effect required in animation and that needed for artwork for print is that airbrushing for animation tends to be simplified, as some detail is lost in shooting on film and an elaborate image is ineffective.

Inevitably, because animation involves multiple images — even a brief animated feature film consumes thousands of artworks — some of the work required is repetitive and rather mechanical, but movement adds literally an extra dimension to the finished product.

MATERIALS AND METHODS

Materials and media for airbrush animation vary according to the purpose of the artwork and the effect to be achieved. Simple background work, for instance, may be on paper and could be sprayed with gouache, inks or arylics. But much artwork for animation sequences is painted directly on to cels (clear acetate sheets) which can be superimposed in layers, each layer carrying a different element of the final animation. Acrylic is the best medium for use on cel, as it is

flexible enough not to crack with any movement of the cel.

A great advantage of airbrushing for painting animation on cels is that the fine spray tends to cling to almost any surface, whereas paint applied with a brush can separate and streak on smooth or glossy-surfaced supports. A slight drawback is the problem of matching paint mixes frame to frame so the quality is continuous, because an airbrush has limited paint-holding capacity. The actual hue and the density of color must be consistent

Sequence for breakfast cereal (right)
Airbrush work is important in advertising animation, especially if products are required to move in unrealistic or fanciful ways. This example (right) of breakfast cereal dropping into a bowl was supposed to create a magical effect as the cereal lightly floated down from above. The ability of the airbrush to create "out of focus" images made the sequence possible — it would have been virtually impossible to film for real.

A frame from an animation sequence
This single frame from an animation sequence comprises an airbrushed background and four hand-painted acetate cells. The background remains consistent for the whole of the sequence but the cells are subtly different in each frame.

1 Base artwork on board
2 Acetate with bare tree
3 Acetate with snow
4 Acetate with fox character
5 Fifth acetate cell of falling snow combined with previous cells and base artwork.

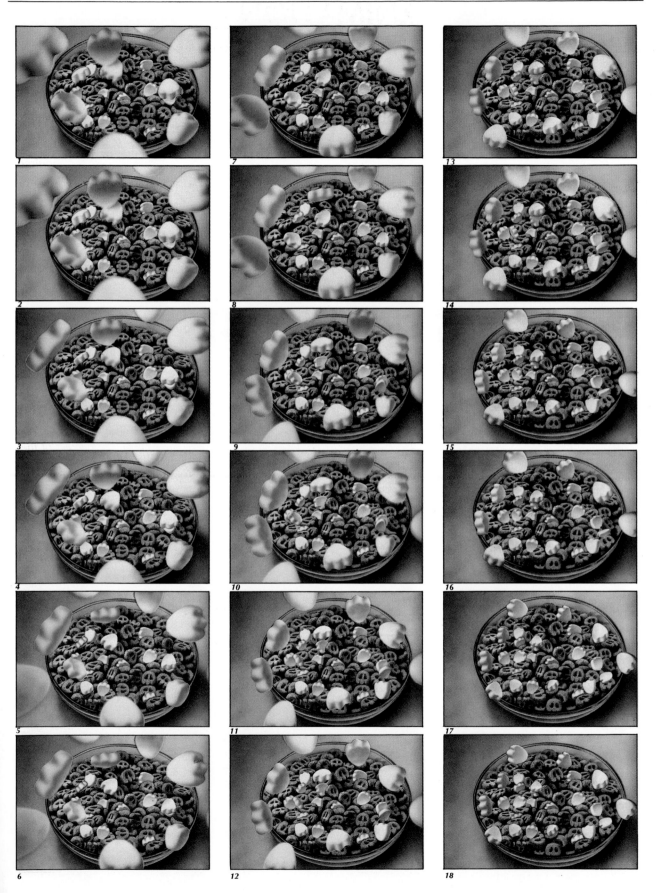

ADVERTISING ANIMATION

Airbrushing techniques offer specific advantages for advertising work. Packshots on camera for a long time, for instance, are carefully scrutinized and must have the kind of perfect finish, which only airbrushing can achieve. Similarly an image which has to be enlarged must retain its quality. Again, only airbrushing is suitable; with handbrush work, the brushmarks show up all too clearly when the picture is blown up. One further strength of airbrushing is that it retains a good deal of its definition and brightness throughout the reprocessing required to animate photographic images.

Airbrush work is often combined with hand-drawn animation and with film camera work used in advertising. Animals required to "talk" in a commercial, for example, can be filmed and edited into the required sequences of movement, but for the effect to look slick and convincing, judicious airbrushing "improvement" of individual frames is vital. It is usually airbrushing that makes their mouths seem to move.

Combining airbrushing and handpainting for advertising

The animation sequence on these pages shows airbrush work combined with hand-painted character animation. The airbrushed packshot does, surprisingly, look more convincing on camera than the real thing. In the early frames there is little movement in the pack, but gradually it leans toward the character introduced from the right. These frames represent the main stages of the action, but many more frames are shot to animate the sequence smoothly.

1

2

3

4

5

6

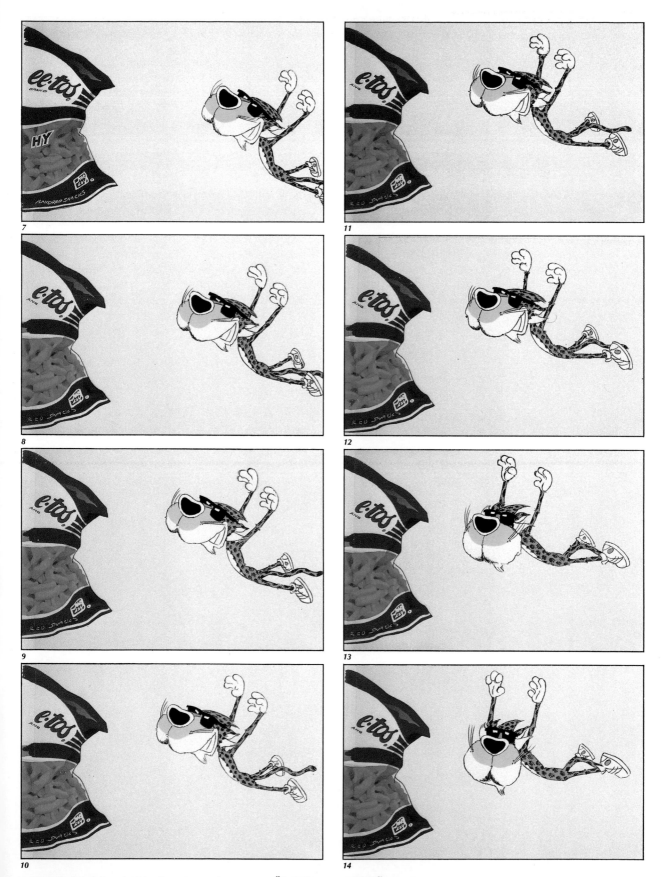

7

8

9

10

11

12

13

14

CERAMIC RESTORATION

The airbrush is much prized in the restoration of china and ceramics, as well as in the decoration of new ceramics. It is used for making all kinds of invisible mends, that simply could not be done by hand. Before the airbrush was taken up by ceramic restorers, invisible repairs on the lines of those described below tended to be somewhat visible.

The studio photographed here employs a team of six china restorers. They have an airbrush booth in a corner of the studio, which houses two airbrush stations. Both airbrushes are in constant use. The booth is fitted with a large air extractor, which is essential in an enclosed working environment. Each member of the team works on several different items at once, employing a variety of tools and substances depending on the stage each job is at. The airbrushes are used mainly for background color and for blurry mottled effects, rather than fine detail which is done with a paintbrush. The walls of the studio are lined with shelves sagging under the weight of plates, ornaments, teapots, vases, dolls and all manner of ceramic and china objects in varying states of repair.

Acrylic stoving enamel is the primary medium used in this business. It is usually mixed with stoving enamel thinner to varying consistencies, depending on the job in hand. Although stoving enamel is touch dry in minutes, it has to be cured in the oven for about half an hour at a low temperature – 220°F/105°C between each coat. Stoving enamel is not a natural airbrush medium and it does tend to clog up the nozzle and needle very easily. As always, cleaning and daily care are essential. A reamer is useful for cleaning out the nozzle (see page 55) but caution is advised.

Before spraying on to a china surface, it must be completely clean, grease-free and even. Very fine grades of sandpaper can be used to smooth filler to the point where you cannot feel it if you run a finger over it.

The spray booth
The studio featured on these pages has a specially constructed spray booth (above) which is where all the airbrushing takes place. This booth is essential because some of the materials used in ceramic restoration are toxic. The booth has a powerful extractor fan to suck out all the noxious fumes.

The studio
This typical ceramic restoration studio looks chaotic but is, in fact, well organized. Some pigments are sprayed on; others are applied by hand.

SPECIFIC TECHNIQUES

Disguising a Join

Feathering out is a technique employed to avoid creating a hard edge where new glaze meets old. There are no hard and fast rules, because each glaze is different in its solidity, gradation of tone and translucency. As you spray toward the join, you lift the airbrush back from the surface of the china, feathering away into nothing, taking great care not to darken the surrounding edges. Feathering can be done by hand but you can never disguise the join properly. Another way of disguising edges is simply to spray thinner over them – it softens edges.

Restoring or Applying a Glaze

One of the most important uses of the airbrush in this field is in recreating an antique color glaze, either touching up an existing glaze where the china has been chipped or damaged in some other way, or starting from scratch. A color glaze, say blue, has to be built up in several layers, starting with a neutral color layer that approximates the color of the original clay. If you were to try spraying blue directly on to a patch of white repaired clay in the middle of an existing blue glaze, you would never achieve a match. Glazes are fairly transparent, and each coat contributes to the final overall color. Three or more coats of blue glaze are then dappled on with the airbrush, each layer thinner than the last, to create an authentic final color.

Color Mixing

For ceramic restoration, colors have to mixed by eye. China colors are infinitely variable and patchy. Two or three coats of varying shades are generally needed before a perfect match can be achieved. When mixing and thinning media, it is a good idea to use a dropper to transfer the liquid to the airbrush bowl. Note down the number drops of each component in the formula, so that the mix can be repeated as necessary.

Spraying enamels (left and below left)
In this series of photographs, stoving enamel is being sprayed on to a repaired ornament. All the spraying takes place in the spray booth which is located at one end of the studio.

Spotting

Spotting is an aging or antiquing trick. Powder pigment is dropped on to a small amount of ceramic glaze in the bowl of the airbrush, but not mixed with it. As the glaze is sprayed through the airbrush the powder spots the surface of the china and is embedded there in the glaze. Spray in quick bursts from a distance of 2-3 in/5-6 cm. The powder tends to clog the workings of the airbrush, and it needs to be flushed out constantly with the appropriate solvent.

Achieving a grainy texture

The airbrush is also useful for creating other types of finish, such as the mat flesh color of a china doll's face and body. Or for a variable texture, sprinkle the surface of the final coat of a mat enamel glaze with talcum powder from a fine brush. The wetter the enamel, the more talc adheres and the more textured the finish. This technique could be adapted for any type of model where a fine, tactile texture is required.

Varied glaze effects

A hazy glaze can be achieved by spraying the final coat from a distance of about 9 in/22 cm. Glaze is a heavy medium, and it will reach the surface more as droplets than a fine spray if the brush is held at a distance. The nearer you hold it, the shinier and more solid the result.

Homemade airbrush holder

At the ceramic restoration studio featured here they have designed a worktop airbrush holder most appropriate for the way they use an airbrush. A block of wood, 4x4x4, with a channel chiseled down the center of the top surface, sits beside each restorer and holds the airbrush when it is not in use. Its advantage over a bench hangar is that you can pick up and put down the brush much more quickly and without having to look up each time.

Ceramic tile as palette

Ceramic tiles are very useful for judging the coarseness of spray and color before spraying the object itself – dark tiles for light colors and white tiles for dark colors. A tissue or piece of paper towel stands by to clean off the tiles after each test.

DETAILED REPAIR WORK

In this example of detailed ceramic repair work, a replacement lizard head is molded and painted to restore a magnificent reptilian scene to its former glory. The replacement piece was crafted from a special epoxy putty which has a secret recipe.

1 The new lizard head is roughly molded and then stuck in place. The initial shaping and carving is done with a riffler (a fine file). In this repair, a similar lizard on the other side of the dish, was used as a model for the new head.

2 Fine sandpaper is used to smooth down the initial shaping. After each sanding, finer details are added with a riffler or needle.

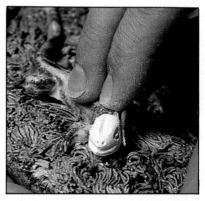

3 When the necessary modeling has been completed, the join between the new head and the original ceramic ware is honed down to a fine line.

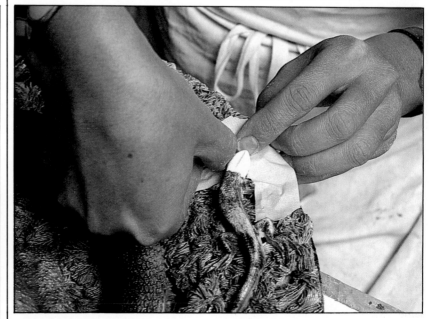

4 A simple paper mask is slipped under the lizards head to protect the ceramic *foundation from overspray that would otherwise spoil the paintwork.*

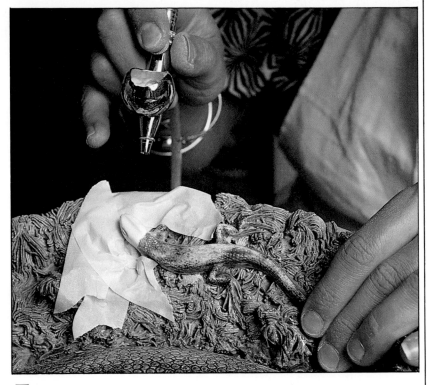

5 *The masking is purposely crude so that any overspray will overlap the original glaze and help to integrate the new head with its surroundings. However, tape is forced into undercuts.*

7 *The undercoat is sprayed on the front of the head first. A smooth undercoat is essential as any dribbles or spatters at* this stage will show through when the final colors are applied, thus ruining the repair.

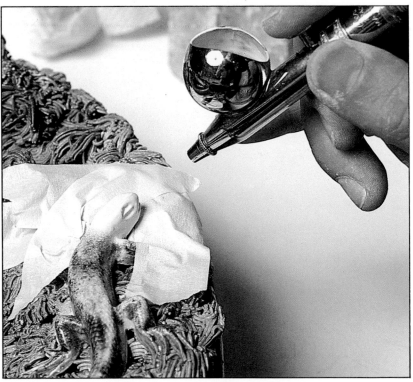

6 *The first coating of color is mixed to match the color of the plate before it was painted. If you don't start with the same base color, there is little hope of being able to match the end result.*

Here, a beige undercoat of stoving enamel is being tested.

8 *Overspray is allowed to fall on to the original ceramic ware – this ensures that* the join between old and new will not be perceptible to sight or touch.

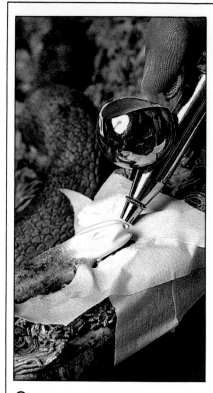

9 *All visible areas are sprayed, including the nostrils.*

10 *A way of disguising the join where the old glaze meets the new, is to spray thinner over it. This softens down the hard edges and smoothes over the join, but care must be taken not to allow the thinner to dribble as this will ruin the finished effect.*

11 *The brown and dark shades on the lizard's skin are spattered on, taking care not to allow too much overspray to fall on to the body of the lizard as this could darken the overall tone. The colors are tested on a clean ceramic tile to judge both the color and the coarseness of the spray.*

12 *Although the undercoat glaze is touch dry in a matter of minutes, the plate has to be stoved before the next coat of color is applied. In most cases, the stoving takes half an hour or so at a temperature of 220°F/430°C.*

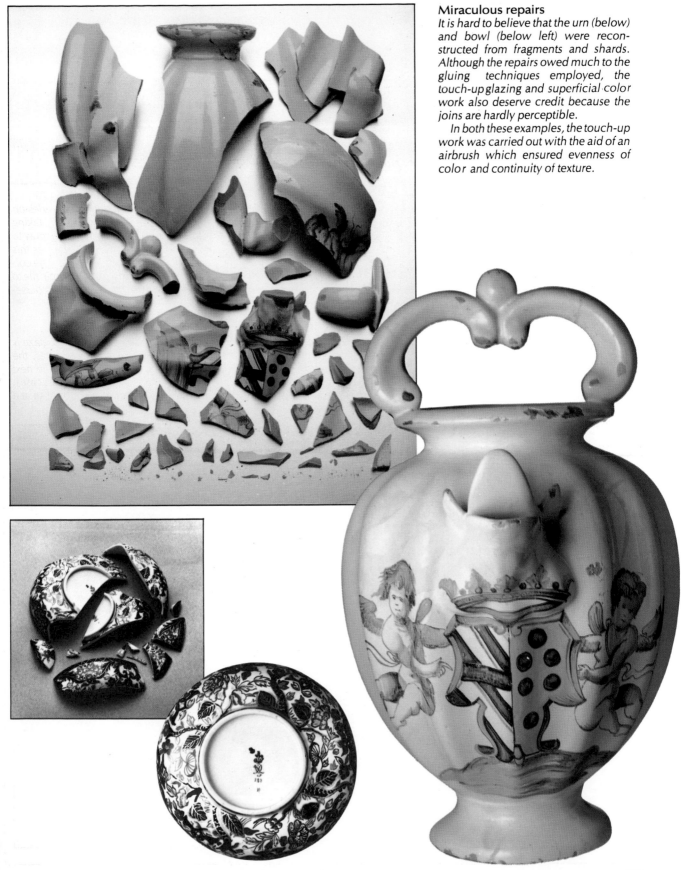

Miraculous repairs

It is hard to believe that the urn (below) and bowl (below left) were reconstructed from fragments and shards. Although the repairs owed much to the gluing techniques employed, the touch-up glazing and superficial color work also deserve credit because the joins are hardly perceptible.

In both these examples, the touch-up work was carried out with the aid of an airbrush which ensured evenness of color and continuity of texture.

TECHNICAL ILLUSTRATION

The development of technical illustration to a high art took place within industrial studios, such as those of automotive manufacturers, where artists would specialize in different aspects of the work – technical drawing, airbrush rendering, or hand-painted detail work. Illustrators now working in this field are usually independent of any particular organization and are likely to have to master all these aspects of the craft, and also the many conventions of technical illustration which have been developed for showing the exterior finish and interior workings of all types of machinery, constructions and technical products.

Technical illustration has its origins in drawings produced for machine manuals, but it now has broader applications in product development, marketing and advertising, and covers a range of work from basic diagrams to prestigious, highly finished color renderings. Airbrushing has an important role across this whole range, and many of the forms of presentation derive directly from the capabilities of the airbrush.

There is often a great deal of complicated information to be conveyed in technical illustration and it is important that this is accurately and descriptively portrayed. External views exploit the flawless surface effects that can be achieved by airbrushing, of gleaming metal and smoothly finished paintwork. But the capacity of airbrush work to explain the three-dimensional quality of an object is also used in exterior and interior renderings.

Two of the most important techniques available to the technical illustrator are ghosting and cut-aways. Ghosting and cut-aways are conventions commonly employed in technical illustration to show the internal components and functions normally concealed by the outer shell. Ghosting shows the inner working as if through a transparent outer layer. Cut-aways reveal internal sections from various angles and in different depths.

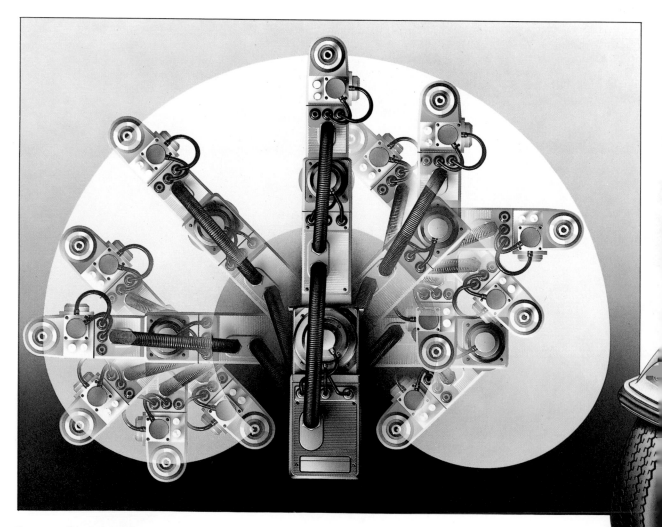

Representing movement
The ghosting in this artwork shows how the parts of an engine move.

GHOSTING

Ghosting to reveal detail hidden below the surface is usually done in one of two ways: by illustrating the components fully and then laying a translucent spray of color overall; or by airbrushing the detail lightly over a ground of opaque color, so the forms are accurately defined but seen as if emerging from the underlayer.

Detailed rendering
The motorcycle (right and below) shows a combination of ghosting and cut-away techniques.

Deciding on techniques
At a very early stage it was decided that the gas tank area should be ghosted but the more detailed engine area should be cut-away.

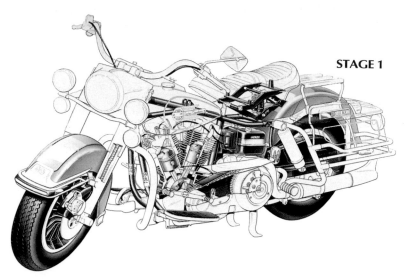

STAGE 1

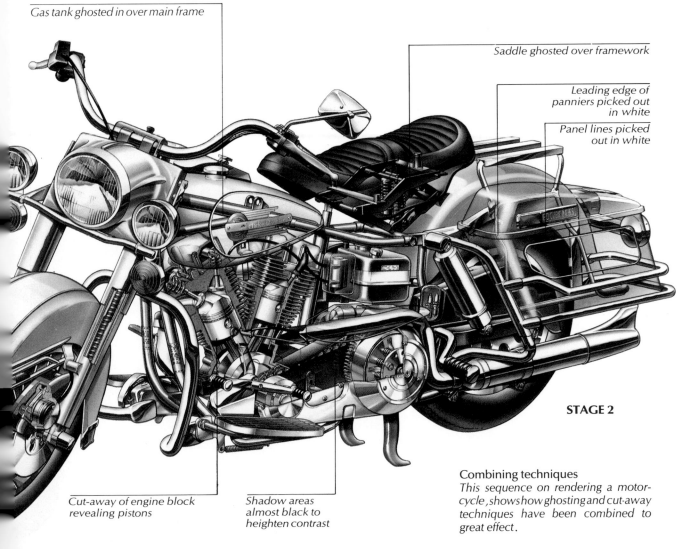

Gas tank ghosted in over main frame

Saddle ghosted over framework

Leading edge of panniers picked out in white

Panel lines picked out in white

STAGE 2

Cut-away of engine block revealing pistons

Shadow areas almost black to heighten contrast

Combining techniques
This sequence on rendering a motorcycle, shows how ghosting and cut-away techniques have been combined to great effect.

CUT-AWAYS

The value of cut-aways for showing internal detail is that the illustrator can portray highly complex structures which contain various levels and internal functions while still showing the overall shape. Cut-aways have to be worked out in great detail. The airbrushing itself is straighforward and standard airbrushing techniques are used – areas of flat and graded color are applied by means of masks which must be cut with absolute precision. But the initial drawing requires enormous skill and patience in working out just how to present these complex invisible structures. The advantage of airbrushing is that it gives a smooth clear finish and rendering of highlights and shadows.

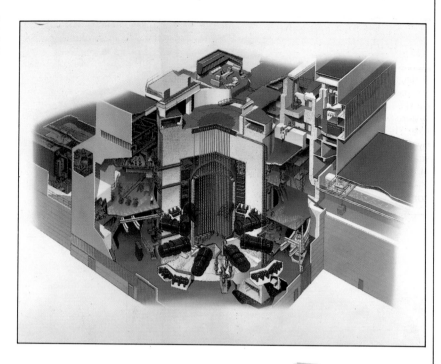

Cut-away angles
The cutaway of the nuclear power station (top) depends on two simple cross-sections, one at 90° and one at 120°, drawn up from the technical plans. Ghosting in of the ring of red components, plus normal perspective drawing completes the effect. The turbine (right) is a more straightforward cut-away. Spattered texture identifies the vertical section and the lines of the section are shown in flame red, a common convention.

SCHEMATIC AND DIAGRAMMATIC RENDERINGS

A diagrammatic approach is appropriate for specific technical functions which must be understood in terms of how the system works, rather than what it looks like. The relationship of parts is shown by a schematic construction that shows scale and continuity without actually illustrating the components.

In the past, this style of drawing was commonly applied in studio work for parts and maintenance manuals to show, for example, the braking systems of cars or electrical circuitry. These were quite distinct from the more lavish airbrush renderings of finished objects. Currently, however, sophisticated schematic artwork showing complex processes and functions is in great demand for advertising and brochure work. As more and more illustrators have become involved in work of this type, more elaborate and slickly finished styles have developed. But they still serve the basic purpose of explaining technical information in a clear and precise manner. Typically, there is a strong linear emphasis in this type of drawing and the color is designed to identify basic elements and trace the continuity of the system.

Line and color

This diagrammatic rendering of an automotive oil system (below) demonstrates a careful line drawing given depth and detail with schematic application of color. The yellow oil flow shows up clearly against a monochrome background

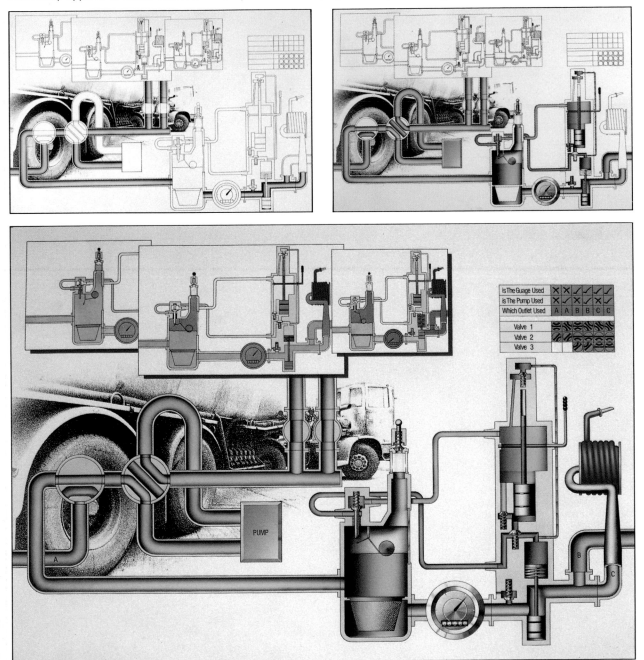

ADVANCED TECHNIQUES FOR FULLY-REALIZED IMAGES

One of the best-known features of airbrush work is the fully-realized, hyper-realistic painting which creates an image almost more convincing than the real thing. This was brought to a very high standard by experienced illustrators and studio managers in the 1950s and 60s and this has been a standard aspired to ever since by all airbrush artists.

The effect of this style is of powerful realism and elaborate detail, but in close up it can be seen that there is actually a great economy of means. There is a crisp clarity to the initial drawing which defines the shape of the object. This can be seen in the inset of the Jaguar car (below), where the construction lines and outline are visible in the partially airbrushed section at the rear. The holding line underpins the three-dimensionality of the object, but it is

completely obliterated by the subsequent airbrushing. The painted effect is solidly three-dimensional, with a sleek surface finish demonstrating some subtle coloration.

The halfway stage of this image also shows the technique of working from front to back of the illustration, building up the layers of color. If one section is too highly rendered in advance of other areas of the image, it unbalances the work and it is difficult to ensure the coherence of the final effect. Similar elements should be worked to the same stage at each new step. The example shows the lit and shadowed areas of the body paintwork extended down the length of the car. The basic structure of one tyre has been worked, so the back tyre will be the next immediate stage, followed by further work on the overall tones. As the final image emerges there is careful attention to hand-painted detail in elements such as the chromework, dashboard and the air vents.

CREATING FULLY-REALIZED ARTWORK

Numbers cut out and left unsprayed

Combined masking techniques

The first stage of this rendering of a camouflaged aircraft involved transparent inks sprayed over linework, working light to dark, followed by opaque gouache sprayed in to adjust the balance of color and tone. Cut film masks and loose masking materials wer both used to differentiate hard and soft edges. The combined masking techniques mean that some hand-applied brushwork was needed to link the elements and bring up the final details

Advantages of artwork

One of the main advantages of fully-realised airbrushed artwork is that it can give a good impression of a new machine which as yet only exists in plan. Similarly, camouflage patterns can be altered and changed to suit, as in the two examples on the right.

Working to a commission

Although the image of the car (below) appears half finished, the artwork is in fact complete. The artist was commissioned to produce such a work.

Feathering-off of line to give the appearance of rounding a corner

Grading color

Opaque gouache is used to obtain the density of color required and to lay light areas over dark to create the shiny effect. Each gradation of color is quite distinct and this apparent complexity was created by a relatively simple masking and airbrushing sequence.

Enlargement of rear wing

Lettering done with technical pen and ink on board before spraying

Loose-paper used to create soft edges to camouflage

All construction lines visible

Dark areas and shadows sprayed at an early stage

Brushed in white highlights

Simple dot/dash technique, if it is regular, is very effective

Lighter tone of green reflected up on underside of car body

STAGE 1

AIRBRUSH AND PAINTBRUSH MIX

Previous examples have shown the way brushwork and pen-drawn detail are often used together to complete an airbrush rendering, but this helicopter illustration relies on a combination of airbrushing and traditional painting techniques throughout. The airbrush is used to give a solid three-dimensional effect for the body; the easy and subtle gradation of tone needed for realistic shadowing can only be achieved with an airbrush. There is plenty of detail here, however, for which hand-painting is not only appropriate but labor-saving. Airbrushing on this scale almost invariably needs elaborate masking every time a new color is applied. But many areas of detail can be carefully and quickly hand-painted to give a finish which complements the airbrushed texture.

STAGE 2

Shadow areas almost black beneath motor

Painting sequence
Most of the first stage (top) was done with one large mask supplemented with a certain amount of torn paper and low-tack masking.

In the second stage (above), the figure was touched up by hand

Tear-shaped highlight on cowl

Firmly sprayed edging highlight

STAGE 4

STAGE 3

Superficial detailing
Highlights and surface details are added at the third stage (above). The interior of the helicopter was largely painted by hand.

Slight darkening along panel lines to add realism

Fine rivet detailing dotted with brush along ruler

Highlights and details
Hand-painted highlights and fine details can provide a certain movement and roughness of texture which contrasts well with the smoother finish of the airbrush work.

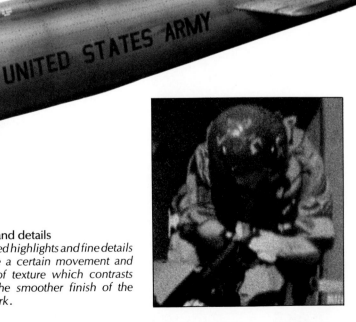

The final image (above)
The final image has a vigorous quality well expressed by the combination of techniques used which are appropriate to the subject. There is an overlap here between technical and editorial illustration. This picture showing the helicopter in action implies a story to be told, but the accurate and detailed rendering of the machine requires technical knowledge. In editorial or movie posterwork, the artist may be required to provide a panoramic background, often hand-painted.

METHODS OF CONSTRUCTION

In many studios, pre-drawn two- and three-point perspective grids are used as aids to drawing (see page 137). When using perspective grids, tracing paper is laid over the grid and the pattern is used as a guide. Once the construction of the image has been completed it is transferred directly on to line or line and wash board (see page 134).

However, in many cases, pre-drawn grids are not suitable, either because the angle is wrong or because the perspective is too extreme. The size of the object being drawn also has a bearing on whether or not a standard grid is suitable. To get around this problem many illustrators construct their own base grids to fit the exact requirements of the subject, often starting with a hand-drawn rough. In the examples on these pages, two different grids were used to construct very similar images. Drawing the larger illustration on a pre-drawn perspective artwork grid would not be possible.

Two approaches to technical illustration

The highly finished and fully rendered technical illustration of a Jaguar engine (left) was commissioned for a glossy brochure. The engine has been split down the middle and the two halves drawn apart. The inner sections of the engine have been carefully sectioned at various angles and planes to give maximum information, yet the basic forms are still maintained.

A more traditional illustration (below), typical of the type that came from the boards of studio managers in the heyday of the aircraft and automobile industries in the 1950s and 1960s, has a different approach. It is lit by a single light source which strikes the image at an angle of 45° and atmospheric perspective has been used. With this rendering of perspective, objects further from the eye appear hazy and less defined. The traditional engineering colors of gray greens and blues have also been used, with the section cuts outlined in red.

PHOTORETOUCHING

The professional retoucher is just as much an artist as the graphic illustrator is, but ironically the retoucher's greatest accolade is when his or her work goes unnoticed – when the alterations to a photograph are completely invisible. The retoucher's skills may be required for a variety of reasons: cosmetic work on a product photograph may be considerably cheaper than reshooting the product; there may be unwanted reflections on a shiny surface – reflections that the photographer could not avoid; a print to be used in a newspaper may need sharpening up so that it will reproduce clearly; the background to an object or person may need changing or eliminating; where the camera cannot lie, the retoucher may be asked to – removing a particular face from a group photograph, for example; an old battered and cracked photograph may need restoring; the joins in a photomontage may need disguising in a similar way.

The techniques of retouching are achieved with the mainstream airbrush skills of accurate masking, vignetting, laying in flat blocks of color and so on. The variable factors include dealing with the photographic surface, color mixing and matching, and most important of all, assessing how to approach each task.

Not all retouching is concerned with disguising alterations. Certain styles, such as the color tinting of black and white prints, or photomontage where the juxtaposition of unrelated subjects may produce surreal or bizarre images, are not intended to look realistic and begin to fall into the category of original art.

Retouching is highly skilled work and first attempts are unlikely to be convincing. Don't be put off further attempts, however – practice and experience will pay off.

PAINTS

The specialist paint and materials you need will depend on the type of retouching you do. The simplest black and white print retouching need involve very little extra equipment. A retoucher's palette of gray tones is available, but most professionals mix their own from black, brown, and white watercolors, and white gouache, to ensure an exact match. The addition of small amounts of brown to a mixed gray counteracts the blue tinge that black and white alone produce. For color retouching, ordinary liquid watercolors and dyes are ideal.

A useful exercise for the retoucher is to mix up a value scale of grays and then to try matching the greys exactly with the tones on a black and white print. The same exercise can be repeated with color scales.

SURFACES

Retouching can be done on black and white and color prints, and on black and white negatives and color transparencies. Prints are much easier to handle and are better for beginners.

Photographic print papers have a fine non-absorbent surface with either a gloss or mat finish. They need to be treated with care.

Mat finish papers are better for first attempts because the contrast between the print and the retouched areas will be less marked than on a glossy finish.

Prints will bend and curl during retouching unless they are securely mounted.

Low-tack masking film is the ideal masking material.

REMOVING BACKGROUNDS

Taking out the background behind an object or person is one of the most common retouching tasks and was required for both the shot of the compressor below and the military vehicle opposite. The technique is simple. First mount the print. Swab the surface of the print with cotton dipped in lighter fuel to remove grease and dust. Lay a sheet of masking film over the entire area of the image including the required background dimensions. With a very sharp rounded scalpel blade, cut around the outline of the object. This is the most crucial stage of the job so take as long as necessary. Any noticeable errors will mean starting again. Use straight edges, ellipse and circle templates, French curves and other cutting edges to guide your blade. Peel off the film to expose the background sections. Start spraying at the darkest area of the original background and begin building up a neutral tone. Build up the background in several layers, allowing each layer to dry thoroughly, rather than spraying thickly at one go.

Spraying shadows
Soft shadows were sprayed on the artwork (below) to ground the image.

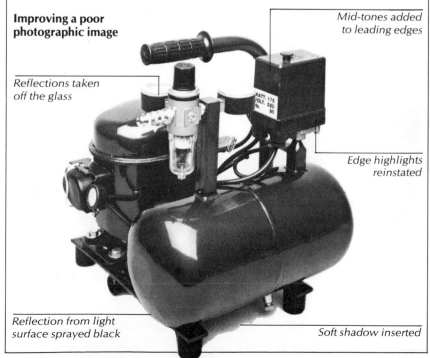

Improving a poor photographic image

Reflections taken off the glass

Mid-tones added to leading edges

Edge highlights reinstated

Reflection from light surface sprayed black

Soft shadow inserted

TOTAL RETOUCH

Occasionally a photograph will need an almost total retouch. Perhaps there is no possibility of reshooting the image – it may be an action shot of a skier in mid-air or it may be an old photograph. The shot of the military vehicle (below) – muddied and set against a distractingly busy background – was the only one available. To add to the problems, the picture was taken in bright conditions under heavy cover.

For the photograph to be used, the background had to be taken out and almost every surface resprayed. The job was tackled in two separate stages – first the background was removed according to the method described opposite, and convincing shadows were inserted to suggest the ground beneath.

The vehicle itself was then cleaned up. The retoucher had made a copy of the print before starting so that the original was always to hand for reference. The image was treated plane by

plane, as if it were being created from scratch. Some of the detail in areas of heavy shadow, particularly under the chassis and around the rear wheel, was completely obscured in the original and had to be reinstated. The retoucher needed additional visual reference here in order to recreate the detail accurately.

Combining techniques
In addition to using an airbrush, the retoucher of the truck (below) used a fine brush for adding details.

BEFORE

AFTER

CLASSIC RETOUCHING TECHNIQUES

These two before-and-after examples (below and right) demonstrate changes the retoucher is commonly asked to make to product photographs for use in brochures and other sales material.

The original studio photograph of the pre-set airbrush handle (right) had several faults: the screw thread and knurling was cleaned up by hand; the texture of the handle, although accurately photographed, was felt to be too grainy and the retoucher used the airbrush to give it a shiny chrome finish; machinery marks visible on the crown cap (inset) were obliterated by a combination of hand and airbrush work; the overall tonal contrast of the photograph was boosted by the addition of a mid-gray tone; and the background and shadows were resprayed to remove the blemishes in both original shots caused by poor studio lighting. The shot of the airbrush and adapter (below) was treated in much the same way.

Adding mid-tones
The image (below) was destined for a manufacturer's catalog but, before it could be inserted, the mid-tones of gray had to be touched up and the image given greater definition (below right). Bad lighting was partly responsible for the weak original.

Correcting bad lighting
The background of the original photograph (top) was corrected to compensate for insufficient lighting.

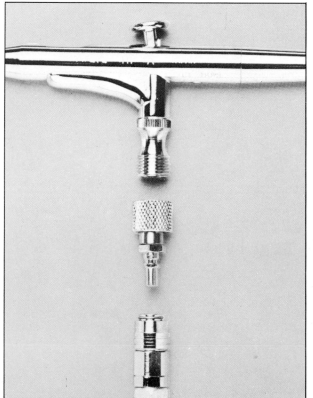

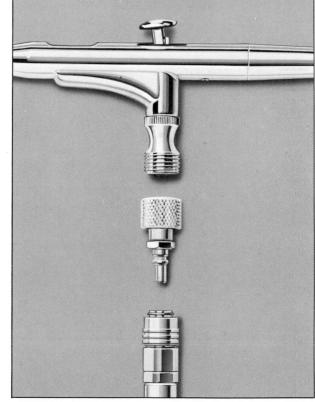

PHOTORETOUCHING OPTIONS

This series of photographs demonstrates three possible ways of retouching an image. In each case, the demands of a hypothetical client have been taken into consideration.

One of the factors that a retoucher must take into account before work commences is the quality of the paper — if paint won't adhere to the surface, there is little that can be done.

Isolating a component
Here, one item has been isolated with white gouache — a technique that is often used if the image is needed for printing.

Selecting a portion
In this photograph, the background vignette has been imitated with an airbrush; the right hand portion is superfluous.

The original image
This is a standard promotional photograph that has not been touched up in any way.

Spraying a new background
The whole background has been obliterated in this example by a carefully sprayed vignette. Accurate masking is essential.

PRINT RESTORATION

Print restoration involves returning old, battered or torn photographs to their original splendor by deft use of airbrush and paintbrush. Very small or miniature photographs can be enlarged, restored and then rephotographed at their original size. It is always a good idea to work on a copy — the surface of an old print is often cracked or even torn and, even more importantly, unless you are very skilled you might ruin the precious original.

The restoration work can be tackled in much the same way as any other retouching project. It will probably help to work on an enlargement. Special problems you may encounter include faded tones, — spotting — particularly on old sepia photographs — and other blemishes. Some of these can be dealt with by scratching out with a scalpel and toning in the damaged area with the airbrush.

PHOTOMONTAGE

Photomontage is a form of collage — elements from different photographs are combined, put together by cutting and pasting, and then rephotographed. The impact of the combined image may be shocking and brutal — a trapped bleeding animal sitting on the lap of a person sporting a fur coat — or comic and light-hearted. The role of the airbrush may be limited to disguising the joins of the cut pieces, or may involve reshaping or toning one or more elements of the montage so that they fit more precisely.

The demands of advertising sometimes involve realistically superimposing one image on another. Here the airbrush may be used extensively to give the new image a coherent visual identity — in fact a total retouch. The airbrush work might actually be done on an acetate overlay, and then combined prints and overlay rephotographed as one image.

COLOR RETOUCHING

Special sets of retouching colors are available from artist's suppliers but are not essential. Watercolors and water-based inks and dyes are all suitable for airbrushing on to photographic papers.

Color retouching falls into two categories: tinting, which is not intended to be realistic, and correcting color on an existing color print in some way. Skill with color matching and balancing is just as important for color retouching as black and white retouching.

The most common commercial demand for color retouching is in correcting, enhancing, or obliterating detail — perhaps a facial imperfection or an unwanted reflection. Such problems can be corrected in exactly the same way as on black and white prints.

FOOD DECORATION

Cake decoration sometimes reaches the status of high art, as demonstrated by this gelatin-iced rich fruit cake depicting a Roman statue. A constantly expanding range of commercially produced food colors and improvements in their quality, combined with the delicate touch of the airbrush, means greater realism and subtlety can be achieved.

Although decorated cakes can be successfully frozen if correctly packaged, the colors sometimes run during the defrosting process. It is better, therefore, to decorate the cake a couple of days in advance, so that the colors can be allowed to dry thoroughly.

An initial background color can be created by mixing color into the icing before rolling it out. Alternatively a flat wash can be sprayed over the iced cake with an airbrush. The pure white of the icing was allowed to form the background in this case.

Ensure that your airbrush has been thoroughly cleaned of any paint, other medium, and solvent before using it to spray food color. Many of the substances sprayed through airbrushes are highly toxic and poisonous if swallowed in however small a quantity.

What you need
Liquid food colors in gray, red, gold and green (edible colors only must be used in food decoration so check the packaging before you start), tracing paper or low-tack masking film, a fine paintbrush, cotton, a ceramic palette or white plate for mixing colors, and a spare piece of white icing for testing colors.

PREPARING THE SURFACE

The surface relief of this design — the torso on a pedestal — is created first with blocks of marzipan which are then covered with white gelatin icing. Gelatin icing is a smoother and more malleable substance than royal icing and is better for this type of work. The icing should be left for at least 12 hours to dry out thoroughly in a dust-free environment, such as a card box with a lid, before any color is sprayed on to it.

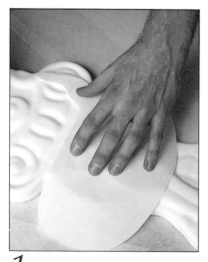

1 Mask off the cake board and sides of the cake with wax or tracing paper to protect them from overspray. Lay a sheet of tracing paper or low-tack masking film over the top of the cake, just larger than the area to be sprayed. Masking film will adhere lightly to dry cake icing without damaging it. Draw on and cut out the area to be sprayed, in this case the column section. Reposition the cut mask.

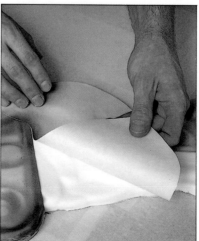

2 Prepare a thin solution of gray liquid food color, diluting it with water to achieve the correct strength. Test the color strength on a spare piece of white icing.

Holding the airbrush about 2 in/5 cm from the surface of the cake, begin spraying freehand, gently at first and then gradually build up detail and shading to create a marbled stone effect.

3 After spraying, peel off the masking. Do this very gently so that the icing underneath doesn't get damaged.

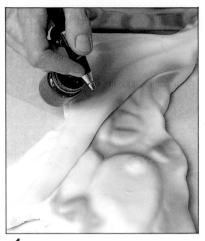

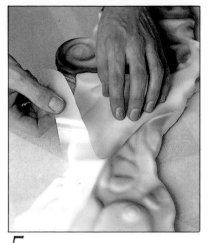

4 *Cut a new mask, this time exposing the torso and covering the column. Again, charge your airbrush with a thin solution of gray food color.*

5 *After spraying the torso, lift off the mask. Underneath you should find pure white icing which can be sprayed red later as the toga.*

BRUSH DETAILING

After the "stone" surface has been sprayed, add the red for the töga. The finishing touches are best applied with a fine paint brush. Detailing of this kind demands a very steady hand.

1 *Add marble veins in both white and black. Don't be tempted into using very strong colors or the effect will look unrealistic. Similarly, if you overdo the marbling, the sense of subtlety will be lost.*

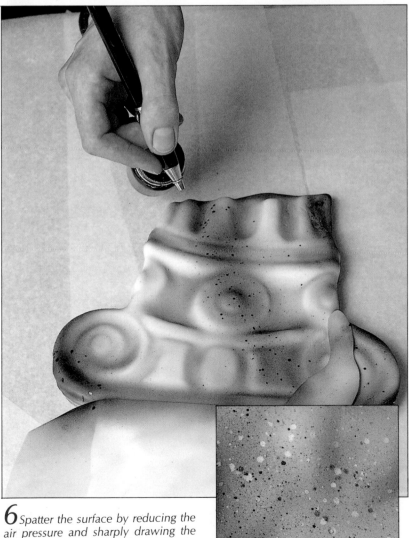

2 *The toga is masked off and sprayed with bright red dye. When the dye is dry, add the details of the gold key design and the border with a very fine brush.*

6 *Spatter the surface by reducing the air pressure and sharply drawing the lever back. Allow to dry thoroughly.*

continued . .

3 The laurel leaves are cut individually from thinly rolled gelatin icing, sprayed with a solution of leaf green, and left to dry. They are fixed in position with small dabs of royal icing around the base of the torso. The final touch is to fix gold berries – little balls of icing painted by hand – to the laurel leaves.

4 The fine detailing on the veins of the leaves is created by dragging the dye on with a dry brush.

The finished icing
The ability to produce a three dimensional illusion is only really made possible by using an airbrush. It is hard to believe that the finished piece (right) is in fact flat.

MEDICAL ILLUSTRATION

Airbrushes have always been used in the field of medical illustration, particularly surgical illustration. The artist can be more discriminating than the photographer — it is often important for the sake of clarity to edit the information and leave out what is not important, for example the background and the instrumentation, homing in on the salient changes at each stage of an operation. There are many branches to medical illustration, each being highly specialized.

PROFESSIONAL BACKGROUND

To be a successful medical illustrator, you have to know about anatomy. Many medical illustrators put in years of medical study as part of their training, concentrating on the aspects of medicine most useful to the illustrator,

such as anatomy and dissection. The illustrator carries into the operating theater a picture in his or her head of the relevant anatomical area in a well state, and then records in sketchnotes what changes take place. Translating this into an artwork sequence, you can start with a master artwork of the area as it should be, and then represent the changes on acetate overlays. In this way you can build up a stock of master artworks of various parts of the anatomy, which can be used time and time again. The graphic interpretation of medical surfaces comes with practice and experience, using reference and a microscope. (Colors used to represent different organs and substances are standardized, although the exact shade may be determined by the approach of the illustrator.)

Clarity with an airbrush

In anatomical illustrations, airbrushed artworks have the edge over photographs because unnecessary bits and pieces can be edited out. In this artwork of muscle structures, blood vessels and other tissues have been left out so that they don't confuse the viewer.

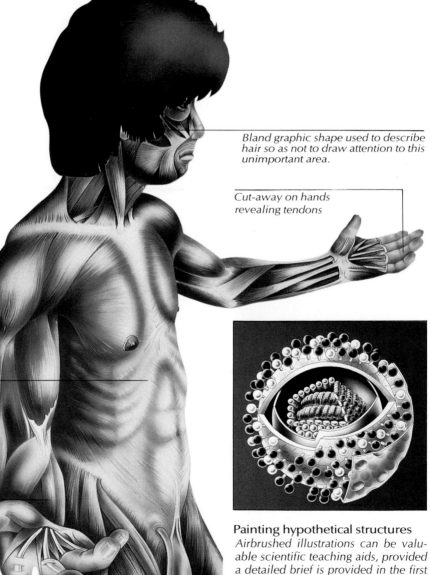

Bland graphic shape used to describe hair so as not to draw attention to this unimportant area.

Cut-away on hands revealing tendons

The basic form of the stomach was sprayed first and line work was added with a paintbrush. The area was then sprayed over quite thickly with gouache to give an impression of the fat layer.

Dark shadow area on the lower arm gives the impression of the hand being thrust toward the viewer.

Painting hypothetical structures

Airbrushed illustrations can be valuable scientific teaching aids, provided a detailed brief is provided in the first place by an expert.

MEDIA

You will probably find you use a variety of media. The illustrator whose work is featured here primes drafting film with a vinyl-based ground and sprays, inks, gouache, acrylics and watercolors on artboard. If you need a lot of the same color, mix up an adequate supply and store it in a sealable jar, such as a pharmacist's pill box. Gouache, for example, can never be mixed to exactly the same consistency twice, so making sure you have enough to complete the job is crucial. When mixing colors that you will want to repeat, measure the ingredients in drops and take a note of the formula. You can get the closest possible match in this way.

Acrylic is not recommended for use on drafting film because it doesn't dry quickly enough. If you put another color on too soon, the colors may run and you will have to retouch. A hair drier can of course be used to speed the process of drying any medium.

The transparency of watercolor can be used to great effect in rendering the layering of human flesh, with for example, the color of blood showing through layers of other colors — structures showing through structures. Transparency techniques are generally important in medical illustration.

MASKING

Low-tack masking film is the only suitable masking material for this very precise type of work. If you are working on an acetate overlay, don't leave masking film on it overnight because it won't come off the next day. This illustrator's method of working is long in the preparation, and works excellently as a result. Lay a piece of masking film over the whole artwork, smoothing it down carefully. Using a magnifying lens on an arm attached to the work surface, cut a very intricate master mask, including all lines that may be needed. Cut carefully and patiently, doing the hard, sharp lines first and then the dark shadow areas. Turn a corner back on each cut piece of mask. Lift and replace each piece as required with the greatest of care. If you are even a pencil-line width out when you replace a piece of mask, you will have hours of retouching ahead of you.

CREATING A MEDICAL ILLUSTRATION

Accuracy is probably more crucial in the field of medical illustration than in any other. For this reason, medical illustrators often use special aids. like powerful benchtop lenses with built-in lighting.

Magnifying the image
A powerful magnifying lens is an essential aid when adding detail. In this case a lens is being used in conjunction with a very fine paint brush.

Spraying freehand
Painting a medical illustration with an airbrush demands a steady hand; masking is usually kept to a minimum.

Applying conventions
Certain conventions are applied to medical illustration, including the use of specific colors for certain organs. In this illustration of a cross-section of human flesh, the glands and blood vessels follow convention.

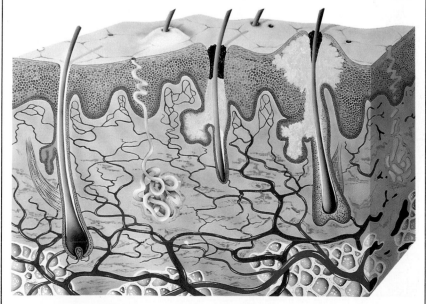

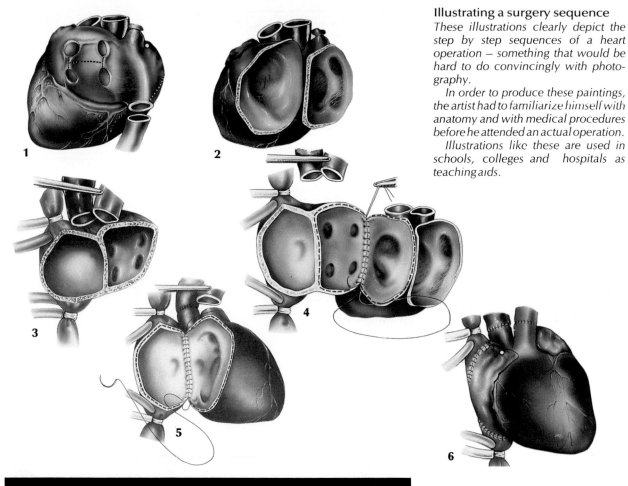

Illustrating a surgery sequence

These illustrations clearly depict the step by step sequences of a heart operation – something that would be hard to do convincingly with photography.

In order to produce these paintings, the artist had to familiarize himself with anatomy and with medical procedures before he attended an actual operation.

Illustrations like these are used in schools, colleges and hospitals as teaching aids.

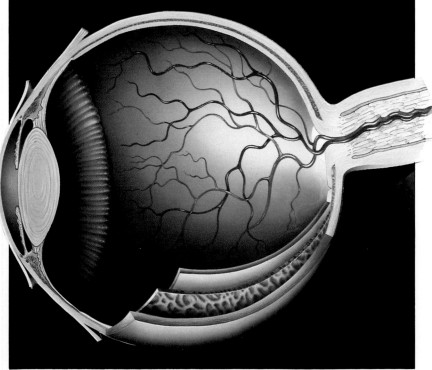

Combining techniques

An airbrush was used to lay down simple, vignetted background colors in this illustration. On top of these colors, the details of the eye were brushed in by hand.

For the sake of clarity, the layers of tissue around the eye have been overlapped – this makes the structure of the eye more readily understood.

223

SPRAYING FABRICS

AIRBRUSHING A T-SHIRT

The airbrush is the ideal tool for applying an image to a T-shirt because of the versatility it offers. Anything from flat carefully masked blocks of color to freehand strokes and spattered backgrounds can in a matter of minutes create a unique garment.

What you need

A good quality 100% cotton T-shirt, an iron, pins or masking tape, a piece of stiff but flexible card larger than the T-shirt, tracing paper, a piece of tough card larger than the area of the image, a craft knife, a weight (anything to hand), spatter cap, textile airbrush colors in violet, blue, magenta, powder blue and yellow, cleaner, and brown paper for heat setting (optional).

Textile Airbrush Colors

Colorfast textile colors, specially formulated for spraying through an airbrush, are the best medium to use on T-shirts. Textile colors are quick-drying, will not bleed and are waterproof, and can be used successfully on most types and colors of fabric. The color can be loaded straight from bottle to airbrush, without thinning or mixing. It comes in plastic bottles fitted with dispensing caps in 1 oz/30 cc and 4 oz/120 cc sizes. Cleaner is available in the same range for removing dried color from the airbrush. Badger produce their Air-Tex Textile Airbrush Color range in 13 colors and black and white, and other manufacturers have comparable ranges in a similar number of colors, so there is no shortage of choice.

STARTING TO SPRAY

1 Use a good quality cotton T-shirt to ensure vibrancy of colors and clarity of effects. Iron the shirt first to give a smooth surface for spraying. Either pin or tape the T-shirt to the work surface and slide a piece of card larger than the area of the image inside the shirt. Or cut a piece of stiff card to a T-shirt shape large enough to stretch the shirt flat, but not to distort it when fitted inside. In this case the shirt was taped to the work surface.

This simple design was drawn freehand straight on to a piece of tracing paper positioned on the shirt, enabling the artist to work out the size and proportion of the finished image.

Special fabric paints

2 The only area that needs masking here is the square. Overspray falling outside the circle area will be part of the design. The mask is made from a piece of tough card much larger than the area of the image. Use the original tracing to transfer the drawing of the square on to the card, and carefully cut out the square with a sturdy craft knife. A scalpel is not usually strong enough for this job. Take care not to damage the square.

3 Load the fabric color directly into the color well or bowl of the airbrush. No thinning or mixing is necessary. Have a bottle of cleaner handy for flushing out the airbrush between colors. The colors used in the circle are violet for the inner circle, blue for coarse spattering into the center of the violet, magneta around the edge of the violet, powder blue around the magneta and finally a yellow outer circle.

4 Position the negative mask (the square of card) at the top right-hand edge of the circle and weight it down with anything suitable to hand – coins, a paper weight, a stone, whatever. Attach the spatter cap to the airbrush, set the pressure on the compressor to 10 psi/0·7 bar and describe a fairly light circle of violet with a fine

The effect of the spatter cap is to disrupt the spray expelled from the tip of the airbrush – the spray hits the edges of the cap on its way out and breaks up. If the spatter cap is clogged up, the effect is even coarser, so it may be an idea not to clean out your spatter cap too regularly or thoroughly. A normal nozzle cap allows the cleanest possible spray to be expelled.

Flush out the airbrush with cleaner. Allow the violet to dry – these colors are quick-drying, so it should only be a matter of a few minutes. Load the color well or cup with blue and, holding the brush about 8 in/25 cm above the shirt, spatter larger blobs of color over the central area.

8 Spray the same order of colors as for the circle – violet, blue, magenta, powder blue, yellow – this time in parallel lines across the square from top right to bottom left, holding the airbrush roughly 4 in/10 cm from the shirt. Hold the airbrush at a slight angle só that the spray hits the surface right to left, in the direction you are laying in the colors. Fade off each color and blend each new color into the previous one. Leave as clean a white stripe as possible – there will inevitably be some overspray – at the bottom left edge, to give the square greater definition and impact. Remove the mask to reveal the design.

5 Flush out the airbrush and load with magenta. Spatter a few coarse blobs in among the blue in the center of the circle and then spray a finer spatter around the edge of the violet circle.

Spray a third circle of powder blue and a final outer circle of yellow, in each case allowing the previous color to dry out first.

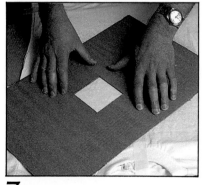

7 Position the positive mask (the large piece of card with the square cut out) exactly over the white space. You should be able to do this by eye. Alternatively, to alter the final image, you might want to position the new mask slightly out of register with the first mask, creating a white drop shadow along two sides of the square. Weight down the mask.

You can mask off any exposed areas of white T-shirt around the edge of the mask with scrap paper to prevent overspray falling where it isn't wanted.

6 Remove the mask to expose the clean white square beneath.

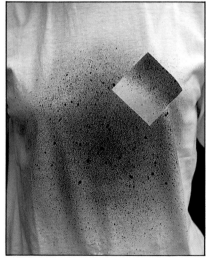

9 The finished garment. Hundreds of variations on this one simple idea are possible, simply by substituting a new range of colors or using different shapes. the whole project took an experienced airbrush artist about 15 minutes to complete.

SPRAYING A TWO-COLOR PATTERN USING A CUT MASK

A stencil mask for airbrushing on fabric needs to be made of a reasonably durable material, but one which is not too difficult to cut cleanly, especially if the pattern is intricate. For this example of an all-over pattern sprayed in two colors, the mask is cut from medium-weight card. The card had to be good quality, as the mask is thoroughly wetted by the airbrush spray each time a color is applied; poor quality card may sag, separate into paper layers or disintegrate when wet.

Detailed floral patterns with a repeating motif like this require crisp cutting. A sharp craft knife with a fairly light blade is used to retain the subtlety of shapes such as the curved petals with their feathery central markings.

Commencing spraying

1 Spray the first pass of color across the masked area. Judge the distribution of color according to the required effect.

2 Repeat the process to apply the second color. Fabric dyes dry quickly but make sure the colors do not blend and merge if they are wet.

Preparing to spray

1 Pin the cut mask securely to the fabric to avoid airbrush spray drifting under the masked areas.

2 Mix the required color and fill the airbrush jar with dye.

3 Allow the color on the mask to dry before lifting it gently to examine the finished effect; if the mask is still wet you may spread the color beyond the masked shapes, or wet dye could penetrate the pinholes as you remove the pins from the mask. Remove the pins carefully to avoid any damage to the fabric of the mask if it is to be used again.

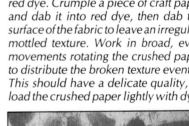

6 *Additional depth is added to the pattern with a lightly textured effect in red dye. Crumple a piece of craft paper and dab it into red dye, then dab the surface of the fabric to leave an irregular, mottled texture. Work in broad, even movements rotating the crushed paper to distribute the broken texture evenly. This should have a delicate quality, so load the crushed paper lightly with dye.*

4 *Weight the fabric flat before vignetting color from the edges of the fabric into the main design.*

7 *The final effect shows the dappling of blue-gray over pink, strengthened by the touches of red texture.*

5 *The vignetted color has the effect of softening and drawing together the different elements of the design. Working freehand, you need to judge the effect finely to avoid overspraying which deadens the pattern quality rather than enhancing it. Keep the fabric stretched flat and taut, using weights or pins as necessary.*

REMAKING DAMAGED MASKS

Fabric patterns often require the same mask to be used several times, to overlay colors, repeat the pattern motifs and to enhance the emphasis of the design. Constant pinning, wetting and peeling mean that sections of the mask may become damaged and ineffective; the patterning must be accurate to ensure a good finish. It may be necessary to recut a whole mask, but sometimes you can get away with reworking only the damaged section.

1 The most accurate way to make a new mask is to spray through the old one on to a clean sheet of card. This gives the exact outline of the pattern.

2 Cutting of a card mask, whether original or remade, must be clean and accurate, with no shreds of card on the edges of the cut to interrupt the outline of airbrush spray.

3 A repeat pattern requires that a careful eye is kept on the continuity between individual motifs.

The benefits of spraying

Sprayed patterning on fabric has a quality quite distinct from that of printed fabric. The linear elements are typically softer, the color blends and overlays mores subtle, and there is a translucency to the color, well served here by the choice of cool and muted hues. An attractive effect is obtained simply by spraying gradated color through a stencil mask, but there is plenty of opportunity for inventiveness with freehand work and overlaid textures to create a unique pattern effect for each fabric length.

Grid pattern printed on to fabric

Spraying fabrics freehand (above)

Virtually no masking was used on these two scarves. The grid pattern that overlays the mottled effect was hand printed on to the silk using a wire mesh.

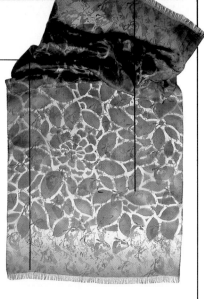

Mask lifted in some areas to soften the
edges of leaves

Vignetted bottom edge

Combining techniques (above)

*A simple leaf pattern was sprayed on
to the scarf first, and the bottom section vignetted. Crumpled paper was
then rolled over the paint to add
texture.*

Simple and complex masking (below)

*The scarf on the left shows simple
masking in diagonal bands with dappled texture created by dabbing with
crumpled paper. A more complicated
mask was used on the scarf on the
right.*

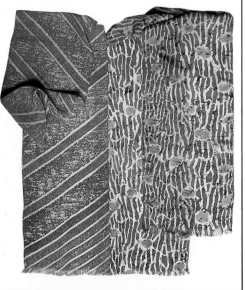

SPRAYING REPLICA MODELS

Building replica models has become a very popular hobby, and many modelers now use an airbrush, or even a small spray gun, to achieve the kind of authentic finish beyond paintbrushing.

Apart from the model itself, the equipment and materials needed are fairly basic. The only essential items of equipment are a good quality airbrush, or spray gun and matching compressor, plus routine spraying accessories such as masking tape, low-tack masking film and liquid masks – all of which are invaluable for model finishing. Paints are a matter of personal choice. Enamels are the most popular paints, but more and more modelers are now trying out modern acrylic finishes. Besides paints, suitable thinners and a cleaning agent such as lighter fuel will be needed.

Ideally, models should be painted in room temperatures about 70 F/21 C to aid paint flow and rapid drying. At anything much cooler, paint may dry so slowly that it is hard to avoid dust settling on it. Paint consistency depends on the type of airbrush used, but should usually be about the same thickness as creamy milk. The amount of thinner you need to add to achieve the right consistency varies with the brand and age of the paint.

All plastic parts should be thoroughly cleaned with soap and water or cleaning fluids before painting to remove all traces of mold release wax before painting – but never use solvents that might damage the plastic surface. It is essential to use masks and films when painting in more than one color, and it is worth trying to paint as much of the body before assembly as possible. A study of the real thing will show which panels can be painted separately and which should be joined and the join line filled prior to painting.

To achieve the overall depth of gloss that makes the model stand out from the crowd finish off with multiple coats of high gloss lacquer.

SPRAYING MODEL RACING CARS

Although the plastic components of most kit cars are supplied in the colors of the real thing, many modelers find that they don't look quite right and they prefer to respray with enamel. It is a good idea to assemble as much as possible of the body sections before spraying – otherwise you may chip the paint as you try to fit the pieces together.

Before spraying the bodywork, degrease the surface with a rag dipped in lighter fuel or thinner; this also takes off any dust and other particles. Spray the bodywork section by section, masking off specific areas with low-tack masking film as necessary.

When the paint is dry, polish the bodywork carefully with a reducing wax; this will give a good shine.

Numbers and details can be added in two ways but before you start, wipe over the model to get rid of any dust. You can either cut stencils from masking film and spray the details, or you can use the transfers supplied with the kit.

Color schemes
The model of a Brabham racing car (top right) sports a simple color scheme of matt white and black; all the details were supplied with the kit. In contrast, the racing colors of the Porsche (right) were created using a combination of masking and spraying, and hand brushwork.

It is common practice among serious modelmakers to adapt and customize existing kits by painting and fabricating structure and detail.

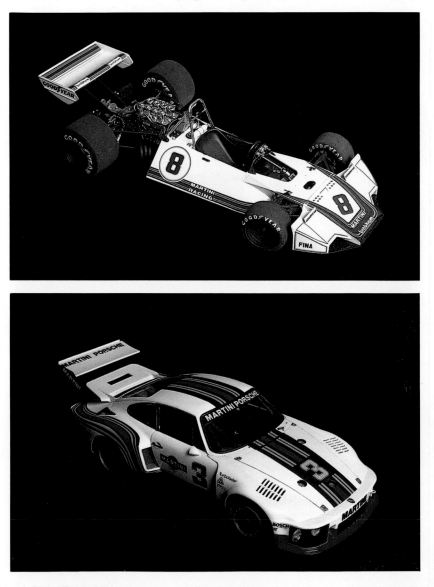

Fine detailing

Attention to fine detail like the gold-painted honeycomb wheels on the white Porsche (below) and the windshield wipers on the red Porsche (right) make all the difference to what would otherwise be straightforward paint jobs. Perfectionists choose colors found on the real thing.

SPRAYING HIGH-GLOSS FINISHES

Fine detailing
A combination of airbrushing and hand-painting is used to create the engine details.

High-gloss paint finish on body relies on the careful spraying of several fine layers of enamel in a dust-free environment

Spraying textures
The appearance of this high-quality model has been enhanced by adding the textures found in the various materials used in racing cars, including mild steel, cast aluminum and even brass.

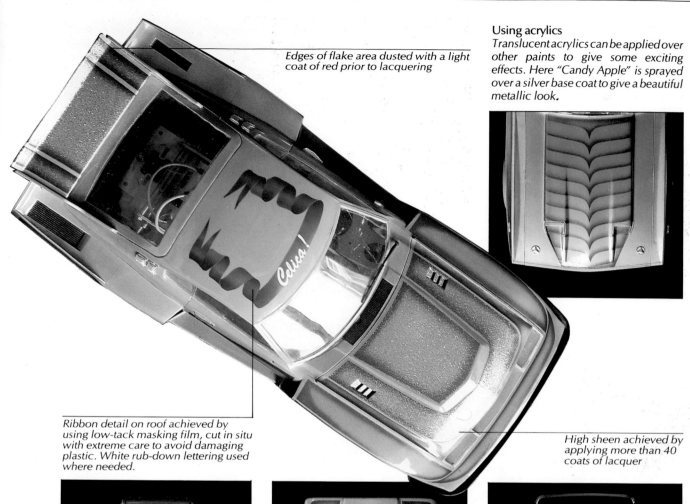

Edges of flake area dusted with a light
coat of red prior to lacquering

Using acrylics
Translucent acrylics can be applied over
other paints to give some exciting
effects. Here "Candy Apple" is sprayed
over a silver base coat to give a beautiful
metallic look.

Ribbon detail on roof achieved by
using low-tack masking film, cut in situ
with extreme care to avoid damaging
plastic. White rub-down lettering used
where needed.

High sheen achieved by
applying more than 40
coats of lacquer

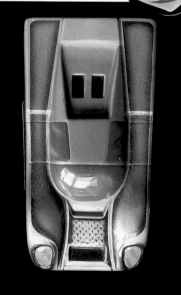

Using primer
Additions such as wide wheel arches
and spoilers should be given a base coat
of primer before painting to ensure the
surface blends in to the main bodywork,
as on this "Snow pearl" and silver flake
Corvette.

Highlights
"Fish scales" on the bonnet, window
and headlight details, sprayed through
simple stencils, provide the finishing
touches. The roof also has interesting
highlights.

Pitfalls
A few plastics are attacked by acrylics
and it is always worth making a few
preliminary tests before starting a
major project. Here, the plastic has
reacted to an "orange peel" effect.

MILITARY MODELS

Some modelers go to quite extraordinary lengths to ensure their models are painted in colors that are truly authentic, and may spend hours or even days researching book references and archives for clues. The search for authenticity can provoke intense rivalry and many a passionate debate has been conducted over the exact color of a 1930 LMS locomotive or the 1985 Formula One Ferrari.

Creating special effects

Achieving a realistic weathered look demands a creative eye and, for these models, the modeler preferred the extra scope, and softer edges, of airbrushing freehand.

Military modelers are no exception and often take great pains to ensure the livery and camouflage follows precisely the same pattern as the original. Some models are painted factory fresh, but many are painted as if they were in action – with mud, dust and all. It is in these weathering effects that the airbrush really comes into its own.

With smaller models, say 1/35th scale, highest finesse, double action airbrushes are needed to give the fine lines of camouflage. With larger, working models, larger airbrushes or small touch-up guns are quite adequate. Bold areas of camouflage and weathering can be marked out with masking tape or crepe paper. More complex shapes need masks made with narrow tape, while for fine or elaborate detailing, liquid masks may be applied.

The type of paints used varies considerably, but for smaller models, small tinlets of accurately matched enamels, such as Precision Paints and Humbrol, are very popular.

Using transfers

Although many working models are original designs, built for out and out performances, some are replicas constructed with great attention to authenticity. Using transfers can make this easier.

Transfer uses
The lifebelts on this ¹/25th scale Dusseldorf fire boat (left) are actual transfers, but many modellers create similar details with paper stencils made by scaling up or down photos and drawings by photocopying.

ARCHITECTURAL MODELS

The kinds of architectural model made by amateurs and professionals are often completely different. Amateurs tend to make buildings to provide a setting for other models, for example, for railways, or battle scenes for military models. Professionally made models are sometimes intended as prototypes of the real thing, perhaps to give a 3-D impression of the architect's design. Naturally, the aims of airbrushing with each type of model tend to be very different.

With amateur models, the idea is usually to make the buildings look weathered, and to help them blend into the landscape. Often, the best way to do this is to use the airbrush freehand, providing you have a steady hand, masking only for distinct color changes or areas such as windows. If the model is lacking in detail, though, this can be airbrushed in using multiple cut paper stencils—the edges of slates and tiles on a roof for example, or shadow painted on window frames, to create a 3-D effect.

Professional models, however, usually need to look smooth and slick rather than realistic. Here, the emphasis is on bold, clearly defined slabs of color rather than fine detail, and tape masking is very much the norm.

MODEL AIRCRAFT

Like racing cars and boats, model aircraft may be either static or working. Builders of static models have long appreciated just how useful a tool the airbrush is, and exploit the full range of graphic effects, using masking tapes, frisk and liquid film to create a thoroughly authentic finish. Builders of working models have been slower to catch on, preferring to concentrate on the practicalities of flying rather than the artistry of paint finishes. But the inspiration of film special effects departments—which use superb models indistinguishable on film from the real thing — combined with frequent articles in the modeling press, have opened their eyes to the possibilities. The remarkable working model Spitfire illustrated here gives an idea of just how impressive a finish can be achieved with an airbrush.

Spraying model aircraft

Spraying base color on to the fuselage of a Spitfire model. For a model this size (¹/₅th scale), it made sense to use a full-size car spray gun and cellulose paint, even though it is not fuel proof. A final coat of lacquer protects the paint.

Spraying architectural models

This architect's impression of the Wonderworld Leisure Complex is typical of professional architectural models in its use of bold blocks of airbrushed color. Indeed, the brightly colored geometrical shapes are crucial to its sense of fantasy and fun. The model is made largely from plexiglass and etched brass, and it was essential to select paint that did not react with the materials. Mat cellulose was the choice throughout, and masking tape was used extensively to ensure distinct color origination. An advantage of mat cellulose is that it dries quickly, reducing the chances of dust settling while it is still wet. It can be glossed over with lacquer if necessary, but most models of this type look better with a smooth, mat finish.

Roundels can be brushed or sprayed. Here, the outline was drawn using a compass, and then filled in by brush.

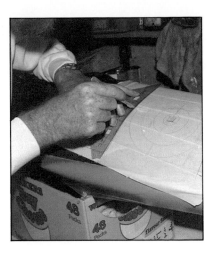

While masking tapes and films are widely used by modellers, you can often get by with simple paper masks made by copying or tracing the plans for the model. The lines are not perfect but the soft airbrushed edges look like natural aging. Here, cutting and folding back allowed the mask to be used repeatedly down one wing, and, then it was turned over for the other.

Where clear lines are needed for lettering, a film mask must be cut using a sharp modeling knife. A flexible plastic rule can be bent to follow the curve of the wing.

Transfers are not always available in the right size, but it may be possible to make a stencil by cutting out a photo-copy enlargement of the transfer numbers. Here, the stencil was held in place using artist's display mount adhesive – typical of the way modelers are learning to exploit artist's techniques.

The finished model

The finished model (left and below, minus engine and retractable landing gear) shows just how effectively an airbrush can be used to create an illusion of detail without adding the weight of real surface detail. One of the most telling details is the rivet line – achieved simply by spraying through the punched edge of computer paper, giving both a row of rivets and the panel edge at the same time. To complete the authentic look, dirt and stains have been painted over the roundels, so that the effect can still be seen when the plane is in the air.

Even though an airbrush is best for small details, using stencils means a spray gun can be used to paint in large areas quickly.

Holes made in the stencil with a leather punch can be sprayed through to depict panel fastenings.

CAMOUFLAGE TECHNIQUES

Camouflage is used on all kinds of military vehicles, from jeeps to jet fighters, to make them less visible, and an effective technique for painting camouflage is an essential part of military modeling. Camouflage depends on carefully worked out, yet apparently random, color patterns – some subtle, some bold and simple – to break up the outline of the vehicle and help it blend into its typical background. There are numerous variations, and careful research is required to find the right pattern for both the vehicle and the kind of terrain it usually operated in.

Airbrushing and spraying is ideally suited to reproduce camouflage patterns on models; many real – life camouflages depend on soft, sprayed edges.

Many patterns are best executed freehand without masks, though on smaller scale models this demands considerable skill and an airbrush of the highest quality and finesse. Even freehand patterns, however, must be carefully thought out in advance. The pattern shown in the pictures below is among the most common and easy to copy, and can often be done freehand using just loose, hand-held masks.

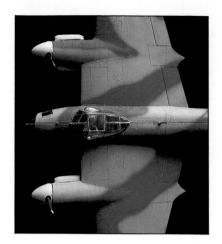

DISGUISING DIFFERENCES

Spraying camouflage
If they are to fly well, model aircraft usually have to be slightly different in scale and detail to the original. A good painted camouflage is one of the most effective ways of disguising these minor differences.

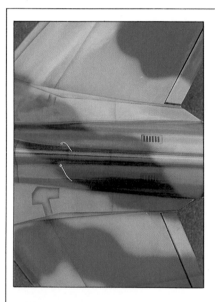

Adding details
Painted panel lines, grilles and so on, add to the illusory effect.

The model was finished off with an overall spray application of clear, fuelproof lacquer .

The "fighting cock" logo of the famous No 43 squadron was reproduced by cutting masks in low-tack masking film and airbrushing. The black outline was made with a technical drawing pen.

Variations on camouflage patterns

Left: Camouflage on World War II 1/32nd scale Mosquito airbrushed freehand

Top right: A recent RAF style (now superseded) using contrasting colors and asymmetric patterns

Centre right: USAF Far East camouflage, typical of the Vietnam War. At such a small scale (1/100th) the realistic brush-painted soft edges in the top model look hard; the airbrushed edges on the lower model are exaggerated but look better.

Bottom right: German World War II "splinter" camouflage on tiny models. For the hard edges on the wings and tails, tape masks were used.

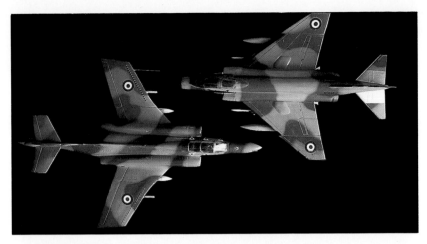

RAF camouflage patterns

Decoration here was a mixture of transfers, rub-on lettering, and airbrush work. The yellow rescue masks around the canopy were made with a masking tape stencil cut in situ and then airbrushed.

USAF Far East camouflage from the Vietnam war

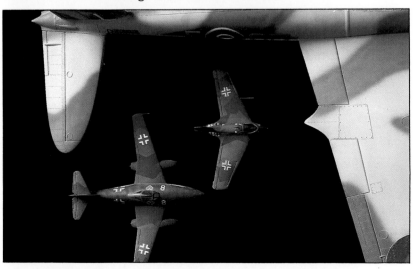

World War II German camouflage

WORKING MODEL AIRCRAFT

Although some working model aircraft are built accurately to scale, exact replicas in miniature of the real thing, the vast majority of "sports" models are approximations, altered in both scale and detail to enable them to fly (near-scale models), or original designs (non-scale models). But all working models, like static models, can be greatly enhanced by an airbrush finish.

With near-scale models, airbrushing helps to disguise the scale and detail differences, making the model look more real. Many non-scale models, meanwhile, rely almost entirely on the paint job to create an impression, since they are constructed very simply to match the novice's pocket and skills in modeling and flying. Often there is no attempt to mimic real planes in these finishes. Instead, the modeler aims to create a striking or attractive color scheme.

The emphasis throughout in painting model aircraft is on keeping them light enough to fly. A heavy paintbrush finish would almost certainly ground many aircraft, and even an airbrush must be used carefully; there is no question of a multi-layer lacquer finish, for instance. Many modelers use ink, rather than paint, to keep the weight added by the finish to the barest minimum. Similarly, they paint in details where adding real surface detail would add unacceptably to the overall weight of the plane. Improvised stencils and templates, and a high finesse airbrush technique, mean these painted details can look surprisingly effective.

An additional requirement for painting powered models is that the paint must be fuel-proof – or covered in a fuel-proof lacquer – for the exhaust waste from the engine attacks many paints. This often means using exotic paints such as epoxides or polyurethanes. These must be completely cleared from the spray gun while still wet, since once dry they are almost impossible to clean off.

Painting working model aircraft

A good paint finish draws attention away from the obvious differences between this model BAe Hawk and the real thing; note the propeller that has been added to this model jet to enable it to fly. This Hawk is not painted in the familiar Red Arrow colors, but in general it pays to use a well-known and obvious color scheme that everyone recognizes, to steer the eye away from any disparities.

Painted details
Above: an illusion of detail is created by airbrushing air intakes, access doors and so on, using cut paper stencils.

Two-tone desert camouflage enhanced with PCB tape panel lines looked a little too harsh; airbrushing the camouflage edges softened the effect.

An overall coat of epoxy lacquer (mat) produces an even finish and protects the paint from fuel waste.

Wooden parts of the model prefinished in polyester surfacing resin to ensure matching surface for painting since the model was made from fiber glass and plastic as well as wood.

DETAILING FLYING MODELS

Although real detail must often be abandoned with flying models to keep weight down to a minimum, judicious airbrushing can at least create an illusion of detail. A high finesse airbrush is usually needed, but simple stencils can be improvised or cut out from tracings or photocopies of pictures of the original. Close up, such painted details may look a little crude, but when the model is flying they can often look remarkably convincing.

Creating illusions
The wheel recesses on the painted aircraft (right) were sprayed.

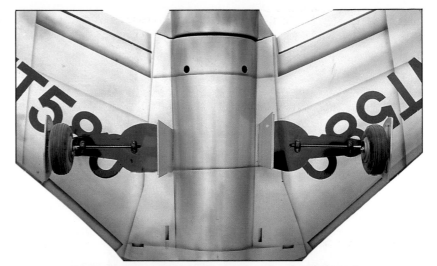

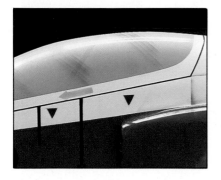

Creative spraying
Above: *simulated plexiglass canopy on a solid wooden model airbrushed using a sheet of writing paper as a mask.*
Right: *Lightweight tissue and balsawood model given an illusion of solidity with airbrushed fuselage details and shadows.*

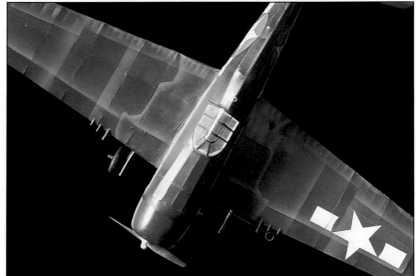

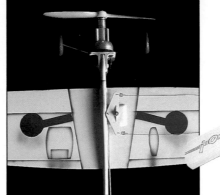

Decoration on a simple fabric model created by airbrushing with a film mask. The mask is cut out on the backing sheet and then transferred to the wing to avoid damaging the wing by cutting in situ.

Above: *The soft edges possible with an airbrush give shadows that look convincing from a distance.*
Right: *Enlarged photocopies of printed letters can be cut out to make stencils for wing markings.*

REFERENCE
SECTION

CONTRIBUTORS' PROFILES

Work by the airbrush artists introduced below is featured in The Complete Manual of Airbrushing Techniques. They have all been extremely generous both with their time and their secrets, and in allowing us to reproduce copyright material.

SHELLEY PAGE

Shelley Page works for the Richard Williams animation studio in London, producing special airbrushed effects for advertising animations and movie feature work. On leaving art college she worked as a freelance illustrator in the UK, Europe and the US, and subsequently joined the Richard Williams studio as a general artist/designer, progressing to art editor in charge of the product side of commercials.

She specialized in pack shots and quickly realized the advantages of her airbrush training in this area, but has found it useful in solving a number of animation problems. The work, she says, tends to evolve because of the capabilities of the airbrush; it is often found to be more versatile, more successful and certainly more economical than other more complex technical solutions. The studio offers her a wide range of creative possibilities which she feels would not be available in other fields of design work.

CRUMBS OF LONDON

Creators of extraordinary cake designs, Greg Robinson and Max Schofield are Crumbs of London. They describe their work as 'cake sculpture' and design to commissions for television, theaters, restaurants and pop groups.

Greg and Max have always rejected traditional approaches to cake decoration, instead exploring new ways of creating decorative finishes. Enter the airbrush, which has alowed them to experiment with food colors on edible media such as cake icing and produce varied and striking effects.

Among their more bizarre commissions have been a plane flying down the Grand Canyon, Noah's Ark, a teddy bears' swimming party, celebrity portraits and a corseted female torso, not to mention the robed Greek torso featured in this book.

STUDIO 1D

Around the back of the church in London's Kensington High Street is Studio 1D—a china and ceramic restoration company. The shelves of the workshop bow under the weight of all kinds of china objects — ordinary and extraordinary plates, bowls and teapots, Victorian dolls' heads, huge vases, jugs and animals.

Among the items waiting to be restored, the extent of the damage varies enormously. With considerable skill and expertise the workforce of Studio 1D can mend a crack in a vase so that you can neither see it nor feel it. They can build up and color a three-dimensional figure that has lost its head until it looks as good as the day it was made. The airbrush is invaluable in this type of work for blending new color into old and for creating a whole variety of finishes. The two airbrushes they share between six are in continuous use.

Studio 1D runs on-site courses for small groups throughout the year, teaching and demonstrating the delicate techniques involved in ceramic restoration.

CYNTHIA CLARKE –
MEDICAL ILLUSTRATOR

With an impressive working background including years spent at medical school studying anatomy, Cynthia Clarke has reached the top of her profession and is currently Chair of the Institute of Medical Illustration. As well as years of illustration work for professional journals and medical textbooks, covering all kinds of medical topics, from heart transplants to pregnancy, she has worked widely in television and film, directing teams of animation artists producing highly complex sequences of the human body in action.

Airbrushes have always been perfectly suited to the demands of medical illustration. With her wealth of experience, Cynthia has all kinds of short-cuts and techniques at her fingertips, some of which are demonstrated on pages 221 to 223. She relies one hundred per cent on her airbrush to achieve the special effects required in medical illustration of translucency, photographic realism and perfect flat tones.

TERRY WEBSTER – MODELER

A visit to Terry Webster's house in Leamington Spa is a bizarre experience. Larger than life punk crocodiles, skinhead pigs and lounging hippopotami populate his studio and adorn his sitting room. Terry started out as an illustrator, becoming known for his "Captain Hippo" series of posters. His separate interests in seaside postcards and modeling gradually came together, combining in his three-dimensional scenes of British caricatures at the seaside, and his modeling career was born. Since then more and more grotesque creations have been brought to life at his hands, some of which are illustrated in this book. His work is sought after and he receives many commissions for one-off pieces.

Terry started using the airbrush about ten years ago when he was looking for a means of achieving a high gloss finish on his seaside models. Many of the effects he wants to create would be difficult or impossible to produce without either his paint-encrusted de Vilbiss Sprite or the larger spray gun which he uses for laying in large areas of color.

IAN PEACOCK

Ian Peacock's career as a modeler reaches back into his childhood when at the age of five a fascination with aircraft was inspired by wartime Spitfires. By profession he has been an electronics design engineer for most of his working life. That is until recently, when his obsession with modeling took over. He now terms himself as a consultant to the model and hobby business and is involved in modeling as writer, practitioner and lecturer. He has written for the modelmaking press for the last twenty-five years, concentrating on spray painting, and has published a book on airbrushing for modelers called The Manual of Airbrushing and Spray Painting (Argus Books). He slots in spraying commissions alongside writing and lecturing – he has just finished spray painting a 9ft 6in/2.85m model of a Boeing 747 for an advertising agency.

Ian came to the spray gun and airbrush via the most tortuous route of all – trial and error, looking for the methods which would best produce the effects he wanted. In the thirty-five years since he first took up an airbrush he has acquired considerable dexterity and technical knowledge, but would not claim to be a creative artist. He insists he has no artistic talent but as an engineer by training can copy and interpret ideas very skilfully. Working on the basis that you can't lecture or write about something you haven't done yourself, he has built up what must be a rare collection of over 65 airbrushes and 40 spray guns, all of which he uses, he says, "equally badly". The examples of his work featured in this book, however, prove otherwise.

WARWICKSHIRE ILLUSTRATIONS LIMITED

Warwickshire Illustrations Limited is now an illustration graphics and typesetting company employing around thirty people. It started out over twenty years ago as a two-man technical illustration partnership specializing in color cutaway illustration. The two founders – John Lowe and R A Jennings – expanded the business gradually and were joined by an airbrush expert, John Beecham, in 1972. John started his professional career as a photoretoucher and then moved on to technical illustration. He uses the airbrush pretty well all the time, finding it the most accurate, reliable and speedy way of producing a perfect finish.

Warwickshire Illustrations Limited enjoys an international reputation for specialist airbrush illustration, with clients throughout Europe, the UK and the US. They are involved mainly in publicity work and advertising.

GLOSSARY OF TERMS

acetate or art cel
A transparent plastic film that comes in sheets or rolls and can be airbrushed on to directly, using appropriate media. Because of its transparency, acetate is used widely in illustration and animation to superimpose one image on another.

acrylic
A twentieth century artist's paint – a plastic paint made up of pigment suspended in polymer emulsion. It is water-based, but can be used thickly like oils or diluted like watercolors. Acrylic is popular for its qualities of versatility, durability, water resistance once dry, fast drying, and toughness. It is used in many areas of airbrush art, from fine art to decorating stage scenery.

adapter
For the airbrush artist, this is used to match almost any type of airbrush with almost any type of air source and air hose. Adapters are available, for example, to run up to five airbrushes off one air source at the same time.

advancing colors
See warm colors.

aerial perspective
In painting, this is a method of suggesting distance with color density and tonal value.

airbrush
For the purposes of this book, the term airbrush encompasses a range of designs from the simplest single action model to the sophisticated Turbo and the more heavy duty spray gun (the air eraser is not included). An airbrush is a precision instrument that produces and directs a spray of atomized paint powered by compressed air.

air eraser
Working on the same principle as an airbrush, the air eraser expels erasing powder which blasts off the surface of whatever is being sprayed. A bit heavy-handed for illustration work, but commonly used for glass etching.

air line
Alternative term for air hose.

art cel
See acetate.

art paper
A hard, smooth, shiny-surfaced paper ideal for airbrush work. The surface of the paper is coated with china clay. When mounted on a pulp base, art paper becomes art board. Common types include Bristol board, CS10 and Schoelleshammer.

atomization
The reduction of a liquid color medium to spray by mixing with compressed air.

A/W
Commonly used abbreviation for artwork.

balance
When referring to a painting or design, balance relates to the harmony of color or of composition; when referring to a book or magazine page layout, it relates to the relative weights of text and pictures, or to the values of color and black and white.

bar
A measure of air pressure; 1 bar = 14.5 psi (pounds per square inch).

base artwork
A piece of artwork that can be used for different purposes in combination with overlays. In medical illustration, for example, a base artwork of the human heart may be used first to demonstrate a heart in good working order and then with an overlay to show the same heart with blocked arteries; in animation a base artwork will be used for the backdrop while the action is superimposed on a series of acetate overlays.

bleaching
In photoretouching a specially prepared photographer's bleach may be used to remove anything from a blemish or scratch to an unwanted backdrop or figure; the airbrush can then be used to tone in or transform the bleached area.

bleed
The area of an illustration that extends beyond the dimensions to be used; also used to describe one color showing through or running into another.

blocking in
An early stage in a painting or illustration where the basic tones, colors and shapes of the final image are laid in.

blocking out
In retouching, removing unwanted sections of a photograph before respraying.

body colour
See gouache.

bowl
Type of color housing on gravity feed airbrushes, also known as the color cup.

Bristol board
A type of art board with a hard, shiny, smooth surface layer mounted on a pulp base, ideal for fine airbrush illustration.

bromide paper
A type of photographic paper with a smooth, shiny, non-absorbent surface which can be airbrushed. The surface is coated with an emulsion of silver bromide.

cel
Sheet of transparent acetate used for overlays, particularly in animation.

collage
An image made up of other images or elements superimposed or juxtaposed; a collage may include paint, photographs, fabric, found objects and so on.

color cup
See bowl.

color separation
The printing process by which an artwork is broken down photographically into a predetermined number of colors usually four or five, for the purposes of reproduction. A separate printing plate is then made for each color.

color wheel
A graphic device which lays out the color primaries, secondaries and tertiaries in a circle, showing their relationship to each other; a useful aid to the artist in indicating which colors to use to achieve various effects.

complementary colors
Pairs of colors opposite each other on the color wheel – green and red or blue and orange – which can be made to produce white or gray if correctly mixed.

compressed air
Air maintained by whatever means at a higher pressure than the atmosphere. Used to atomize paint whithin an airbrush.

contour masking
Masking with a flexible medium, such as masking film or liquid masking, where the mask follows the ups and downs of the surface, for example on a model car hood or a ceramic statue.

cool or receding colors
The blues and greens from the "cool" side of the color wheel appear to recede from the viewer, whereas the "warm" reds, pinks and oranges appear to advance towards the viewer.

crown cap
An accessory available for some airbrush models to replace the needle cap. It protects the needle from damage and, when you are laying in large areas of color prevents the build-up of pigment and spattering.

CS10
See art board.

cutaway
In technical illustration, the surface covering of a machine may be partly removed or cut away to expose the inner workings.

cyan
The blue used in four-color printing is always referred to as cyan; the other three colors are magenta, yellow and black.

diffuser
An elementary form of airbrush. A metal tube hinged in the middle operated by blowing through one end while the other end is immersed in color The air and paint meet at the break in the tube and the paint is scattered by the air onto the surface.

diorama
Three-dimensional background setting for models, such as a Wild West landscape complete with tumbleweed and cactus as a setting for a gold rush wagontrain.

double action
The most widely used and sophisticated design of airbrush, the double action airbrush gives the artist the facility to control both the flow of color and the flow of air delivered to the needle while spraying

drop shadow
A shadow painted behind a flat image to bring it away from the page and suggest substance; display lettering is often given a drop shadow. A simple masking technique can be used to produce drop shadows in airbrushing: The mask used for the image itself is shifted sideways and down, exposing the drop shadow area. The exposed areas of the actual image are then remasked and the remaining exposed area, the drop shadow, is sprayed in producing an exact match with the actual image.

dry transfers
Sheets of ready-made letters, symbols, patterns, borders and technical illustrations that are simply rubbed down on to almost any dry, clean surface as required.

emulsion
The light sensitive coating on photographic paper or film made of fine grains of silver bromide suspended in gelatin.

exploded view
A technical illustration of, say, an airbrush with all its components arranged as in their assembled state but separated so that each single component is completely visible.

ferrule
Seamless on more expensive paintbrushes, the ferrule is the metal tube encasing and holding in position the hairs of the paintbrush.

fixed double action
The less versatile of the two types of double action airbrush (see also independent double action); the flow of color and the flow of air expelled from the airbrush can be independently determined, unlike on the simpler single action models, but not while spraying. The ratio of paint to air is infinitely variable but must be worked out and set before spraying.

fixing
A method of covering finished artwork with an appropriate medium to render the color permanent and to protect them.

found objects or objets trouvés
Any ordinary object used for an aesthetic purpose, for example a comb used as an airbrush mask or a leaf used in a collage.

freehand airbrushing
The techniques of spraying without masking.

Frisk film
A brand of low-tack masking film which has come to be used as a generic term by many airbrush artists.

fugitive colors
Colors which will fade in natural light.

ghosting
In technical illustration, the method of showing the internal workings of a machine through a transparently rendered casing — a difficult effect to achieve.

gouache
Water based paint that can be used transparently or opaquely; also known as body color.

gravity feed
Describes the method by which color is delivered to the airbrush needle from the paint well, jar, cup or bowl attached to the top of the body in gravity-feed designs (see also suction feed); many models are available with either gravity or suction feed — design can operate with a greater capacity color housing and is more practical for large scale work.

ground
A term used in fine art for anything that you spray on to — glass, masonite, or canvas; and in graphics and fine art, the support.

hard edge
In airbrushing, the edge created by spraying over a hard mask – a sharp, crisp edge.

hard mask
As opposed to a loose mask, a mask that is fixed to the surface so that no spray can creep beneath, such as low-tack masking film or frisk film or liquid masking.

highlight
Where an object picks up and reflects a point or area of light of greater intensity than the local brightness. In airbrushing, highlights are generally added at the end of a piece of work, when the artist is able to judge how much highlight the final image needs.

independent double action
The most versatile of all airbrush designs; the flow of colour and the flow of air expelled from the airbrush can be independently controlled to an infinitely variable ratio while spraying (see also fixed double action).

knifing
Using a blade to scratch into colour to create highlights or texture, or to remove blemishes and unwanted colour.

lever
Finger-operated control level which controls the flow of air and colour through the airbrush; also known as the button, finger lever, and trigger.

linear perspective
The system of technical drawing where parallel lines appear to recede until they converge on one point; see also vanishing point.

local colour
The colour of an object in ordinary light conditions when it is not affected by very bright light, shadow, reflection from an adjacent object or distance: It is important to take into account local colour when analysing light and shadow.

loose mask
A mask that is not fixed to the surface being sprayed: A loose mask may be a hand held French curve, a weighted down piece of tissue paper, a ball of cotton wool, or a cardboard template; see also hard mask.

magenta
The red used in four colour printing; the other three are yellow, black and cyan.

marker
A thick-nibbed felt or fibre pen widely used for colouring up roughs and presentations. In airbrushing, markers are convenient tools for quickly working out a colour, masking, and spraying sequence.

mask
Anything that gets in the way of airbrush spray reaching the surface being sprayed – a finger, a comb or a piece of masking film all become masks when they interrupt the spray.

medium (pl. media)
Anything that is sprayed through an airbrush – artist's paints such as watercolours, oils and acrylics, specially developed photoretouching inks, and fabric colours.

mixed media
The technique of executing a painting with more than one medium, say gouache, acrylic, and graphite pencil.

moisture trap
An accessory to an airbrush air source which filters moisture droplets from the air being fed to the airbrush to prevent spattering caused by air bubbles coming through the air hose.

monochrome
A monochrome painting is one executed in varying tones of a single colour, sometimes with the addition of black and white.

mouth diffuser
See diffuser.

mural
A wall painting; in car customizing, a scene painted on to the body of a vehicle.

needle
An important airbrush component in all "with needle" designs, the needle controls the flow of medium through the nozzle: The needle in an airbrush needs regularly cleaning and checking for damage, and is the component which most commonly needs replacing. Many airbrushes are packaged with a supply of spare needles.

negative mask
A mask which blocks out the object itself allowing the area around to be sprayed; opposite of positive mask.

nozzle
One of the most delicate components of the airbrush, the nozzle contains and protects the tip of the needle and in most designs is where the air and colour meet and are atomized.

opacity
A paint characteristic which enables it to block out completely whatever is beneath; gouache, acrylic and oil, for example, have the quality of opacity, where watercolour, ink and dye do not.

overspray
In airbrushing, the spray which falls around the area at which the airbrush nozzle is actually directed; many airbrush techniques rely on overspray creating the required effect.

photomontage
The creation of a single image from two or more existing images; the method of superimposition can vary, but the airbrush is very useful for disguising joins and blending one image into another.

photoretouching
A profession in itself, much used in the newspaper and advertising businesses throughout this century, photoretouching is the art of altering an existing photographic image, for example adding colour to a black and white image, sharpening tonal contrast, obliterating an element of a picture altogether, introducing a new element, or simply tidying up a messy image. Fine airbrush spray is ideally suited to these demands.

positive mask
A mask which blocks out the background around an object, exposing the object itself to spray; opposite of negative mask.

process white
A white gouache used for correction on both illustration and text artwork.

psi (pounds per square inch)
Imperial measure of air pressure; 1 psi is equivalent to 0.007 bar.

pulsing
Unevenness in the air flow supplied by a diaphragm compressor to the airbrush, sometimes bad enough to cause spattering. An anti-pulsation device is available which can be fitted to a compressor to counteract this problem.

reamer
Similar to a filed-down needle, a reamer has three flat sides meeting at a sharp point. It can be used (with great care) for cleaning an airbrush nozzle assembly.

register
A term used in colour printing. Separate plates are used for printing each colour and each plate must be positioned exactly over the others – in register. The slightest overlap will cause the final image to be blurred – out of register (see also registration marks).

registration marks
Small marks (a circle with a cross through it) made at the four corners of a piece of artwork to facilitate the matching of the printing plates (see also register).

regulator
A combined pressure control and moisture trap which can be attached to any of the storage compressors.

retouching
See photoretouching.

scamp
In graphics, a rough initial sketch of an idea.

scratching back
Using a scalpel blade to scratch out colour to create highlights or texture; also removing blemishes and blots.

single action
A broad category of airbrush including several variations – the common feature is that you cannot control the amount of air and paint expelled separately during spraying, unlike with the more sophisticated double action designs. On models at the top end of the range, you can adjust the ratio of paint to air before spraying, but the only action involved in producing the spray is pressing down the control lever.

sizing
A method of preparing a canvas or board support ready for painting.

soft edge
In airbrushing, the edge created by spraying over a loose mask – a soft, undefined edged.

spatter
A very coarse spray effect made up of unevenly sized and irregularly spaced dots of colour. Style and density of spatter can range from almost invisible speckle to a large blob pattern. Spatter effect is achieved by dropping the air pressure.

spidering
An unwanted firework of colour, often at the end of a line. Spidering can be caused by several things including too much colour or too much air.

spray gun
One down from the airbrush, a spray gun is useful for covering large areas with colour. Much used in painting scenery and large murals.

stencilling
Creating pattern by spraying through a pre-cut loose mask made of cardboard, acetate, metal etc. weighted or taped in position.

stipple
A textured spray effect made up of evenly sized dots achieved by dropping the air pressure and holding the airbrush nozzle further from the surface while spraying. It may be applied by hand with a stippling paintbrush.

stoving enamel
A type of enamel used in ceramic decoration made heatproof by baking at a low temperature.

suction feed
This describes a method by which colour is delivered to the airbrush needle from the paint housing. In suction feed designs, colour is sucked into the body of the airbrush from a jar, cup or bowl attached to the side or underneath of the body. The simplest single action models are generally suction feed while many of the more sophisticated double action models are available with either gravity or suction feed colour housing (see also gravity feed).

support
A term used in graphics and fine art for anything that you spray on to – acetate, canvas, wood etc.

surface
A general term for anything that you spray on to – artboard, pottery, cake icing, or a car bonnet.

tack
In airbrushing the adhesive quality of masking film. Low-tack masking film is the most useful for graphic and illustration work because it can be used over a painted surface without damaging it .

template
A shape or series of shapes that can be used as a mask or traced around. A template can be made of anything from tissue paper to cardboard to plastic, and may be homemade or shop bought. An ellipse template, for example, is a plastic rectangle with several different sized ellipses cut from it.

tonal value
The degree of density of a tone; tonal value scales can be mixed – a useful exercise for the photoretoucher who has to match tones exactly.

trigger
See lever.

trim masks
Marks used on printing proofs to indicate the four corners of the actual page size, the size to which the final page will be trimmed.

vanishing point
In perspective drawing, the point on the horizon at which receding parallel lines meet.

vignette
A graduated tone or area of colour that gently fades from solid colour at one extreme to no colour at the other; a technique which the airbrush is ideally suited to produce.

wash
An evenly laid area of transparent colour that can be achieved with water-based paints such as watercolour and gouache. The desire to lay a perfect wash spurred Charles Burdick to invent the airbrush .

well
A colour housing on some airbrush designs that is recessed into the body of the airbrush.

INDEX

CREDITS

The publishers would like to thank the following for their help in the production of this book. **Editorial contributor** Judy Martin, **Studio photography** Mark French, **Practical photography** Ian Howes, **Graphic art suppliers** Langford & Hill Ltd., Peter Owen, **Illustration consultant** Ken Warner (Head of illustration, Falmouth College of Art). **Demonstrators** John Beecham (technical illustration), Terry Webster (glass fibre models), Eleanor Allit (fabrics), Ian Peacock (models), Roger Goode (models), Julian Short (3-D caricatures), Greg Robinson and Max Schofield (cake decoration), the staff at Studio 1D (ceramic restoration), Eye Media International Ltd. (Aerosonic Print System), Shelley Page (animation), Cynthia Clarke (medical illustration),

The following companies have assisted in the production of the book. Warwickshire Illustrations Ltd. of Coventry (technical artwork), Richard Williams Animation Ltd (animation), Spitting Image Productions Ltd. (3-D caricatures). The Publishers would also like to thank the following for allowing artwork to be reproduced. Rolls Royce (Motor Cars) Ltd. (pages 84/85, 212/213), Thames Television Ltd. (pages 194), General Mills Inc. New York (USA) (page 195), Frito-Lay Inc. USA; (pages 196/7).

Artwork credits
(Where necessary, the position of illustrations on each page is indicated by the following letters: L = Left; R = Right; TL = top left; TR = top right; BL = bottom left; BR = bottom right; and C = center.)

10/11 Peter Owen; 12 TL Paul Allen, BL Bob Murdoch; 13 Dave Willardson; 14/15 Hajime Sorayama; 16 Norbert Cames; 20 Mark Thomas; 35 Norbert Cames; 43 Morris & Ingram (London) Ltd.; 44/45 ICO s.r.l., Italy; 79 TL Norbert Cames, L Norbert Cames, BR Colin Elgie; 80 Mark Thomas; 80/81 Warwickshire Illustrations Ltd.; 83 Mark Thomas; 84/85 T Roger Stewart, B Warwickshire Illustrations Ltd.; 86 John Harwood; 87 Oliver Kidd; 88/89 Norbert Cames; 119 Peter Owen; 129 Oliver Kidd; 131 Mark Thomas; 133 Mark Thomas; 139 TL Michael Cacy, TC Mike Hollifield, TR Mark Thomas, B Mark Thomas; 150 T John Harwood, B John Harwood; 151 Hajime Sorayama; 152-157 Warwickshire Illustrations Ltd.; 181 Dennis Gilbert; 183 Spitting Image Productions Ltd.; 187 Spitting Image Productions Ltd.; 193 Jaques Gastineau; 194 Shelley Page; 195 Shelley Page; 196/7 Frito-Lay Inc USA; 204 John Harwood; 205 Gary Weller; 206 Warwickshire Ilustrations Ltd.; 207 David Brailsford; 208/9 Warwickshire Illustrations Ltd.; 209 T Alan Clark, C Stuart Johnson; 210/211 Pete Serjeant; 212/213 Warwickshire Illustrations Ltd.; 215 Falmouth College of Art; 221-223 Cynthia Clarke; 230/231 Roger Goode; 232 Ian Peacock; 233 TL TR John Wyte, B Model Boats Magazine; 234 TL Peacock; 235 Ian Peacock; 236/237 Ian Peacock; 238/239 Ian Peacock

Filmsetting Text Filmsetters Ltd., **Lithographic reproduction** Universal Colour Scanning Ltd.